Grandma's
ITALIAN
Kitchen

Publications International, Ltd.

Favorite Brand Name Recipes at www.fbnr.com

All recipes and photographs that contain specific brand names are copyrighted by those companies and/or associations, unless otherwise specified. All recipe photographs *except* those on pages 205, 223, 237, 245, 269, 289, 327 and 351 copyright © Publications International, Ltd.

Nestlé and Toll House are registered trademarks of Nestlé.

Butter Flavor CRISCO® all-vegetable shortening and Butter Flavor CRISCO® No-Stick Cooking Spray are artificially flavored.

Some of the products listed in this publication may be in limited distribution.

Introduction and text on pages 20–21, 58–59, 112–113, 140–141, 182–183, 224–225, 254–255, 296–297, 346–347 and 362–363 written by Elizabeth A. Matlin.

Photo credits: © CORBIS: Owen Franken: 88; Todd Gipstein: 62, 210; John Heseltine: 363; Mimmo Jodice: 224; Michael Lewis: 10, back cover bottom; Dennis Marsico: 296; Vittoriano Rastelli: 116; **Dave Darian:** 42, 120, 134, 268, 337, 347; © **Suzanne Plunkett:** front cover inset.

Illustrations by Roger Gorringe.

Front cover food photography by Proffitt Photography, Ltd., Chicago.

Pictured on the front cover *(clockwise from top left):* Cannoli Pastries *(page 358),* Focaccia *(page 256),* Shellfish Cioppino *(page 54),* Greens and Gemelli *(page 130)* and Chicken Cacciatore *(page 154).*

Pictured on the back cover *(top to bottom):* Rigatoni Salad *(page 342)* and Parmesan Polenta *(page 24).*

ISBN: 0-7853-8054-X

Library of Congress Control Number: 2003100973

Manufactured in China.

8 7 6 5 4 3 2 1

Microwave Cooking: Microwave ovens vary in wattage. Use the cooking times as guidelines and check for doneness before adding more time.

Preparation/Cooking Times: Preparation times are based on the approximate amount of time required to assemble the recipe before cooking, baking, chilling or serving. These times include preparation steps such as measuring, chopping and mixing. The fact that some preparations and cooking can be done simultaneously is taken into account. Preparation of optional ingredients and serving suggestions is not included.

Contents

Introduction

Despite being a very narrow peninsula not more than a few hundred miles wide, the Italy's topography varies greatly from its northernmost regions to its southernmost tip. These geographical variances result in a vast range of culinary diversity.

THE ITALIAN NORTH

Northern Italy, known for cream-based sauces, bustling industry and rich natural resources, differs greatly from its regions to the south. The geography, climate, culture and history each add their unique fingerprint to the food, creating a groaning board of culinary treasures.

From the alps of the far north to the uplands and central Italian plains, the fare changes along with the land. Stretching across northernmost Italy is the Alpine Slope, a landscape of towering mountains, deep valleys, grasslands and forests. The Apennine mountains form a rocky spine that extends almost the entire length of Italy. The Po Valley is a low-lying area that runs between the Alps in

the north and the Apennine Mountains in the south. Rice paddies irrigated by the Po River yield short-grained arborio rice, the main ingredient in risotto. North of the Adriactic Sea is a narrow strip of land, the Adriatic Plain, located in the Friuli-Venezia region. This chalky limestone plateau is not suitable for farming or livestock but does provide a unique environment for wine-making. The Western Uplands and Plains span the Tyrrhenian Sea from north to south. Second only to the Po Valley in agricultural prosperity, the northern portion of this bountiful area includes the hill country of Tuscany and Umbria and is well-known for grain and livestock production.

The Italian economy was once agriculturally based, but Italian manufacturing has become a major player in the world's industrial market. While agricultural is responsible for only a small portion of Italy's economy today, it is still more modernized in the north than the south.

THE ITALIAN SOUTH

Known as the Mezzogiorno to natives, southern Italy is a land of tomato-based sauces, rural economy and ancient traditions. Unlike the abundant north, southern cuisine is imbued with the creativity that comes from inventing flavorful dishes despite tough farming conditions and little pastureland for cattle.

Historical domination by the Greeks, Arabs and Spanish is reflected in the spices, tomatoes and other vegetables grown throughout the area. As the Apennine Mountains continue their run down through central and southern Italy, forests and pastures dramatically give way to farmland and then high mountains, plateaus and volcanoes. Pasta, bread and seafood are highlighted in the cuisine of Apulia, which owes most

of its culinary heritage to Greece. This region, along with the Southeastern Plains, form the heel of Italy's boot and border the Adriatic Sea. While large farming estates harvest vegetables, fruit, wheat and corn, the region also produces more wine than any other area in Italy. The fishing industry ranks as the fourth largest in Italy. The south end of the Western Uplands and Plains boasts a warm climate and fertile volcanic soil making for a rich agricultural area. Fruit, vegetables, wheat, tobacco and vineyards abound. The hill region is noted for its fine extra-virgin olive oils and pork products. Fish and shellfish from the Tyrrhenian Sea are a mainstay along the coast. Sicily, the largest island in the Mediterranean Sea, is separated from mainland Italy by the Strait of Messina. The northern part of the island is mountainous while the southern portion has hills and plains. Farmers grow wheat, almonds, grapes, citrus fruit and olives in the rich volcanic soil. Seafood, eggplants and tomatoes are also abundant.

Despite government efforts to develop greater industry in the south, the majority of Italy's manufacturing still resides in the north. Recently some southern farms and vinyards have upgraded their agricultural and winemaking technologies, ensuring a prosperous future for all of Italy.

L'Antipasto

*T*he first course in an Italian dinner generally includes meats, cheeses, some vegetables and, of course, breads. Arranged in small, bite-size portions, antipasto wakens a diner's taste buds. Roughly translated, antipasto means "before pasta," which suggests it is typically eaten as a precursor to the pasta course, although often enough Italians can make a snack or an entire meal out of these appetizers. Prepared cold or hot, and frequently containing cold cut meats, olives, eggplant, tomatoes, and cheese, antipasto in Italian restaurants shows the pride Italian chefs take in their presentation of this appetizer, relishing in the colorful appearance almost as much as in the succulent tastes.

Artichoke Crostini (page 43)

Roasted Eggplant Spread with Focaccia

1 eggplant (1 pound)
1 medium tomato
1 tablespoon fresh lemon juice
1 tablespoon chopped fresh basil *or* 1 teaspoon dried basil leaves
2 teaspoons chopped fresh thyme *or* ¾ teaspoon dried thyme leaves
1 clove garlic, minced
¼ teaspoon salt
1 tablespoon extra virgin olive oil
Focaccia (recipe page 10)

1. Preheat oven to 400°F. Poke holes in several places in eggplant with fork. Cut stem end from tomato and place in small baking pan. Place eggplant on oven rack; bake 10 minutes. Place tomato in oven with eggplant. Bake vegetables 40 minutes.

2. Cool vegetables slightly, then peel. Cut eggplant into large slices. Place tomato and eggplant in food processor or blender. Add lemon juice, basil, thyme, garlic and salt; process until well blended. Slowly drizzle oil through feed tube and process until mixture is well blended. Refrigerate 3 hours or overnight.

3. To serve, spread 1 tablespoon on each focaccia wedge. Garnish with cherry tomato wedges and additional fresh basil, if desired. *Makes 10 appetizer servings*

Eggplants originated in Asia, probably India, but most Americans associate them with the cuisine of southern Italy where they have been popular for hundreds of years. Many varieties of eggplants have been cultivated since ancient times. The most common variety in America is the large, elongated dark purple eggplant. The pale yellowish-white flesh, which becomes soft when cooked, has a mild almost bland taste that combines well with many flavors.

Roasted Eggplant Spread with Focaccia

Focaccia

¾ cup warm water (110° to 115°F)
1½ teaspoons sugar
1 teaspoon active dry yeast
1 tablespoon extra virgin olive oil
1 teaspoon salt
1 teaspoon dried rosemary
1 cup all-purpose flour
1 cup whole wheat flour
Nonstick cooking spray

1. Pour water into large bowl. Dissolve sugar and yeast in water; let stand 10 minutes or until bubbly. Stir in oil, salt and rosemary. Add flours, ½ cup at a time, stirring until dough begins to pull away from side of bowl and forms a ball.

2. Turn dough onto lightly floured surface and knead 5 minutes or until smooth and elastic, adding more flour if necessary. Place dough in bowl lightly sprayed with cooking spray and turn dough so all sides are coated. Cover with towel or plastic wrap and let rise in warm draft-free place about 1 hour or until doubled in bulk.

3. Turn dough onto lightly floured surface and knead 1 minute. Divide into 3 balls; roll each into 6-inch circle. Using fingertips, dimple surfaces of dough. Place on baking sheet sprayed with cooking spray; cover and let rise 30 minutes more.

4. Preheat oven to 400°F. Spray tops of dough circles with cooking spray; bake about 13 minutes or until golden brown. Remove from oven and cut each loaf into wedges.   *Makes 10 servings*

Fra Diavolo Antipasto Salad

1 cup prepared Italian salad dressing
3 to 4 tablespoons *Frank's® RedHot®* Cayenne Pepper Sauce or to taste
1/4 cup chopped fresh Italian parsley
6 cups assorted vegetables, such as cauliflower, carrots, tomatoes, celery, zucchini and/or mushrooms, cut into bite-size pieces
1 jar (6 ounces) Tuscan peppers, drained
1/4 pound mild provolone cheese, cut into small sticks
1/4 pound fresh mozzarella cheese, cut into small cubes*
1/4 pound hard salami, cut into small cubes
  Romaine lettuce leaves

Look for fresh mozzarella in the deli section of your supermarket.

Whisk together salad dressing, *Frank's RedHot* Sauce and parsley in small bowl. Place vegetables, peppers, cheeses and salami in large bowl. Add dressing; toss well to coat evenly. Cover and marinate in refrigerator 1 hour. Arrange lettuce on large platter. Spoon salad over lettuce just before serving.   *Makes 6 appetizer servings*

Prep Time: 20 minutes
Marinate Time: 1 hour

Oysters Romano

12 oysters, shucked and on the half shell
2 slices bacon, cut into 12 (1-inch) pieces
1/2 cup Italian-seasoned dry bread crumbs
2 tablespoons butter or margarine, melted
1/2 teaspoon garlic salt
6 tablespoons grated Romano, Parmesan or provolone cheese
  Fresh chives for garnish

Preheat oven to 375°F. Place shells with oysters on baking sheet. Top each oyster with 1 piece bacon. Bake 10 minutes or until bacon is crisp. Meanwhile, combine bread crumbs, butter and garlic salt in small bowl. Spoon mixture over oysters; top with cheese. Bake 5 to 10 minutes or until cheese melts. Garnish with chives, if desired. Serve immediately.   *Makes 4 appetizer servings*

Mozzarella & Tomato with Lemon Dijon Dressing

1/3 cup olive oil
1/4 cup GREY POUPON® COUNTRY DIJON® Mustard
2 tablespoons lemon juice
2 teaspoons finely chopped fresh basil leaves
1/2 teaspoon sugar
3 medium tomatoes, sliced
6 ounces mozzarella cheese, sliced
2 cups mixed salad greens
1/4 cup coarsely chopped pitted ripe olives
Chopped fresh basil leaves

Whisk oil, mustard, lemon juice, basil and sugar in small bowl; set aside. Arrange tomatoes and cheese slices over salad greens on serving platter. Top with chopped olives and basil leaves; garnish as desired. Drizzle with prepared dressing before serving.

Makes 6 appetizer servings

Fast Pesto Focaccia

1 can (10 ounces) pizza crust dough
2 tablespoons prepared pesto
4 sun-dried tomatoes packed in oil, drained

Preheat oven to 425°F. Lightly grease 8×8×2-inch pan. Unroll pizza dough; fold in half and pat into pan. Spread pesto evenly over dough. Chop tomatoes or snip with kitchen scissors; sprinkle over pesto. Press tomatoes into dough. Make indentations in dough every 2 inches using wooden spoon handle. Bake 10 to 12 minutes or until golden brown. Cut into squares and serve warm or at room temperature.

Makes 16 squares

Prep and Cook Time: 20 minutes

Mozzarella & Tomato with
Lemon Dijon Dressing

Mediterranean Frittata

¼ cup olive oil

5 small yellow onions, thinly sliced

1 can (14½ ounces) whole peeled tomatoes, drained and chopped

¼ pound prosciutto or cooked ham, chopped

¼ cup grated Parmesan cheese

2 tablespoons chopped fresh parsley

½ teaspoon dried marjoram leaves

¼ teaspoon dried basil leaves

¼ teaspoon salt

Generous dash black pepper

6 eggs

2 tablespoons butter or margarine

Italian parsley leaves for garnish

1. Heat oil in medium skillet over medium-high heat. Cook and stir onions in hot oil 6 to 8 minutes until soft and golden. Add tomatoes. Cook and stir over medium heat 5 minutes. Remove tomatoes and onions to large bowl with slotted spoon; discard drippings. Cool tomato-onion mixture to room temperature.

2. Stir prosciutto, cheese, parsley, marjoram, basil, salt and pepper into cooled tomato-onion mixture. Whisk eggs in small bowl; stir into prosciutto mixture.

3. Preheat broiler. Heat butter in large broilerproof skillet over medium heat until melted and bubbly; reduce heat to low.

4. Add egg mixture to skillet, spreading evenly. Cook over low heat 8 to 10 minutes until all but top ¼ inch of egg mixture is set; shake pan gently to test. *Do not stir.*

5. Broil egg mixture about 4 inches from heat 1 to 2 minutes until top of egg mixture is set. (Do not brown or frittata will be dry.) Frittata can be served hot, at room temperature or cold. To serve, cut into wedges. Garnish, if desired.

Makes 6 to 8 appetizer servings

Mediterranean Frittata

Sausage Pizza Piena

1 tablespoon olive oil
1 onion, chopped
1 red bell pepper, diced
1 green bell pepper, diced
1 pound turkey sausage, casing removed
1 teaspoon dried marjoram leaves
1 pound thawed frozen bread dough, at room temperature
2 cups (8 ounces) shredded mozzarella cheese
2 eggs, lightly beaten
3 tablespoons *Frank's® RedHot®* Cayenne Pepper Sauce
1 tablespoon milk
   Grated Parmesan cheese
   Sesame seeds

1. Heat oil in large nonstick skillet. Add onion and bell peppers; cook 5 minutes or until tender. Add sausage and marjoram. Cook and stir 5 minutes or until meat is no longer pink. Drain well; cool.

2. Preheat oven to 375°F. Cut dough in half. Roll half of dough into 14×10-inch rectangle on lightly floured board. (Let dough rest 5 minutes if dough springs back when rolling.) Pat onto bottom and 1 inch up sides of greased 13×9×2-inch baking pan. Roll out remaining half of dough to 13×9-inch rectangle; keep covered.

3. Stir cheese, eggs and *Frank's RedHot* Sauce into sausage mixture; toss to coat evenly. Spoon evenly over bottom dough. Cover sausage mixture with top half of dough. Pinch top and bottom edges of dough to seal. Brush top lightly with milk. Sprinkle with Parmesan cheese and sesame seeds.

4. Bake 25 minutes or until golden and bread sounds hollow when tapped. Let stand 10 minutes. Cut into squares to serve. *Makes 6 to 8 servings*

Prep Time: 30 minutes
Bake Time: 25 minutes

Toasted Pesto Rounds

- 1/4 cup thinly sliced fresh basil or chopped fresh dill
- 1/4 cup (1 ounce) grated Parmesan cheese
- 1 medium clove garlic, minced
- 3 tablespoons reduced-calorie mayonnaise
- 12 French bread slices, about 1/4 inch thick
- 4 teaspoons chopped tomato
- 1 green onion with top, sliced
  Black pepper

Preheat broiler. Combine basil, cheese, garlic and mayonnaise in small bowl; mix well. Arrange bread slices in single layer on large nonstick baking sheet or broiler pan. Broil, 6 to 8 inches from heat, 30 to 45 seconds or until bread slices are lightly toasted. Turn bread slices over; spread evenly with basil mixture. Broil 1 minute or until lightly browned. Top evenly with tomato and green onion. Season to taste with pepper. Transfer to serving plate. *Makes 12 servings*

Stuffed Portobello Mushrooms

- 4 portobello mushrooms (4 ounces each)
- 1/4 cup olive oil
- 2 cloves garlic, pressed
- 6 ounces crumbled goat cheese
- 2 ounces prosciutto or thinly sliced ham, chopped
- 1/4 cup chopped fresh basil
  Mixed salad greens

Remove stems and gently scrape gills from underside of mushrooms; discard stems and gills. Brush mushroom caps with combined oil and garlic. Combine cheese, prosciutto and basil in medium bowl. Grill mushrooms, top side up, on covered grill over medium KINGSFORD® Briquets 4 minutes. Turn mushrooms over; fill caps with cheese mixture, dividing equally. Cover and grill 3 to 4 minutes longer until cheese mixture is warm. Remove mushrooms from grill; cut into quarters. Serve on mixed greens. *Makes 4 servings*

Tuscan Tuna Stuffed Pasta Salad

16 uncooked jumbo pasta shells
½ cup balsamic vinaigrette salad dressing
¼ cup chopped fresh basil or parsley
½ teaspoon salt
⅛ teaspoon ground black pepper
1 can (15 ounces) white kidney beans, rinsed and drained
1 can (6 ounces) white tuna packed in water, drained and flaked
1 jar (4 ounces) chopped pimiento, rinsed and drained
1⅓ cups *French's*® French Fried Onions, divided

Cook pasta shells according to package directions using shortest cooking time. Drain; rinse under cold running water. Set aside.

Combine salad dressing, basil, salt and pepper in medium bowl; whisk until well blended. Stir in beans, tuna, pimiento and *⅔ cup* French Fried Onions. Spoon 3 tablespoons bean mixture into each pasta shell. Sprinkle with remaining *⅔ cup* onions. *Makes 4 main course or 8 appetizer servings*

Prep Time: 20 minutes
Cook Time: 10 minutes

Tuscan Tuna Stuffed Pasta Salad

Lucca •
Florence •
Pisa •
TUSCANY
• Siena

Tuscany

AS A LEADING CENTER FOR ITALIAN AND EUROPEAN CULTURE, IT COMES AS NO SURPRISE THAT TUSCAN CUISINE IS CONSIDERED ONE OF THE WORLD'S FINEST.

Tuscany is named after the Estruscans, an ancient tribe that settled the Florence area in the seventh century B.C. Famous for its green hills, olive groves and vineyards, Tuscany depicts the quintessential Italian countryside. The varied landscape of the Apennine Mountains and the Tyrrhenian seacoast interspersed with lakes, rivers and wooded valleys makes this one of the most beautiful regions in Italy. As a leading center for Italian and European culture (even the Italian language evolved from a Tuscan dialect), it comes as no surprise that Tuscan cuisine is considered one of the world's finest. What is surprising is that its appeal lies not in artistic flourishes but in utter simplicity. During the fifteenth century there were actually Tuscan laws forbidding extravagant dinner parties of more than three courses. In a land where culinary opulence was once a crime, it's understandable that frugality and a dislike for haute cuisine still lingers.

The simplicity of Tuscan cooking succeeds only because the finest seasonal ingredients are used. Their purity and natural flavor render extensive sauces and seasonings pointless. The only essential seasoning is olive oil. Without it the dishes are not truly Tuscan. The nation's best bread and purest olive oil form the foundation of the cuisine. Bread is the pasta of Tuscany and is often used as an ingredient. Thrifty Tuscans incorporate crusty pieces of day-old loaves into panzanella (tomato, onion and basil bread salad) and ribollita (vegetable soup thickened with bread).

The use of olive oil over butter indicates the region's proximity to central Italy. Olive groves replace dairy cows and the pervasive oil is drizzled over soups and salads, simmered with beans and basted over roasting meats. There is a bold fruitiness to Tuscan olive oil and both quality and flavor vary with the trees' location. The province of Lucca is renown for its delicate, golden oil that pairs well with fish while the Chianti hills yield a dark, intensely flavored oil. Herbs also play a starring role on the Tuscan stage. Nowhere else in Italy are they so widely used. Rosemary is especially favored, its branches used as basting brushes or stripped of their leaves and skewered with sausages for grilling. Rounding out the region's specialties are legumes (chick-peas, fava and cannellini beans), panforte (Siena's dark fruit and nut cake), seafood from the Tyrrhenian coast and the magnificent Florentine dish bistecca alla fiorentina, a hefty steak from the famed Chianina beef grilled over wood coals.

The food of Tuscany is said to exist only to complement its amazing wines. Tuscan vineyards were first planted by the ancient Estruscans and the region has become one of Italy's premium wine producers. Classic Chianti is still the dominant red wine, but aromatic Brunello, made from Grosso grapes, and Vino Nobile, from a type of Sangiovese grape, are also favored. Until recently Tuscan whites held less prestige. An exception is Vernaccia di San Gimignano, a crisp, light wine produced from a grape of the same name in the medieval town of San Gimignano.

Florence, Tuscany's capital, has ruled the region's politics, art, culture and cuisine for more than six hundred years. Some of the world's greatest artists, Leonardo da Vinci and Michelangelo among them, have lived and worked in Florence. While tourism plays an important economic role in both the province and region, clothing, glass, plastics and pharmaceuticals are also manufactured. Tuscany also produces some of the world's finest white marble from quarries located in the Apuan Alps. In addition to Florence's many artistic and cultural jewels, the region draws tourists to Pisa's famous leaning tower and Siena's illustrious medieval Gothic cathedral.

Tuscan White Bean Crostini

2 cans (15 ounces each) white beans (such as Great Northern or
   cannellini), rinsed and drained

$\frac{1}{2}$ large red bell pepper, finely chopped *or* $\frac{1}{3}$ cup finely chopped roasted red
   bell pepper

$\frac{1}{3}$ cup finely chopped onion

$\frac{1}{3}$ cup red wine vinegar

3 tablespoons chopped fresh parsley

1 tablespoon olive oil

2 cloves garlic, minced

$\frac{1}{2}$ teaspoon dried oregano leaves

$\frac{1}{4}$ teaspoon black pepper

18 French bread slices, about $\frac{1}{4}$ inch thick

1. Combine beans, bell pepper and onion in large bowl.

2. Whisk together vinegar, parsley, oil, garlic, oregano and black pepper in small bowl. Pour over bean mixture; toss to coat. Cover; refrigerate 2 hours or overnight.

3. Arrange bread slices in single layer on large nonstick baking sheet or broiler pan. Broil, 6 to 8 inches from heat, 30 to 45 seconds or until bread slices are lightly toasted. Remove; cool completely.

4. Top each toasted bread slice with about 3 tablespoons of bean mixture.

Makes 6 servings

If using dried beans, rinse under running water and pick out any debris or blemished beans. Dried beans should soak in water for several hours or overnight to soften before cooking. To soak, place the beans in a large saucepan or bowl and cover with 3 inches of water. Let stand, covered, for 6 hours or overnight. Do not soak beans longer than 12 hours or they may begin to ferment. Drain beans before cooking.

Tuscan White Bean Crostini

Parmesan Polenta

4 cups chicken broth

1¼ cups yellow cornmeal

1 small onion, minced

4 cloves garlic, minced

1 tablespoon minced fresh rosemary *or* 1 teaspoon dried rosemary

½ teaspoon salt

6 tablespoons grated Parmesan cheese

1 tablespoon olive oil, divided

1. Spray 11×7-inch baking pan with nonstick cooking spray; set aside. Spray one side of 7-inch-long sheet of waxed paper with cooking spray; set aside. Combine chicken broth, cornmeal, onion, garlic, rosemary and salt in medium saucepan. Cover and bring to a boil over high heat. Reduce heat to medium and simmer 10 to 15 minutes or until mixture has consistency of thick mashed potatoes. Remove from heat and stir in cheese.

2. Spread polenta evenly in prepared pan; place waxed paper, sprayed-side down, on polenta and smooth. (If surface is bumpy, it is more likely to stick to grill.) Cool on wire rack 15 minutes or until firm. Remove waxed paper; cut into 6 squares. Remove squares from pan.

3. To prevent sticking, spray grid with cooking spray. Prepare coals for grilling. Brush tops of squares with half the oil. Grill oil-side down on covered grill over medium to low coals for 6 to 8 minutes or until golden. Brush with remaining oil and gently turn over. Grill 6 to 8 minutes more or until golden. Serve warm.

Makes 6 servings

Parmesan Polenta

Marinated Antipasto

1 cup julienne-sliced carrots
1 cup fresh green beans, cut into 2-inch pieces
1 cup fresh brussels sprouts, quartered
1 cup thinly sliced baby yellow squash
1/2 cup thinly sliced red bell pepper
1/2 cup thinly sliced yellow bell pepper
1 can (9 ounces) artichoke hearts, drained and quartered
2 cups water
1/2 cup white wine vinegar
1 tablespoon olive oil
1 teaspoon sugar
2 bay leaves
1 clove garlic
6 sprigs fresh thyme
1/4 teaspoon black pepper
1/2 cup chopped green onions with tops
1/2 cup minced parsley
Peel of 2 oranges, cut into thin strips

1. Bring 4 cups water to a boil in large saucepan over high heat. Add carrots, beans and brussels sprouts; cover and simmer 1 minute. Add squash and bell peppers; cover and simmer 1 minute or until vegetables are crisp-tender. Remove from heat; drain. Place vegetables and artichoke hearts in heatproof bowl.

2. Combine 2 cups water, vinegar, oil, sugar, bay leaves, garlic, thyme and black pepper in medium saucepan. Bring to a boil over medium heat. Pour over vegetables; mix well. Cool completely. Cover and refrigerate 12 hours or up to 3 days before serving.

3. Before serving, drain vegetables. Discard bay leaves, garlic and thyme. Toss vegetables with onions, parsley and orange peel.   *Makes 8 servings*

Marinated Antipasto

Bruschetta

1 can (14½ ounces) DEL MONTE® Diced Tomatoes, drained
2 tablespoons chopped fresh basil *or* ½ teaspoon dried basil
1 small clove garlic, finely minced
½ French bread baguette, cut into ⅜-inch-thick slices
2 tablespoons olive oil

1. Combine tomatoes, basil and garlic in 1-quart bowl; cover and refrigerate at least ½ hour.

2. Preheat broiler. Place bread slices on baking sheet; lightly brush both sides of bread with oil. Broil until lightly toasted, turning to toast both sides. Cool on wire rack.

3. Bring tomato mixture to room temperature. Spoon tomato mixture over bread and serve immediately. Sprinkle with additional fresh basil leaves, if desired.

Makes 8 appetizer servings

Note: For a fat-free version, omit olive oil. For a lower-fat variation, spray the bread with olive oil cooking spray.

Prep Time: 15 minutes
Cook Time: 30 minutes

Elegant Shrimp Scampi

6 tablespoons butter
6 to 8 large cloves garlic, minced
1½ pounds large raw shrimp (about 16), peeled and deveined
6 green onions, thinly sliced
¼ cup dry white wine
   Juice of 1 lemon (about 2 tablespoons)
¼ cup chopped fresh parsley
   Salt and black pepper to taste
   Lemon slices and fresh parsley sprigs for garnish (optional)

1. Clarify butter by melting it in small saucepan over low heat. *Do not stir.* Skim off white foam that forms on top. Strain clarified butter through cheesecloth into glass measuring cup to yield ⅓ cup. Discard milky residue at bottom of pan.

2. Heat clarified butter in large skillet over medium heat. Add garlic; cook and stir 1 to 2 minutes until softened but not brown.

3. Add shrimp, green onions, wine and lemon juice; cook and stir until shrimp turn pink and are firm and opaque, 1 to 2 minutes on each side. *Do not overcook.*

4. Just before serving, add chopped parsley and season with salt and pepper. Serve on individual shell-shaped or small gratin dishes. Garnish, if desired.

Makes 8 servings

To peel shrimp, remove legs by gently pulling shell. Loosen shell with your fingers, then slide it off. To devein shrimp, cut a shallow slit along back of shrimp with paring knife. Lift out vein. (This is easier to do under cold running water.)

Onion and Pepper Calzones

1 teaspoon vegetable oil
$1/2$ cup chopped onion
$1/2$ cup chopped green bell pepper
$1/4$ teaspoon salt
$1/8$ teaspoon dried basil leaves
$1/8$ teaspoon dried oregano leaves
$1/8$ teaspoon black pepper
1 can (12 ounces) country biscuits (10 biscuits)
$1/4$ cup (1 ounce) shredded mozzarella cheese
$1/2$ cup prepared spaghetti or pizza sauce
2 tablespoons grated Parmesan cheese

1. Preheat oven to 400°F. Heat oil in medium nonstick skillet over medium-high heat. Add onion and bell pepper. Cook 5 minutes, stirring occasionally. Remove from heat. Add salt, basil, oregano and black pepper; stir to combine. Cool slightly.

2. While onion mixture is cooling, flatten biscuits into $3^{1}/_{2}$-inch circles about $1/8$ inch thick using palm of hand.

3. Stir mozzarella cheese into onion mixture; spoon 1 teaspoonful onto each biscuit. Fold biscuits in half, covering filling. Press edges with tines of fork to seal; transfer to baking sheet.

4. Bake 10 to 12 minutes or until golden brown. While calzones are baking, place spaghetti sauce in small microwavable bowl. Cover with vented plastic wrap. Microwave at HIGH 3 minutes or until hot.

5. To serve, spoon spaghetti sauce and Parmesan cheese evenly over each calzone. Serve immediately. *Makes 10 appetizers*

Prep and Cook Time: 25 minutes

Onion and Pepper Calzones

Sesame Italian Breadsticks

1/4 cup grated Parmesan cheese
3 tablespoons sesame seeds
2 teaspoons Italian seasoning
1 teaspoon kosher salt (optional)
12 frozen bread dough dinner rolls, thawed
1/4 cup butter, melted

Preheat the oven to 425°F. Spray large baking sheet with nonstick cooking spray. In small bowl, combine cheese, sesame seeds, Italian seasoning and salt, if desired. Spread out on plate. On lightly floured surface, roll each bread piece into a rope, about 8 inches long and 1/2 inch thick. Place on baking sheet and brush tops and sides with butter. Roll each buttered rope in seasoning, pressing seasoning into sides. Return ropes to baking sheet, placing 2 inches apart. Twist each rope 3 times pressing both ends of rope down on baking sheet. Bake 10 to 12 minutes, or until golden brown.

Makes 12 bread sticks

Crostini

1/4 loaf whole wheat baguette (4 ounces)
4 plum tomatoes
1 cup (4 ounces) shredded part-skim mozzarella cheese
3 tablespoons prepared pesto sauce

1. Preheat oven to 400°F. Slice baguette into 16 very thin, diagonal slices. Slice each tomato vertically into four 1/4-inch slices.

2. Place baguette slices on nonstick baking sheet. Top each with 1 tablespoon cheese, then 1 slice tomato. Bake about 8 minutes or until bread is lightly toasted and cheese is melted. Remove from oven; top each crostini with about 1/2 teaspoon pesto sauce.

Makes 8 appetizer servings

Antipasto with Marinated Mushrooms

1 recipe Marinated Mushrooms (recipe follows)
4 teaspoons red wine vinegar
1/2 teaspoon *each* dried basil leaves *and* dried oregano leaves
  Generous dash black pepper
1/4 cup olive oil
4 ounces mozzarella cheese, cut into 1/2-inch cubes
4 ounces prosciutto or cooked ham, thinly sliced
4 ounces provolone cheese, cut into 2-inch sticks
1 jar (10 ounces) pepperoncini peppers, drained
8 ounces hard salami, thinly sliced
2 jars (6 ounces each) marinated artichoke hearts, drained
1 can (6 ounces) pitted ripe olives, drained

Prepare Marinated Mushrooms; set aside. Combine vinegar, basil, oregano and black pepper in small bowl. Whisk in oil until well blended. Add mozzarella cubes; stir to coat. Marinate, covered, in refrigerator at least 2 hours. Drain mozzarella cubes; reserve marinade. Wrap 1/2 of prosciutto slices around provolone sticks; roll up remaining slices separately. Arrange mozzarella cubes, prosciutto-wrapped provolone sticks, prosciutto rolls, Marinated Mushrooms, pepperoncini, salami, artichoke hearts and olives on large platter lined with lettuce, if desired. Drizzle reserved marinade over pepperoncini, artichoke hearts and olives.

Makes 6 to 8 servings

Marinated Mushrooms

3 tablespoons lemon juice
2 tablespoons chopped fresh parsley
1/2 teaspoon salt
1/4 teaspoon dried tarragon leaves
1 clove garlic, slightly crushed
1/8 teaspoon black pepper
1/2 cup olive oil
1/2 pound small or medium fresh mushrooms, stems removed

Combine all ingredients except oil and mushrooms in medium bowl. Whisk in oil until well blended. Add mushrooms; stir to coat. Marinate, covered, in refrigerator 4 hours or overnight, stirring occasionally.

Antipasto with Marinated Mushrooms

$\mathcal{F}$ried Calamari with Tartar Sauce

1 pound fresh or thawed frozen squid
1 egg
1 tablespoon milk
³/₄ cup fine dry unseasoned bread crumbs
Vegetable oil
Tartar Sauce (recipe page 38)
Lemon wedges (optional)

1. To clean each squid, hold body of squid firmly in one hand. Grasp head firmly with other hand; pull head, twisting gently from side to side. (Head and contents of body should pull away in one piece.) Set aside tubular body sac. Cut tentacles off head; set aside. Discard head and contents of body.

2. Grasp tip of pointed, thin, clear cartilage protruding from body; pull out and discard. Rinse squid under cold running water. Peel off and discard spotted outer membrane covering body sac and fins. Pull off side fins; set aside. Rinse inside of squid body thoroughly under running water. Repeat with remaining squid.

3. Cut each squid body crosswise into ¹/₄-inch rings. Cut reserved fins into thin slices. (Body rings, fins and reserved tentacles are all edible parts.) Pat pieces thoroughly dry with paper towels.

4. Beat egg with milk in small bowl. Add squid pieces; stir to coat well. Spread bread crumbs on plate. Dip squid pieces in bread crumbs; place in shallow bowl or on waxed paper. Let stand 10 to 15 minutes before frying.

5. To deep fry squid,* heat 1¹/₂ inches oil in large saucepan to 350°F. (Caution: Squid will pop and spatter during frying; do not stand too close to pan.) Adjust heat to maintain temperature. Fry 8 to 10 pieces of squid at a time in hot oil 45 to 60 seconds until light brown. Remove with slotted spoon; drain on paper towels. Repeat with remaining squid pieces.

6. Serve hot with Tartar Sauce and lemon wedges. Garnish as desired.

Makes 2 to 3 servings

*To shallow fry squid, heat about ¹/₄ inch oil in large skillet over medium-high heat; reduce heat to medium. Add as many pieces of squid in single layer without crowding to hot oil. Cook, turning once with 2 forks, 1 minute per side or until light brown. Proceed as directed in step 5. (This method uses less oil but requires slightly more hand work.)

Fried Calamari with Tartar Sauce

Tartar Sauce

1 green onion
1 tablespoon drained capers
1 small sweet gherkin or pickle
2 tablespoons chopped fresh parsley
1 ⅓ cups mayonnaise

1. Thinly slice green onion. Mince capers and gherkin.

2. Fold green onion, capers, gherkin and parsley into mayonnaise. Cover and refrigerate until ready to serve.

Makes about 1 ⅓ cups

Quattro Formaggio Pizza

1 (12-inch) Italian bread shell
½ cup prepared pizza or marinara sauce
4 ounces shaved or thinly sliced provolone cheese
1 cup (4 ounces) shredded smoked or regular mozzarella cheese
2 ounces Asiago or brick cheese, thinly sliced
¼ cup freshly grated Parmesan or Romano cheese

1. Heat oven to 450°F.

2. Place bread shell on baking sheet. Spread pizza sauce evenly over bread shell.

3. Top sauce with provolone, mozzarella, Asiago and Parmesan cheese.

4. Bake 14 minutes or until bread shell is golden brown and cheese is melted.

5. Cut into wedges; serve immediately.

Makes 4 servings

Prep and Cook Time: 26 minutes

Marinated Antipasto Kabobs

1/2 (9-ounce) package spinach three-cheese tortellini or plain tortellini
1 package (9 ounces) frozen artichoke hearts, thawed
20 small fresh mushrooms, stems removed
1 large red bell pepper, cut into 20 equal-sized pieces
1/2 cup white balsamic or white wine vinegar
1/4 cup (1 ounce) grated Parmesan cheese
1/4 cup minced fresh basil
2 tablespoons Dijon mustard
1 tablespoon olive oil
1/2 teaspoon sugar
1/4 teaspoon black pepper
20 cherry tomatoes

1. Cook tortellini according to package directions. Drain well. Cool slightly; cover and refrigerate until ready to assemble kabobs.

2. Cook artichokes according to package directions; drain. Immediately add artichokes to bowl of ice water to stop cooking process. Let stand 1 to 2 minutes; drain well. Place artichokes in large resealable plastic food storage bag. Add mushrooms and bell pepper.

3. Combine vinegar, cheese, basil, mustard, oil, sugar and black pepper in small bowl; mix well. Add to vegetable mixture in plastic bag; seal bag. Turn bag over several times to coat ingredients evenly. Refrigerate several hours or overnight, turning bag occasionally.

4. Remove vegetables from marinade, reserving marinade. Arrange vegetables on skewers alternately with tortellini and tomatoes; place on serving platter. Drizzle with reserved marinade, if desired. *Makes 20 kabobs*

Cook's Notes: Don't clean mushrooms until just before you're ready to use them (they will absorb water and become mushy). Wipe them with a damp paper towel or rinse them under cold running water and blot dry.

Grilled Garlic & Herb Pizzas

Homemade Pizza Dough (recipe page 42)
8 cloves Grilled Garlic (recipe page 42)
1 medium yellow onion
Olive oil
1 medium red, yellow or orange bell pepper
1 cup crumbled goat cheese
¼ cup chopped fresh herb mixture (thyme, basil, oregano and parsley) *or*
   4 teaspoons dry herb mixture
¼ cup grated Parmesan cheese

Prepare Homemade Pizza Dough. While dough is rising, light KINGSFORD® Briquets in covered grill. Arrange medium-hot briquets on one side of grill. Prepare Grilled Garlic. Lightly oil grid to prevent sticking. Cut onion into ½-inch-thick slices. Insert wooden picks into onion slices from edges to prevent separating into rings. (Soak wooden picks in hot water 15 minutes to prevent burning.) Brush onion lightly with oil. Place whole bell pepper and onion slices on grid around edge of briquets. Grill on covered grill 20 to 30 minutes until tender, turning once or twice. Remove picks from onion slices and separate into rings. Cut pepper in half and remove seeds; slice pepper halves into strips.

Roll or gently stretch each ball of dough into 7-inch round. Brush lightly with oil on both sides. Grill dough on grid directly above medium-hot KINGSFORD® Briquets 1 to 3 minutes or until dough starts to bubble and bottom is lightly browned. Turn; grill 3 to 5 minutes or until second side is lightly browned and dough is cooked through. Remove from grill. Spread 2 cloves Grilled Garlic onto each crust; top with onion, pepper, goat cheese, herbs and Parmesan cheese, dividing equally. Place pizzas around edge of coals; grill covered 5 minutes until bottom crust is crisp, cheese melts and toppings are heated through.

Makes 4 individual pizzas

Note: A 1-pound loaf of frozen bread dough, thawed, can be substituted for Homemade Pizza Dough. Or, substitute 4 pre-baked individual Italian bread shells, add toppings and warm on the grill.

Grilled Garlic & Herb Pizzas

Homemade Pizza Dough

2³⁄₄ cups all-purpose flour, divided
1 package quick-rising yeast
³⁄₄ teaspoon salt
1 cup water
1¹⁄₂ tablespoons vegetable oil

Combine 1¹⁄₂ cups flour, yeast and salt in food processor. Heat water and oil in small saucepan until 120° to 130°F. With food processor running, add water and oil to flour mixture; process 30 seconds. Add 1 cup flour; process until dough comes together to form ball. Knead on floured board 3 to 4 minutes or until smooth and satiny, kneading in as much of the remaining ¹⁄₄ cup flour as needed to prevent dough from sticking. Place dough in oiled bowl, turning once. Cover with towel; let rise in warm place 30 minutes until doubled in bulk. Divide dough into 4 equal balls.

Grilled Garlic

1 or 2 heads garlic
Olive oil

Peel outermost papery skin from garlic heads. Brush heads with oil. Grill heads at edge of grid on covered grill over medium-hot KINGSFORD® Briquets 30 to 45 minutes or until cloves are soft and buttery. Remove from grill; cool slightly. Gently squeeze softened garlic heads from root end so that cloves slip out of skins into small bowl. Use immediately or cover and refrigerate up to 1 week.

Caponata Spread

1½ tablespoons BERTOLLI® Olive Oil
1 medium eggplant, diced (about 4 cups)
1 medium onion, chopped
1½ cups water
1 envelope LIPTON® RECIPE SECRETS® Savory Herb with Garlic Soup Mix
2 tablespoons chopped fresh parsley (optional)
Salt and ground black pepper to taste
Pita chips or thinly sliced Italian or French bread

In 10-inch nonstick skillet, heat oil over medium heat and cook eggplant with onion 3 minutes. Add ½ cup water. Reduce heat to low and simmer covered 3 minutes. Stir in soup mix blended with remaining 1 cup water. Bring to a boil over high heat. Reduce heat to low and simmer uncovered, stirring occasionally, 20 minutes. Stir in parsley, salt and pepper. Serve with pita chips.

Makes about 4 cups spread

Artichoke Crostini

1 jar (6 ounces) marinated artichoke hearts, drained and chopped
3 green onions, chopped
5 tablespoons grated Parmesan cheese, divided
2 tablespoons mayonnaise
12 slices French bread (½ inch thick)

Preheat broiler. Combine artichokes, green onions, 3 tablespoons cheese and mayonnaise in small bowl; mix well. Arrange bread slices on baking sheet. Broil 4 to 5 inches from heat source 2 to 3 minutes on each side or until lightly browned. Remove baking sheet from broiler. Spoon about 1 tablespoon artichoke mixture on each bread slice and sprinkle with remaining 2 tablespoons cheese. Broil 1 to 2 minutes or until cheese is melted and lightly browned. *Makes 4 servings*

Tip: Garnish crostini with red bell pepper, if desired.

Prep and Cook Time: 25 minutes

Tortellini Teasers

Zesty Tomato Sauce (recipe follows)
1/2 (9-ounce) package refrigerated cheese tortellini
1 large red or green bell pepper, cut into 1-inch pieces
2 medium carrots, peeled and sliced 1/2 inch thick
1 medium zucchini, sliced 1/2 inch thick
12 medium fresh mushrooms
12 cherry tomatoes

1. Prepare Zesty Tomato Sauce; keep warm.

2. Cook tortellini according to package directions; drain.

3. Alternate 1 tortellini and 2 to 3 vegetable pieces on long frilled wooden picks or wooden skewers. Serve as dippers with tomato sauce. *Makes 6 servings*

Zesty Tomato Sauce

1 can (15 ounces) tomato purée
2 tablespoons finely chopped onion
2 tablespoons chopped fresh parsley
1 teaspoon dried oregano leaves
1/4 teaspoon dried thyme leaves
1/4 teaspoon salt
1/8 teaspoon black pepper

Combine tomato purée, onion, parsley, oregano and thyme in small saucepan. Heat thoroughly, stirring occasionally. Stir in salt and pepper. Garnish with carrot curl, if desired.

Tortellini Teasers

La Zuppa

Italians eat dinners made up of 4 or 5 courses rather than one main course. Soup is often served as one of the first courses. While antipasti ready the palate, soup prepares the diner's stomach for the pasta dish to follow. Locals in Calabria believe soup does even more; a local song suggests soup appeases hunger and thirst, fills the stomach, cleanses the palate, allows for better sleep, facilitates digestion and puts a little color in the cheeks. Ranging from vegetable minestrones to fish soups, each region of Italy has a traditional soup made from locally available ingredients.

Italian-Style Meatball Soup (page 57)

Roman Spinach Soup

6 cups ⅓-less-salt chicken broth
1 cup cholesterol-free egg substitute
¼ cup minced fresh basil
3 tablespoons freshly grated Parmesan cheese
2 tablespoons lemon juice
1 tablespoon minced fresh parsley
¼ teaspoon white pepper
⅛ teaspoon ground nutmeg
8 cups fresh spinach, washed, stems removed, chopped

1. Bring broth to a boil in 4-quart saucepan over medium heat.

2. Beat together egg substitute, basil, Parmesan cheese, lemon juice, parsley, white pepper and nutmeg in small bowl. Set aside.

3. Stir spinach into broth; simmer 1 minute. Slowly pour egg mixture into broth mixture, whisking constantly so egg threads form. Simmer 2 to 3 minutes or until egg is cooked. Garnish with lemon slices, if desired. Serve immediately.

Makes 8 (¾-cup) servings

Note: Soup may look curdled.

If choosing loose spinach, look for leaves with good color and a crisp texture. Avoid limp, wilted, bruised, spotted or discolored leaves. The leaves should have a fresh aroma, not a sour or musty odor. Avoid leaves with thick coarse stems, a sign of overgrown spinach, which can be tough and bitter. Thick stems also mean more waste, since they are removed and discarded. If purchasing prepackaged, squeeze the bag to check if the contents are resilient and thus fresh and crisp.

Roman Spinach Soup

Pasta e Fagioli

½ cup chopped onion
½ cup sliced carrot
½ cup sliced celery
4 tablespoons extra-virgin olive oil
2 cloves garlic, finely chopped
2 cups reduced-sodium chicken broth or more as needed
1 can (15 ounces) cannellini beans, rinsed and drained
1 can (14½ ounces) Italian plum tomatoes with juices
1 cup BARILLA® Ditalini or other small pasta shape
1 cup cut green beans (fresh or frozen)
1 cup frozen small lima beans
2 cups packed dark leaves of escarole or Swiss chard, cut into small pieces
  Salt and pepper
¼ cup grated Romano cheese, plus more to taste

1. Combine onion, carrot, celery, olive oil and garlic in large broad saucepan. Cover and cook over low heat about 10 minutes until vegetables are tender but not browned.

2. Stir in broth, beans and tomatoes with liquid. Cover and cook about 15 minutes until flavors are blended.

3. Add ditalini, green beans, lima beans and escarole to saucepan. Cook, uncovered, 10 to 12 minutes or until vegetables are very tender and mixture is thick. Add salt and pepper to taste. Stir in cheese. Ladle into bowls; serve with additional cheese.

Makes 4 to 6 servings

Milan Chickpea Soup

1 can (6 ounces) CONTADINA® Tomato Paste
4 cups water or chicken broth
2 cans (15 ounces each) chickpeas or garbanzo beans, undrained
½ pound mild Italian sausage, casing removed, sliced ½ inch thick
1 cup sliced fresh mushrooms
1 cup chopped onion
1½ teaspoons salt
¼ teaspoon ground black pepper
¼ teaspoon marjoram
2 teaspoons grated Parmesan cheese

1. Combine tomato paste and water in large saucepan; stir until well blended.

2. Add chickpeas and liquid, sausage, mushrooms, onion, salt, pepper and marjoram; stir.

3. Cover. Bring to a boil. Reduce heat to low; simmer 30 minutes or until sausage is no longer pink in center. Sprinkle with Parmesan cheese just before serving.

Makes about 10 cups

Prep Time: 6 minutes
Cook Time: 35 minutes

Fresh Tomato Pasta Soup

1 tablespoon olive oil
½ cup chopped onion
1 clove garlic, minced
3 pounds fresh tomatoes, coarsely chopped
3 cups fat-free reduced-sodium chicken broth
1 tablespoon minced fresh basil
1 tablespoon minced fresh marjoram
1 tablespoon minced fresh oregano
1 teaspoon fennel seed
½ teaspoon black pepper
¾ cup uncooked rosamarina or other small pasta
½ cup (2 ounces) shredded part-skim mozzarella cheese

1. Heat oil in large saucepan over medium heat. Add onion and garlic; cook and stir until onion is tender. Add tomatoes, broth, basil, marjoram, oregano, fennel seed and black pepper.

2. Bring to a boil; reduce heat. Cover; simmer 25 minutes. Remove from heat; cool slightly.

3. Puree tomato mixture in food processor or blender in batches. Return to saucepan; bring to a boil. Add pasta; cook 7 to 9 minutes or until tender. Transfer to serving bowls. Sprinkle with mozzarella. Garnish with marjoram sprigs, if desired.

Makes 8 (¾-cup) servings

Tomatoes and Italian cuisine have long been associated with one another because of the variety of uses Italians have found for the South American native. A member of the nightshade family, tomatoes were brought to Europe by Spanish explorers returning from New World journeys. Originally thought by Europeans to be poisonous, the pommes d'amour, *or love apples as the French called them, tomatoes eventually gained worldwide popularity.*

Fresh Tomato Pasta Soup

Shellfish Cioppino

12 cherrystone clams
   Salt
4 tablespoons olive oil
2 cups chopped onions
2 red bell peppers, seeded and chopped
1 green bell pepper, seeded and chopped
8 cloves garlic, minced
2 cups Fish Stock (recipe page 56)
2 cups vermouth or white wine
2 cans (16 ounces each) tomatoes, drained and coarsely chopped
1 tablespoon dried basil leaves
1 teaspoon dried thyme leaves
1 bay leaf
$1/4$ teaspoon red pepper flakes
$3/4$ pound raw large shrimp, peeled and deveined
$1/2$ pound sea scallops
8 crab claws or claw-shaped surimi
   Fresh bay leaves for garnish

1. To prepare clams,* discard any that remain open when tapped with fingers. To clean clams, scrub with stiff brush under cold running water. Soak clams in mixture of $1/3$ cup salt to 1 gallon water 20 minutes. Drain water; repeat 2 more times.

2. To steam clams, place 1 cup water in large stockpot. Bring to boil over high heat; add clams. Cover; reduce heat to medium. Steam 5 to 7 minutes or until clams open. Remove from stockpot with tongs; set aside. Discard any clams that remain unopened.

3. Heat oil in stockpot over medium-high heat. Add onions, bell peppers and garlic. Cover; reduce heat to low. Cook 20 to 25 minutes or until tender, stirring occasionally. Add Fish Stock, vermouth, tomatoes, basil, thyme, bay leaf and red pepper. Partly cover; simmer 30 minutes. Add clams, shrimp, scallops and crab claws to tomato mixture. Cover; remove from heat. Let stand until shrimp turn pink and scallops turn opaque. Remove bay leaf; discard. Ladle into large pasta or soup bowls. Garnish, if desired. *Makes 4 servings*

If fresh clams in shells are not available, substitute $1/2$ pint shucked clams. Steam in vegetable steamer until firm. Omit steps 1 and 2.

Shellfish Cioppino

Fish Stock

1³⁄₄ pounds fish skeletons and heads from lean fish, such as red snapper, cod, halibut or flounder
  2 medium onions
  3 ribs celery, cut into 2-inch pieces
10 cups cold water
  2 slices lemon
³⁄₄ teaspoon dried thyme leaves, crushed
  8 black peppercorns
  3 fresh parsley sprigs
  1 bay leaf
  1 clove garlic

1. Rinse fish skeletons; cut out gills and discard.

2. Trim tops and roots from onions, leaving most of the dried outer skin intact; cut into wedges.

3. Combine fish skeletons and heads, onions and celery in stockpot or Dutch oven. Add water, lemon, thyme, peppercorns, parsley, bay leaf and garlic. Bring to a boil over high heat. Reduce heat to medium-low; simmer, uncovered, 30 minutes, skimming foam that rises to the surface.

4. Remove stock from heat and cool slightly. Strain stock through large sieve or colander lined with several layers of dampened cheesecloth, removing all bones, vegetables and seasonings; discard.

5. Use immediately or refrigerate stock in tightly covered container up to 2 days or freeze stock in freezer containers for several months.   *Makes about 10 cups*

Stocks are an integral part of traditional cooking. They are the basis for sauces, soups and stews. Because of the time needed to make stocks, they are used less frequently in everyday cooking. Instead canned broth and bouillon are used, but they are not as rich and flavorful as a good homemade stock. Stocks are not difficult to make. Since most recipes make large quantities, they can be frozen in small batches for later use.

Italian-Style Meatball Soup

½ pound lean ground beef
¼ pound ground Italian sausage
⅓ cup fine dry bread crumbs
1 egg
1 large onion, finely chopped and divided
½ teaspoon salt
4 cups canned beef broth
2 cups water
1 can (8 ounces) stewed tomatoes
1 can (8 ounces) pizza sauce
1 can (15½ ounces) kidney beans, drained
2 cups sliced cabbage
2 medium carrots, sliced
½ cup frozen Italian green beans

1. Combine beef, sausage, bread crumbs, egg, 2 tablespoons onion and salt in large bowl; mix with hands until thoroughly blended. Shape into 32 (1-inch) meatballs.

2. Brown half the meatballs in large skillet over medium heat, turning frequently and shaking skillet to keep meatballs round. Remove from skillet and drain meatballs on paper towels. Repeat with remaining meatballs.

3. Heat broth, water, tomatoes and pizza sauce in 5-quart Dutch oven over high heat until boiling. Add meatballs, remaining onion, kidney beans, cabbage and carrots. Bring to a boil. Reduce heat to medium-low; simmer, uncovered, 20 minutes. Add green beans; simmer, uncovered, 10 minutes more. *Makes 8 servings*

FRIULI-VENEZIA

Trieste

Friuli-Venezia

UNLIKE ANY OTHER IN ITALY, THIS REGION HAS BEEN SHAPED AS MUCH BY HISTORY AS GEOGRAPHY.

First-time visitors to the region of Friuli-Venezia Giulia might not be sure they are in Italy as plates of pasta are the exception rather than rule. Located in the northeastern corner of the country, this alpine region shares borders with Austria and Slovenia. Unlike any other region in Italy, it has been shaped as much by history as geography. From the fall of the Western Roman Empire to the twentieth century, Friuli-Venezia Giulia has been controlled off and on by Austria, Germany, Hungary and Yugoslavia. (In recent history, it was actually part of Austria until World War I.) This multicultural element is evident in almost every aspect of daily life, including language, customs and cuisine. Once two territories separated by the Isonzo River, the region's present boundary was imposed in 1954, formally joining the areas of Friuli and Venezia Giulia.

Regional culinary differences between Friuli and Venezia Giulia are driven by their distinct cultures. In the inland region of Friuli, cooking is tied to Venetian peasant roots and has a homespun character while the cuisine of Venezia Giulia is more refined and cosmopolitan, reflecting Austrian and Slavic influences. The basic dishes on Friulan tables include exquisite prosciutto from the town of San Daniele, pork sausage called musett served with turnip sauerkraut, cumin-scented bean and cabbage soup named jota, and the staple of polenta made with white and yellow corn. In Venezia Giulia where the seaside province and capital of Trieste resides, beef goulash, wursts, sauerkraut with horseradish sour cream, salted codfish, fish chowders, and strucolo or ricotta-cheese-filled strudel are the local specialties.

The region's eastern areas produce popular local wines, including the sweet dessert wine, Picolit, as well as some of Italy's best whites, such as Tocai Friulano, Pinot Grigio and Pinot Bianco. Central and western areas offer a wide variety of wines, although they are mainly known for their extensive production of Merlot. The limestone Carso hills near Trieste are noted for the red Refosco Istriano and white Malvasia Istriano.

Trieste, the capital of Friuli-Venezia Giulia, borders Slovenia. While it is one of the smallest provinces in Italy, it is also one of the country's largest ports, which plays an important role in the town's economy. Commerce-related activities, such as shipping and banking, are key there as are the metalworking, steel, paper, shipbuilding, pharmaceutical and foodstuff industries. The best-preserved Roman structure in Trieste is the Ricardo Arch, built in 33 B.C. Its basilica dates back to the fifth century and is dedicated to San Giusto, the town's patron. Trieste's diverse heritage of the Austrian Empire is reflected in significant Greek, Serbian and Lutheran churches. One of the largest Jewish synagogues in Europe also resides there.

Friuli-Venezia's eastern areas produce popular local wines, including the sweet dessert wine, Picolit, as well as some of Italy's best whites, such as Tocai Friulano, Pinot Grigio and Pinot Bianco. Central and western areas offer a wide variety of wines, although they are mainly known for their extensive production of Merlot.

Sausage Minestrone Soup

2 tablespoons olive oil
1 large onion, chopped
3 cloves garlic, minced
3 cups water
1 can (14$\frac{1}{2}$ ounces) stewed tomatoes, undrained
1 can (10$\frac{1}{2}$ ounces) kosher condensed beef or chicken broth
1 teaspoon dried basil leaves
1 teaspoon dried oregano leaves
$\frac{1}{4}$ teaspoon crushed red pepper
1 package (12 ounces) HEBREW NATIONAL® Beef Polish Sausage
$\frac{1}{2}$ cup small pasta such as ditalini or small bow ties
1 can (16 ounces) cannellini beans, drained

Heat oil in large saucepan over medium heat. Add onion and garlic; cook
8 minutes, stirring occasionally. Add water, tomatoes with liquid, broth, basil,
oregano and red pepper; bring to a boil.

Meanwhile, cut sausage crosswise into $\frac{1}{2}$-inch slices. Cut each slice into quarters.
Stir sausage and pasta into soup; simmer 15 minutes or until pasta is tender. Add
beans; cook until heated through.   *Makes 6 servings*

Sausage Minestrone Soup

Southern Italian Clam Chowder

2 slices bacon, diced
1 cup chopped onion
½ cup chopped peeled carrots
½ cup chopped celery
2 cans (14.5 ounces each) CONTADINA® Recipe Ready Diced Tomatoes, undrained
1 can (8 ounces) CONTADINA® Tomato Sauce
1 bottle (8-ounces) clam juice
½ teaspoon chopped fresh rosemary *or* ¼ teaspoon dried rosemary leaves, crushed
⅛ teaspoon ground black pepper
2 cans (6½ ounces each) chopped clams, undrained

1. Sauté bacon in large saucepan until crisp. Add onion, carrots and celery; sauté for 2 to 3 minutes or until vegetables are tender.

2. Stir in undrained tomatoes, tomato sauce, clam juice, rosemary and pepper. Bring to a boil.

3. Reduce heat to low; simmer, uncovered, for 15 minutes. Stir in clams and juice. Simmer for 5 minutes or until heated through.   *Makes 8 cups*

Prep Time: 8 minutes
Cook Time: 23 minutes

Hearty Fettuccine, Ham and Bean Soup

2 tablespoons olive oil
1 cup canned chunky Italian tomato sauce
1 cup diced cooked ham
2 cloves garlic, chopped
4 cups canned fat-free, low-salt chicken broth, divided
1 (15-ounce) can garbanzo beans, drained, divided
4 ounces fettuccine (broken in thirds), elbows or rotini
Parmesan cheese

Heat oil in saucepan over medium heat. Add tomato sauce, ham and garlic. Simmer 5 minutes. Add 3 cups broth; stir to blend. Purée remaining broth and 1 cup garbanzo beans in blender. Add to saucepan; add remaining garbanzo beans. Bring to a boil, reduce heat and simmer 10 minutes. Add pasta; cook until tender, about 10 minutes. Serve, passing Parmesan cheese separately.   *Makes 4 to 6 servings*

Favorite recipe from *North Dakota Wheat Commission*

Noodle Soup Parmigiano

3 cups water
$\frac{1}{2}$ pound boneless skinless chicken breast halves, cut into $\frac{1}{2}$-inch pieces
1 cup chopped fresh tomatoes or 1 can (8 ounces) whole peeled tomatoes, undrained and chopped
1 pouch LIPTON® Soup Secrets Noodle Soup Mix with Real Chicken Broth
$\frac{1}{2}$ teaspoon LAWRY'S® Garlic Powder with Parsley (optional)
$\frac{1}{2}$ cup shredded mozzarella cheese (about 2 ounces)
Grated Parmesan cheese (optional)

In medium saucepan, combine all ingredients except cheeses; bring to a boil. Reduce heat and simmer uncovered, stirring occasionally, 5 minutes or until chicken is done. To serve, spoon into bowls; sprinkle with cheeses.

Makes about 5 (1-cup) servings

Chickpea and Shrimp Soup

1 tablespoon olive or vegetable oil
1 cup diced onion
2 cloves garlic, minced
4 cans (10.5 ounces each) beef broth
1 can (14.5 ounces) CONTADINA® Recipe Ready Diced Tomatoes with Roasted Garlic, undrained
1 can (15 ounces) chickpeas or garbanzo beans, drained
1 can (6 ounces) CONTADINA® Italian Paste with Italian Seasonings
8 ounces small cooked shrimp
2 tablespoons chopped fresh Italian parsley *or* 2 teaspoons dried parsley flakes, crushed
1/2 teaspoon salt
1/4 teaspoon ground black pepper

1. Heat oil over medium-high heat in large saucepan. Add onion and garlic; sauté for 1 minute.

2. Stir in broth, undrained tomatoes, chickpeas and tomato paste. Bring to boil.

3. Reduce heat to low; simmer, uncovered, 10 minutes. Add shrimp, parsley, salt and pepper; simmer 3 minutes or until heated through. Stir before serving.

Makes 8 to 10 servings

Chickpea and Shrimp Soup

Hearty Pasta and Chick-Pea Chowder

6 ounces uncooked rotini pasta
2 tablespoons olive oil
³/₄ cup chopped onion
¹/₂ cup thinly sliced carrot
¹/₂ cup chopped celery
2 cloves garlic, minced
¹/₄ cup all-purpose flour
1¹/₂ teaspoons dried Italian seasoning
¹/₈ teaspoon red pepper flakes
¹/₈ teaspoon black pepper
2 cans (13³/₄ ounces each) chicken broth
1 can (19 ounces) chick-peas (garbanzo beans), rinsed and drained
1 can (14¹/₂ ounces) Italian-style stewed tomatoes, undrained
6 slices bacon

1. Cook rotini according to package directions. Rinse, drain and set aside.

2. Meanwhile, heat oil in 4-quart Dutch oven over medium-high heat until hot. Add onion, carrot, celery and garlic. Cook and stir over medium heat 5 to 6 minutes or until vegetables are crisp-tender.

3. Remove from heat. Stir in flour, Italian seasoning, red pepper flakes and black pepper until well blended. Gradually stir in broth. Return to heat and bring to a boil, stirring frequently. Boil, stirring constantly, 1 minute. Reduce heat to medium. Stir in cooked pasta, chick-peas and tomatoes. Cook 5 minutes or until heated through.

4. Meanwhile, place bacon between double layer of paper towels on paper plate. Microwave at HIGH 5 to 6 minutes or until bacon is crisp. Drain and crumble.

5. Sprinkle each serving with bacon and grated cheese. Serve immediately.

Makes 6 servings (about 7 cups)

Serving Suggestion: Top with grated Parmesan cheese and serve with crusty bread, salad greens tossed with Italian dressing, and fruit cobbler.

Prep and Cook Time: 30 minutes

Hearty Pasta and Chick-Pea Chowder

Cioppino

1 teaspoon olive oil
1 large onion, chopped
1 cup sliced celery, with celery tops
1 clove garlic, minced
4 cups water
1 fish flavor bouillon cube
1 tablespoon salt-free Italian herb seasoning
¼ pound cod or other boneless mild-flavored fish fillets
¼ pound small shrimp, peeled and deveined
¼ pound bay scallops
1 large tomato, chopped
¼ cup flaked crabmeat or crabmeat blend
1 can (10 ounces) baby clams, rinsed and drained (optional)
2 tablespoons fresh lemon juice

1. Heat olive oil in large saucepan over medium heat until hot. Add onion, celery and garlic. Cook and stir 5 minutes or until onion is soft. Add water, bouillon cube and Italian seasoning. Cover and bring to a boil over high heat.

2. Cut cod fillets into ½-inch pieces. Add cod, shrimp, scallops and tomato to saucepan. Reduce heat to medium-low; simmer 10 to 15 minutes or until seafood is opaque. Add crabmeat, clams and lemon juice. Heat through. Garnish with lemon wedges, if desired.

Makes 4 servings

Prep and Cook Time: 30 minutes

Tuscan Pasta and Beans

1 package (8 ounces) pasta, uncooked
2 to 3 teaspoons minced garlic
1 tablespoon vegetable oil
1 can (14³/₄ ounces) chicken broth
1 box (10 ounces) BIRDS EYE® frozen Chopped Spinach
1 can (15 ounces) white beans, drained
    Crushed red pepper flakes
    Grated Parmesan cheese

⇛ In large saucepan, cook pasta according to package directions; drain.

⇛ In large skillet, saute garlic in oil over medium-high heat until garlic is tender. Add broth and spinach; cook according to spinach package directions.

⇛ Stir in beans and pasta. Cook, uncovered, over medium-high heat until heated through.

⇛ Season with pepper flakes and cheese to taste.

Makes 4 servings

Variation: Add ¹/₂ pound Italian sausage, casings removed and sliced, with the garlic. Cook until sausage is browned. Continue as directed.

Serving Suggestion: Offer crusty Italian bread to soak up this flavorful broth.

Prep Time: 5 minutes
Cook Time: 20 minutes

Pesto & Tortellini Soup

1 package (9 ounces) fresh cheese tortellini
3 cans (about 14 ounces each) chicken broth
1 jar (7 ounces) roasted red peppers, drained and slivered
$^3/_4$ cup frozen green peas
3 to 4 cups fresh spinach, washed and stems removed
1 to 2 tablespoons pesto *or* $^1/_4$ cup grated Parmesan cheese

Cook tortellini according to package directions; drain. While pasta is cooking, bring broth to a boil over high heat in covered Dutch oven. Add cooked tortellini, peppers and peas; return broth to a boil. Reduce heat to medium and simmer 1 minute. Remove soup from heat; stir in spinach and pesto. *Makes 6 servings*

Prep and Cook Time: 14 minutes

Lentil Soup

1 tablespoon FILIPPO BERIO® Olive Oil
1 medium onion, diced
4 cups beef broth
1 cup dried lentils, rinsed and drained
$^1/_4$ cup tomato sauce
1 teaspoon dried Italian herb seasoning
    Salt and freshly ground black pepper

In large saucepan, heat olive oil over medium heat until hot. Add onion; cook and stir 5 minutes or until softened. Add beef broth; bring mixture to a boil. Stir in lentils, tomato sauce and Italian seasoning. Cover; reduce heat to low and simmer 45 minutes or until lentils are tender. Season to taste with salt and pepper. Serve hot.
Makes 6 servings

Pesto & Tortellini Soup

Roast Tomato-Basil Soup

  2 cans (28 ounces each) peeled whole tomatoes, drained, seeded and liquid reserved
2½ tablespoons packed dark brown sugar
  1 medium onion, finely chopped
  3 cups tomato liquid reserved from canned tomatoes
  3 cups chicken broth
  3 tablespoons tomato paste
¼ teaspoon ground allspice
  1 can (5 ounces) evaporated milk
¼ cup shredded fresh basil leaves (about 10 large)
    Salt and black pepper

SLOW COOKER DIRECTIONS

1. To roast tomatoes, preheat oven to 450°F. Line cookie sheet with foil; spray with nonstick cooking spray. Arrange tomatoes on foil in single layer. Sprinkle with brown sugar and top with onion. Bake about 25 to 30 minutes or until tomatoes look dry and light brown. Let tomatoes cool slightly; finely chop.

2. Place tomato mixture, 3 cups reserved liquid, chicken broth, tomato paste and allspice in slow cooker. Mix well.

3. Cover and cook on LOW 8 hours or on HIGH 4 hours.

4. Add evaporated milk and basil; season with salt and pepper. Cook 30 minutes or until hot. Garnish as desired.

Makes 6 servings

Additional cut fresh basil can be stored by placing stems in a glass of cool water with a plastic bag over the leaves for up to one week, replacing the water every other day.

Roast Tomato-Basil Soup

Hearty Minestrone Soup

2 cans (10¾ ounces each) condensed Italian tomato soup
3 cups water
3 cups cooked vegetables, such as zucchini, peas, corn or beans
2 cups cooked ditalini pasta
1⅓ cups *French's*® French Fried Onions

Combine soup and water in large saucepan. Add vegetables and pasta. Bring to a boil. Reduce heat. Cook until heated through, stirring often.

Place French Fried Onions in microwavable dish. Microwave on HIGH 1 minute or until onions are golden.

Ladle soup into individual bowls. Sprinkle with French Fried Onions.

Makes 6 servings

Prep Time: 10 minutes
Cook Time: 5 minutes

Quick & Easy Meatball Soup

1 package (15 to 18 ounces) frozen Italian sausage meatballs without sauce
2 cans (about 14 ounces each) Italian-style stewed tomatoes
2 cans (about 14 ounces each) beef broth
1 can (about 14 ounces) mixed vegetables
½ cup uncooked rotini or small macaroni
½ teaspoon dried oregano leaves

1. Thaw meatballs in microwave oven according to package directions.

2. Place remaining ingredients in large saucepan. Add meatballs. Bring to boil. Reduce heat; cover and simmer 15 minutes or until pasta is tender.

Makes 4 to 6 servings

Hearty Minestrone Soup

Cheesy Polenta with Zucchini Stew

$2^{1}/_{4}$ cups water, divided

1 cup stone-ground or regular yellow cornmeal

2 eggs

2 egg whites

$^{3}/_{4}$ cup reduced-fat sharp Cheddar cheese

1 jalapeño pepper,* minced

1 teaspoon margarine

$^{1}/_{2}$ teaspoon salt, divided

1 tablespoon olive oil

1 cup chopped onion

2 cups coarsely chopped, peeled eggplant

3 cloves minced garlic

3 cups chopped zucchini

1 cup chopped tomato

$^{1}/_{2}$ cup chopped yellow bell pepper

2 tablespoons minced fresh parsley

1 tablespoon minced fresh oregano

$^{1}/_{4}$ teaspoon minced fresh rosemary

$^{1}/_{4}$ teaspoon red pepper flakes

$^{1}/_{4}$ teaspoon ground pepper blend

*Jalapeño peppers can sting and irritate the skin; wear rubber gloves when handling peppers and do not touch eyes. Wash hands after handling.

1. Bring 2 cups water to a boil. Slowly add cornmeal, stirring constantly. Bring to a boil, stirring constantly, until mixture thickens. Lightly beat eggs and egg whites with remaining $^{1}/_{4}$ cup water. Add to cornmeal; cook and stir until bubbly. Remove from heat; stir in cheese, jalapeño pepper, margarine and $^{1}/_{4}$ teaspoon salt. Pour into 9-inch square baking pan. Cover and refrigerate several hours or until firm.

2. Heat olive oil in medium saucepan over medium heat until hot. Cook and stir onion, eggplant and garlic 5 minutes or until onion is transparent. Add zucchini, tomato, bell pepper, parsley, oregano, rosemary, remaining $^{1}/_{4}$ teaspoon salt, red pepper and pepper blend. Simmer, uncovered, 1 hour.

3. Spray large nonstick skillet with nonstick vegetable cooking spray. Heat skillet over medium heat until hot. Cut polenta in 6 rectangles. Cook over medium heat 8 minutes on each side or until crusty and lightly browned. Serve zucchini stew over polenta.   *Makes 6 servings*

Cheesy Polenta with Zucchini Stew

Minute Minestrone with Bays® Crostini

2 cans (15 ounces each) country vegetable soup
2 leaves romaine lettuce, chopped
2 slices prosciutto, chopped (optional)
½ medium zucchini, sliced
2 tablespoons grated Asiago cheese
1 cup leftover cooked pasta
   Olive oil
4 teaspoons prepared pesto
   Chopped Italian parsley
   Grated lemon peel
   BAYS® Crostini (recipe follows)

In a large saucepan, combine soup, romaine, prosciutto, zucchini and cheese. Heat over low heat, stirring occasionally, until hot and bubbly. In a skillet over low heat, toss pasta with oil to heat thoroughly. Ladle soup mixture into individual bowls. Stir one teaspoonful of prepared pesto into each serving. Spoon pasta on top; sprinkle with parsley and lemon peel. Serve with Bays® Crostini.   *Makes 4 servings*

Other additions: Leftover cooked sugar snap peas or green beans, cut up; pepperoni or chopped ham.

Bays® Crostini

2 tablespoons olive oil
1 teaspoon dry Italian salad dressing mix
4 BAYS® English muffins, split
2 tablespoons grated Asiago cheese
1 tablespoon grated Romano cheese

Combine oil and dressing mix; brush on both sides of muffin halves. Place on baking sheet. Bake in a preheated 325°F oven for 15 minutes. Remove from oven; sprinkle with cheeses. Serve warm or at room temperature.

Italian Tomato and Dandelion Greens Soup

2 cans (14½ ounces each) no-salt-added stewed tomatoes, undrained
1 cup loose-pack frozen zucchini, carrots, cauliflower, lima beans and
   Italian beans
1 cup low sodium tomato juice
1 cup water
1 tablespoon onion powder
1 teaspoon sugar
1 teaspoon dried oregano leaves, crushed
½ teaspoon dried basil leaves, crushed
¼ teaspoon garlic powder
¼ teaspoon black pepper
2 cups packed torn stemmed washed dandelion greens
¼ cup grated Parmesan cheese

Combine stewed tomatoes with juice, frozen vegetables, tomato juice, water, onion powder, sugar, oregano, basil, garlic powder and pepper in large saucepan. Bring to a boil over high heat. Reduce heat to low. Simmer, covered, 4 to 5 minutes or until vegetables are tender, stirring occasionally.

Stir in dandelion greens. Cook about 1 minute or until greens wilt. Top each serving with Parmesan cheese.   *Makes 4 servings*

The dandelion is much more than an unwanted weed in your backyard. It's been used for centuries to make dandelion wine and dandelion honey. Originally, the French called it dent de lion, *or lion's tooth, becasue of the tooth-like edge of the leaf. Available in many salad mixes, as well as fresh in produce aisles, dandelion's slightly tangy, bitter taste can add complexity to the simplest of salads.*

Classic Meatball Soup

2 pounds beef bones
3 ribs celery
2 carrots
1 medium onion, cut in half
1 bay leaf
6 cups cold water
1 egg
4 tablespoons chopped fresh parsley, divided
1 teaspoon salt, divided
$^1/_2$ teaspoon dried marjoram leaves, crushed
$^1/_4$ teaspoon black pepper, divided
$^1/_2$ cup soft fresh bread crumbs
$^1/_4$ cup grated Parmesan cheese
1 pound ground beef
1 can (14$^1/_2$ ounces) whole peeled tomatoes, undrained
$^1/_2$ cup uncooked rotini or small macaroni

For stock, rinse bones and combine with celery, carrots, onion and bay leaf in 6-quart stockpot. Add water. Bring to boil; reduce heat to low. Cover partially and simmer 1 hour, skimming foam occasionally. Preheat oven to 400°F. Spray 13×9-inch baking pan with nonstick cooking spray. Combine egg, 3 tablespoons parsley, $^1/_2$ teaspoon salt, marjoram and $^1/_8$ teaspoon pepper in medium bowl; whisk lightly. Stir in bread crumbs and cheese. Add beef; mix well. Place meat mixture on cutting board; pat evenly into 1-inch-thick square. With sharp knife, cut meat into 1-inch squares; shape each square into a ball. Place meatballs in prepared pan; bake 20 to 25 minutes until brown on all sides and cooked through, turning occasionally. Drain on paper towels.

Strain stock through sieve into medium bowl. Slice celery and carrots; reserve. Discard bones, onion and bay leaf. To degrease stock, let stand 5 minutes to allow fat to rise. Holding paper towel, quickly pull across surface only, allowing towel to absorb fat. Discard. Repeat with clean paper towels to remove all fat. Return stock to stockpot. Drain tomatoes, reserving juice. Chop tomatoes; add to stock with juice. Bring to a boil; boil 5 minutes. Stir in rotini, remaining $^1/_2$ teaspoon salt and $^1/_8$ teaspoon pepper. Cook 6 minutes, stirring occasionally. Add reserved vegetables and meatballs. Reduce heat to medium; cook 10 minutes until hot. Stir in remaining 1 tablespoon parsley. Season to taste. *Makes 4 to 6 servings*

Classic Meatball Soup

Primavera Tortellini en Brodo

2 cans (about 14 ounces each) reduced-sodium chicken broth
1 package (9 ounces) refrigerated fresh tortellini (cheese, chicken or sausage)
2 cups frozen mixed vegetables, such as broccoli, green beans, onions and red bell peppers
1 teaspoon dried basil leaves
  Dash hot pepper sauce or to taste
2 teaspoons cornstarch
1 tablespoon water
¼ cup grated Romano or Parmesan cheese

1. Pour broth into large deep skillet. Cover and bring to a boil over high heat. Add tortellini; reduce heat to medium-high. Cook, uncovered, until pasta is tender, stirring occasionally. (Check package directions for approximate timing.)

2. Transfer tortellini to medium bowl with slotted spoon; keep warm.

3. Add vegetables, basil and hot pepper sauce to broth; bring to a boil. Reduce heat to medium; simmer about 3 minutes or until vegetables are crisp-tender.

4. Blend cornstarch and water in small cup until smooth. Stir into broth mixture. Cook about 2 minutes or until liquid thickens slightly, stirring frequently. Return tortellini to skillet; heat through. Ladle into shallow soup bowls; sprinkle with cheese.

Makes 2 servings

Serving suggestion: Serve with salad and crusty Italian bread.

Prep and Cook Time: 20 minutes

Primavera Tortellini en Brodo

Summer Minestrone

Olive oil-flavored nonstick cooking spray
2 carrots, sliced
1 cup halved green beans
$^{1}/_{2}$ cup sliced celery
$^{1}/_{2}$ cup thinly sliced leek
2 cloves garlic, minced
1 tablespoon fresh sage *or* $^{1}/_{2}$ teaspoon dried sage leaves
1 tablespoon fresh oregano *or* $^{1}/_{2}$ teaspoon dried oregano leaves
3 cans (14 $^{1}/_{2}$ ounces each) fat-free reduced-sodium chicken broth
1 zucchini, halved lengthwise and cut into $^{1}/_{2}$-inch slices
1 cup quartered mushrooms
8 ounces cherry tomatoes, halved
$^{1}/_{4}$ cup minced fresh parsley
3 ounces uncooked small rotini
Salt and black pepper
8 teaspoons grated Parmesan cheese

1. Spray large saucepan with cooking spray. Heat over medium heat until hot. Add carrots, green beans, celery, leek, garlic, sage and oregano. Cook and stir 3 to 5 minutes. Add chicken broth; bring to a boil. Reduce heat and simmer about 5 minutes or until vegetables are just crisp-tender.

2. Add zucchini, mushrooms, tomatoes and parsley; bring to a boil. Stir in pasta. Reduce heat and simmer, uncovered, about 8 minutes or until pasta and vegetables are tender. Season to taste with salt and pepper. Ladle soup into bowls; sprinkle each with 1 teaspoon Parmesan cheese. *Makes 8 first-course servings (about 1 cup each)*

Summer Minestrone

Tuscan White Bean Soup

  6 ounces smoked bacon, diced
 10 cups chicken broth
  1 bag (16 ounces) dried great northern beans, rinsed
  1 can (14$\frac{1}{2}$ ounces) diced tomatoes, undrained
  1 large onion, chopped
  3 carrots, peeled and chopped
  4 cloves garlic, minced
  1 fresh rosemary sprig or 1 teaspoon dried rosemary
  1 teaspoon black pepper

SLOW COOKER DIRECTIONS

Cook bacon in medium skillet over medium-high heat until just cooked; drain and transfer to slow cooker. Add remaining ingredients. Cover and cook on LOW 8 hours or until beans are tender. Remove and discard rosemary sprig before serving.

Makes 8 to 10 servings

Place slices of toasted Italian bread in the bottom of individual soup bowls. Drizzle with olive oil. Pour soup over bread and serve.

Hearty Minestrone Gratiné

1 cup diced celery
1 cup diced zucchini
1 can (28 ounces) tomatoes with liquid, chopped
2 cups water
2 teaspoons sugar
1 teaspoon dried Italian herb seasoning
1 can (15 ounces) garbanzo beans, drained
4 (½-inch) slices French bread, toasted
1 cup (4 ounces) SARGENTO® Light Mozzarella Shredded Cheese
2 tablespoons SARGENTO® Fancy Parmesan Shredded Cheese
  Freshly chopped parsley

Spray large saucepan with nonstick cooking spray. Over medium heat, sauté celery and zucchini until tender. Add tomatoes, water, sugar and herb seasoning. Simmer, uncovered, 15 to 20 minutes. Add garbanzo beans and heat an additional 10 minutes. Meanwhile, heat broiler. Place toasted French bread on broiler pan. Top with Mozzarella cheese. Broil until cheese melts. Ladle soup into bowls and top with French bread. Sprinkle with Parmesan cheese and garnish with parsley.

Makes 4 servings

Chicken Tortellini Soup

1 can (49½ ounces) chicken broth
1 package PERDUE® SHORT CUTS® Fresh Italian Carved Chicken Breast
1 package (9 ounces) fresh pesto or cheese tortellini, or tortelloni
1 cup fresh spinach or arugula leaves, shredded
¼ to ½ cup grated Parmesan cheese

In large saucepan over medium-high heat, bring broth to a boil. Add chicken and tortellini; cook 6 to 8 minutes, until pasta is tender, reducing heat to keep a gentle boil. Just before serving, stir in fresh spinach. Ladle soup into bowls and sprinkle with Parmesan cheese.

Makes 4 servings

Prep Time: 5 minutes
Cook Time: 15 minutes

Ravioli Stew

1 tablespoon olive or vegetable oil
3 medium carrots, chopped
2 medium ribs celery, chopped
1 medium onion, chopped
1 jar (26 to 28 ounces) RAGÚ® Robusto!™ Pasta Sauce
1 can (14½ ounces) chicken broth
1 cup water
1 package (12 to 16 ounces) fresh or frozen mini ravioli, cooked and
    drained

1. In 6-quart saucepot, heat oil over medium-high heat and cook carrots, celery and onion, stirring occasionally, 8 minutes or until golden.

2. Stir in Ragú Pasta Sauce, broth and water. Bring to a boil over high heat. Reduce heat to low and simmer covered 15 minutes.

3. Just before serving, stir in hot ravioli and season, if desired, with salt and ground black pepper. Garnish, if desired, with fresh basil.   *Makes 6 servings*

Prep Time: 10 minutes
Cook Time: 30 minutes

Ravioli Stew

Tomato Pastina Soup

2 teaspoons olive oil
$^2/_3$ cup coarsely chopped green bell pepper
$^1/_2$ cup coarsely chopped onion
$^1/_2$ cup coarsely chopped cucumber
3 cloves garlic, minced
$1^1/_2$ pounds fresh tomatoes, coarsely chopped
1 can ($14^1/_2$ ounces) whole tomatoes, undrained
2 tablespoons balsamic vinegar
2 teaspoons ground cumin
1 teaspoon coriander seeds
$^1/_2$ teaspoon black pepper
$^1/_4$ teaspoon salt
1 ounce uncooked pastina
1 cup water

1. Heat oil in large saucepan over medium heat until hot. Add green pepper, onion, cucumber and garlic; cook and stir until pepper and onion are tender. Add fresh and canned tomatoes, vinegar, cumin, coriander, pepper and salt. Bring to boil over high heat. Reduce heat to low; simmer, covered, 15 minutes. Remove from heat; cool.

2. Place tomato mixture in food processor or blender; process in small batches until smooth. Return to saucepan. Bring to boil over high heat. Add pastina; cook 4 to 6 minutes or until pastina is tender. Stir in water; transfer to serving bowls.

Makes 6 ($^3/_4$-cup) servings

Tomato Pastina Soup

La Pasta

Pasta is synonymous with Italian food. While it is believed that Marco Polo brought noodles to Italy from the Orient, Italians can claim to have popularized as well as perfected them. Romans refined pasta and worked it into their daily cuisine. With an almost endless variety of possible shapes and sizes, pasta can be tailored to the needs of any specific dish. Long thin spaghetti for marinara, pockets for ravioli filling, or shells for a rich cream sauce. The flour- and egg-based dough, when cooked in boiling water, allows Italian cooks to minimize the amount of protein served for the main course to ensure that no one leaves the table hungry.

Ravioli with Creamy Spinach Sauce
(page 100)

Angel Hair with Roasted Red Pepper Sauce

1 package (16 ounces) BARILLA® Angel Hair
1 jar (12 ounces) roasted red peppers with juice, divided
1 tablespoon olive or vegetable oil
3 cloves garlic, minced
2 cups heavy cream
1½ teaspoons salt
1 teaspoon pepper
½ cup (2 ounces) grated Romano cheese, divided
3 tablespoons fresh basil leaves, cut into thin strips (optional)

1. Cook angel hair according to package directions; drain.

2. Meanwhile, chop ¼ cup roasted peppers; set aside. Purée remaining peppers and juice in food processor or blender.

3. Heat oil in large nonstick skillet. Add garlic; cook and stir 2 minutes over medium-low heat. Add pepper purée, cream, salt and pepper; cook over medium heat, stirring frequently, about 6 minutes or until hot and bubbly. Stir in ¼ cup cheese.

4. Combine hot drained angel hair with pepper mixture. Top with reserved chopped peppers, ¼ cup cheese and basil, if desired.   *Makes 6 to 8 servings*

To roast bell peppers, preheat the broiler. Place whole peppers on a foil-covered broiler pan 4 inches from the heat source. Broil 15 to 20 minutes until blackened on all sides, turning the peppers every 5 minutes with tongs. To loosen their skins, steam blackened peppers by placing them in a paper bag immediately after roasting. Close the bag and set it aside to cool for 15 to 20 minutes. The blackened skins will peal off easily.

*Angel Hair with Roasted
Red Pepper Sauce*

Rigatoni with Four Cheeses

3 cups milk
1 tablespoon chopped carrot
1 tablespoon chopped celery
1 tablespoon chopped onion
1 tablespoon fresh parsley sprigs
$1/4$ teaspoon black peppercorns
$1/4$ teaspoon hot pepper sauce
$1/2$ bay leaf
    Dash nutmeg
$1/4$ cup Wisconsin butter
$1/4$ cup flour
$1/2$ cup (2 ounces) grated Wisconsin Parmesan cheese
$1/4$ cup (1 ounce) grated Wisconsin Romano cheese
12 ounces rigatoni, cooked, drained
$1^{1}/2$ cups (6 ounces) shredded Wisconsin Cheddar cheese
$1^{1}/2$ cups (6 ounces) shredded Wisconsin Mozzarella cheese
$1/4$ teaspoon chili powder

In a 2-quart saucepan, combine milk, carrot, celery, onion, parsley, peppercorns, hot pepper sauce, bay leaf and nutmeg. Bring to boil. Reduce heat to low; simmer 10 minutes. Strain, reserving liquid. Melt butter in 2-quart saucepan over low heat. Blend in flour. Gradually add reserved liquid; cook, stirring constantly, until thickened. Remove from heat. Add Parmesan and Romano cheeses; stir until blended. Pour over pasta; toss well. Combine Cheddar and Mozzarella cheese. In buttered 2-quart casserole, layer $1/2$ of pasta mixture, Cheddar cheese mixture and remaining pasta mixture. Sprinkle with chili powder. Bake at 350°F for 25 minutes or until hot.

Makes 6 servings

Favorite recipe from *Wisconsin Milk Marketing Board*

Rigatoni with Four Cheeses

Cannelloni with Tomato-Eggplant Sauce

  1 package (10 ounces) fresh spinach
  1 cup fat-free ricotta cheese
  4 egg whites, beaten
  1/4 cup (1 ounce) grated Parmesan cheese
  2 tablespoons finely chopped fresh parsley
  1/2 teaspoon salt (optional)
  8 manicotti (about 4 ounces), cooked and cooled
    Tomato-Eggplant Sauce (recipe follows)
  1 cup (4 ounces) shredded reduced-fat mozzarella cheese

Preheat oven to 350°F. Wash spinach; do not pat dry. Place spinach in saucepan; cook, covered, over medium-high heat 3 to 5 minutes or until spinach is wilted. Cool slightly and drain; chop finely.

Combine ricotta cheese, spinach, egg whites, Parmesan cheese, parsley and salt in large bowl; mix well. Spoon mixture into manicotti shells; arrange in 13×9-inch baking pan. Spoon Tomato-Eggplant Sauce over manicotti; sprinkle with mozzarella cheese. Bake manicotti, uncovered, 25 to 30 minutes or until hot and bubbly.

Makes 4 servings (2 manicotti each)

Tomato-Eggplant Sauce

    Olive oil-flavored nonstick cooking spray
  1 small eggplant, coarsely chopped
  1/2 cup chopped onion
  2 cloves garlic, minced
  1/2 teaspoon dried tarragon leaves
  1/4 teaspoon dried thyme leaves
  1 can (16 ounces) no-salt-added whole tomatoes, undrained and coarsely
    chopped
    Salt and black pepper

Spray large skillet with cooking spray; heat over medium heat until hot. Add eggplant, onion, garlic, tarragon and thyme; cook and stir about 5 minutes or until vegetables are tender. Stir in tomatoes with juice; bring to a boil. Reduce heat and simmer, uncovered, 3 to 4 minutes. Season to taste with salt and pepper.

Makes about 2 1/2 cups

Cannelloni with Tomato-Eggplant Sauce

Ravioli with Creamy Spinach Sauce

1 package (24 ounces) frozen beef ravioli
1 box (10 ounces) BIRDS EYE® frozen Chopped Spinach
1 jar (14.5 ounces) alfredo pasta sauce*
¼ teaspoon ground nutmeg
1 cup chopped tomato or roasted red pepper

Or, substitute 1 packet (1.6 ounces) alfredo pasta sauce mix prepared according to package directions.

✒ In large saucepan, cook ravioli according to package directions; drain and set aside.

✒ Cook spinach according to package directions; place in strainer. Press excess water from spinach with back of spoon.

✒ In same saucepan, place spinach, alfredo sauce and nutmeg; cook over medium heat until heated through.

✒ Add ravioli and tomato; toss together. *Makes 4 servings*

Prep Time: 5 minutes
Cook Time: 20 minutes

Albacore Salad Puttanesca with Garlic Vinaigrette

2 cups cooked angel hair pasta, chilled
2 cups chopped peeled plum tomatoes
1 cup Garlic Vinaigrette Dressing (recipe page 101)
1 can (4¼ ounces) chopped* ripe olives, drained
1 (3-ounce) pouch of STARKIST® Premium Albacore Tuna
¼ cup chopped fresh basil leaves

If you prefer, the olives may be sliced rather than chopped.

In large bowl, combine chilled pasta, tomatoes, Garlic Vinaigrette Dressing and olives. Add tuna and basil leaves; toss. Serve immediately. *Makes 2 servings*

Garlic Vinaigrette Dressing

- ⅓ cup red wine vinegar
- 2 tablespoons lemon juice
- 1 to 2 cloves garlic, minced or pressed
- 1 teaspoon freshly ground black pepper
- Salt to taste
- 1 cup olive oil

In small bowl, whisk together vinegar, lemon juice, garlic, pepper and salt. Slowly add oil, whisking continuously, until well blended. Refrigerate leftover dressing.

Prep Time: 10 minutes

Fettuccine Aldana

- ¾ cup butter, divided
- 8 ounces fresh mushrooms, sliced
- ⅔ cup chopped green onions, including tops
- 2½ cups heavy cream, divided
- 6 ounces plain fettuccine, cooked and drained
- 6 ounces spinach fettuccine, cooked and drained
- 1½ cups (6 ounces) grated BELGIOIOSO® Romano Cheese, divided
- ¼ teaspoon ground nutmeg
- ⅓ pound prosciutto ham, julienned
- White pepper to taste

Melt ¼ cup butter in large skillet over medium-high heat. Add mushrooms and onions; cook and stir until tender. Remove from skillet; set aside. Add remaining ½ cup butter to skillet; heat until lightly browned. Add 1 cup cream; bring to a boil. Reduce heat to low; simmer until slightly thickened, about 5 minutes. Add pasta, 1 cup cream, 1 cup BelGioioso Romano Cheese and nutmeg; mix lightly. Combine remaining ½ cup cream and romano cheese with mushroom mixture and prosciutto. Pour over hot pasta mixture; toss lightly. Season with pepper to taste.

Makes 4 to 6 servings

Garden Farfalle

8 ounces BARILLA® Farfalle
2 tablespoons olive oil
1 cup sliced onion
4 ounces sliced portobello mushrooms
2 tablespoons chopped fresh garlic
1 cup white wine
3 tablespoons fresh thyme *or* 1 tablespoon dried thyme
2 cans (6 ounces each) light or white tuna packed in water, drained and chunked
4 cups frozen carrot-broccoli-cauliflower mix, steamed
Salt and pepper
1/2 cup grated Parmesan cheese

1. Cook farfalle according to package directions; drain.

2. Heat olive oil in large skillet over medium-high heat. Add onion, mushrooms and garlic; cook and stir 3 to 5 minutes. Add white wine and continue cooking 2 minutes. Add thyme, tuna and vegetables; mix gently.

3. Stir in hot drained farfalle and salt and pepper to taste; cook 3 to 4 minutes. Serve with cheese. *Makes 6 to 8 servings*

Garden Farfalle

Tuscan Pasta & Beans

2 tablespoons margarine or olive oil
2 cloves garlic, minced
$^{1}/_{2}$ cup milk
1 (4.8-ounce) package PASTA RONI® Parmesano
1 (15-ounce) can cannellini or Great Northern beans, rinsed and drained
1 medium tomato, chopped
$^{1}/_{3}$ cup sliced pitted kalamata or ripe olives
2 teaspoons chopped fresh rosemary *or* 1 teaspoon dried rosemary, crushed
$^{1}/_{2}$ cup crumbled feta cheese
$^{1}/_{2}$ cup croutons, coarsely chopped

1. In medium saucepan over medium-high heat, melt margarine. Add garlic; sauté 1 minute.

2. Add 1$^{1}/_{3}$ cups water and milk; bring to a boil. Slowly stir in pasta, beans, tomato, olives, rosemary and Special Seasonings; return to a boil. Reduce heat to medium-low. Gently boil uncovered, 5 to 6 minutes or until pasta is tender, stirring frequently.

3. Stir in cheese. Serve in bowls, topped with croutons.   *Makes 4 servings*

Tip: This dish is reminiscent of *pasta e fagioli,* a Tuscan soup made with pasta and white beans.

Prep Time: 5 minutes
Cook Time: 15 minutes

Classic Fettuccine Alfredo

³/₄ pound uncooked dry fettuccine
  6 tablespoons unsalted butter
²/₃ cup heavy or whipping cream
¹/₂ teaspoon salt
      Generous dash white pepper
      Generous dash ground nutmeg
  1 cup freshly grated Parmesan cheese (about 3 ounces)
  2 tablespoons chopped fresh parsley
      Fresh Italian parsley sprig for garnish

1. Cook fettuccine in large pot of boiling salted water 6 to 8 minutes just until al dente; remove from heat. Drain well; return to dry pot.

2. Place butter and cream in large, heavy skillet over medium-low heat. Cook and stir until butter melts and mixture bubbles. Cook and stir 2 minutes more. Stir in salt, pepper and nutmeg. Remove from heat. Gradually stir in cheese until thoroughly blended and smooth. Return briefly to heat to completely blend cheese if necessary. (Do not let sauce bubble or cheese will become lumpy and tough.)

3. Pour sauce over fettuccine in pot. Stir and toss with 2 forks over low heat 2 to 3 minutes until sauce is thickened and fettuccine is evenly coated. Sprinkle with chopped parsley. Garnish, if desired. Serve immediately. *Makes 4 servings*

Stuffed Shells Florentine

 1 cup (about 4 ounces) coarsely chopped mushrooms
 ½ cup chopped onion
 1 clove garlic, minced
 1 teaspoon Italian seasoning
 ¼ teaspoon ground black pepper
 1 tablespoon FLEISCHMANN'S® Original Margarine
 1 (16-ounce) container fat-free cottage cheese
 1 (10-ounce) package frozen chopped spinach, thawed and well drained
 ½ cup EGG BEATERS® Healthy Real Egg Product
 24 jumbo pasta shells, cooked in unsalted water and drained
 1 (15¼-ounce) jar reduced-sodium spaghetti sauce

In large skillet, over medium-high heat, sauté mushrooms, onion, garlic, Italian seasoning and pepper in margarine until tender. Remove from heat; stir in cottage cheese, spinach and Egg Beaters®. Spoon mixture into shells.

Spread ½ cup spaghetti sauce in bottom of 13×9×2-inch baking dish; arrange shells over sauce. Top with remaining sauce; cover. Bake at 350°F for 35 minutes or until hot.

Makes 7 servings

Prep Time: 30 minutes
Cook Time: 40 minutes

Stuffed Shells Florentine

Shrimp & Asparagus Fettuccine

12 ounces uncooked fettuccine
1 box (10 ounces) BIRDS EYE® frozen Asparagus Cuts*
1 tablespoon vegetable oil
1 package (16 ounces) frozen, uncooked cocktail-size shrimp
1 jar (12 ounces) prepared alfredo sauce
1 jar (4 ounces) sliced pimiento, drained

*Or, substitute 1½ cups Birds Eye® frozen Green Peas or Birds Eye® frozen Broccoli Cuts.

Cook pasta according to package directions, adding asparagus to water 8 minutes before pasta is done. Drain; keep warm.

Meanwhile, heat oil in large skillet over medium-high heat. Add shrimp; cover and cook 3 minutes or until shrimp turn pink. Drain excess liquid, leaving shrimp and about 2 tablespoons liquid in skillet. Reduce heat to low. Stir in alfredo sauce and pimiento. Cover; cook 5 minutes. *Do not boil.*

Toss fettuccine and asparagus with shrimp mixture.   *Makes about 4 servings*

Prep Time: 5 minutes
Cook Time: 20 minutes

Asparagus, once an anxiously awaited harbinger of spring, is now available year-round. However, springtime does bring a plentiful supply at reasonable prices. Whether it's grown wild, cultivated in plots, or carefully tended underground so shoots are completely void of color, asparagus never fails to excite its fans. Orignally called sparrowgrass, which suggests the name we know it by, asparagus is the tender shoot of a perennial vegetable from the lily family.

Shrimp & Asparagus Fettuccine

Angel Hair and Artichokes with Gorgonzola Butter

1 package (16 ounces) BARILLA® Angel Hair
½ cup (1 stick) butter
3 cloves garlic, minced
1 can (14½ ounces) artichokes, drained and quartered
1 can (14½ ounces) chicken broth
8 ounces Gorgonzola or other blue cheese, crumbled

1. Cook angel hair according to package directions; drain.

2. Meanwhile, melt butter in large nonstick skillet over low heat. Add garlic, artichokes, broth and cheese; cook about 5 minutes or until hot and bubbly, stirring frequently.

3. Combine hot drained angel hair with artichoke mixture; toss to coat.

Makes 6 to 8 servings

Spaghetti Bolognese

1 pound lean ground beef (or ¹/₂ pound ground beef and ¹/₂ pound bulk Italian sausage)
¹/₃ cup CRISCO® Oil,* divided
¹/₂ pound mushrooms, cleaned, stems trimmed, and sliced
1 large onion, peeled and diced
1 tablespoon jarred minced garlic (or 2 large garlic cloves, peeled and minced)
1 teaspoon salt, divided
1 teaspoon freshly ground black pepper, divided
1 can (14¹/₂ ounces) tomatoes packed in tomato purée
1 can (8 ounces) tomato paste
1 to 2 teaspoons Italian herb seasoning
³/₄ pound spaghetti
Freshly grated Parmesan cheese (optional)

*Use your favorite Crisco Oil product.

1. Heat large skillet on medium-high heat. Add beef. Break up lumps with fork. Cook 3 to 4 minutes, or until beef is no longer pink. Remove beef from pan with slotted spoon. Set aside. Discard drippings from pan.

2. Return skillet to medium-high heat. Add three tablespoons oil. Add mushrooms, onion and garlic. Sauté 2 minutes. Sprinkle with ¹/₂ teaspoon salt and ¹/₂ teaspoon pepper. Cook 3 minutes, or until onion is translucent.

3. Return beef to pan. Add tomatoes, tomato sauce, Italian seasoning and remaining ¹/₂ teaspoon salt and ¹/₂ teaspoon pepper. Bring to a boil. Reduce heat to low. Simmer sauce 30 to 40 minutes, or until it reaches desired consistency. Stir occasionally.

4. While sauce simmers, cook pasta in large pot of salted water with remaining oil, according to package directions. Drain. Top with sauce. Serve with cheese, if desired.

Makes 8 servings

Note: The sauce can be prepared up to 2 days in advance and refrigerated, tightly covered. Reheat it over low heat or in microwave oven; do not cook pasta until just before serving. For future dinners, you can make a double batch of this sauce and freeze half for up to three months.

EMILIA-ROMAGNA

Bologna

Emilia-Romagna

GEOGRAPHIC DIFFERENCES ASIDE, LOCALS IN EMILIA AND ROMAGNA KNOW HOW TO EAT WELL.

Framed by the Po River, Apennine Mountains and Adriatic Sea, Emilia-Romagna is one of the flattest and most fertile regions in Italy. As its double name suggests, Emilia (in the west) and Romagna (in the east) were once separate states. Formally unified in 1948, it is the transition region from Italy's alpine and Po areas to that of the peninsula. The capital city of Bologna is considered the gateway to Romagna, an area that is totally different in character from its neighbor to the west. Emilia is dominated by cities and plains with the prosperous provinces of Modena, Reggio nell'Emilia and Parma strung like pearls along the ancient Emilian Way while Romagna is defined by the

Apennines and Adriatic coast. These geographic differences are reflected in local dishes (Emilia is known for pork, Parmigiano-Reggiano and balsamic vinegar; Romagna for seafood, game and chestnuts). But the people of both areas share a common culinary outlook: they know how to eat well and serve the best of the harvest.

A leader in Italy's food production, Emilia-Romagna provides one fifth of the nation's wheat. Fruits and vegetables grow in profusion. Pork and beef are mainstays along with their by-products of butter and lard. The region's cuisine, marked by Old World excellence, generates many specialties associated with classic Italian cooking. Wheat harvests make pasta the king, ruling over rice and polenta. Pasta dough is made with fresh eggs and hand rolled into infinite shapes, including lasagna, ravioli, tortellini and cappelletti. Stuffed pastas dominate with fillings reflecting local ingredients. Sauces feature meat (ragù), cream and unsmoked bacon (pancetta). The provinces of Modena, Parma and Reggio nell'Emilia are known for balsamic vinegar, prosciutto and Parmigiano-Reggiano respectively, each adding its stellar essence to local dishes. Parmigiano-Reggiano, the most famous cheese worldwide, has been made for over 700 years and is so revered that it is one of the first foods given to babies. The capital city of Bologna, nicknamed la grassa (the fat), is home to a number of regional delights: ragù Bolognese (meat sauce); mortadella (pork sausage); costoletta alla Bolognese (veal cutlet stuffed with cheese and truffle); lasagne verdi (spinach noodles layered with ragù and béchamel sauces); tortellini in brodo (tortellini served in broth). On the Romagna coast, fish, eel and wild duck are used in pasta dishes, soups and stews. The area is also known for piadina, a round crisp focaccia bread filled with prosciutto, cheese or greens.

Although more well known for its food than wine, Emilia-Romagna does boast a few specialties. Emilia produces sparkling red, dry Lambrusco, the perfect foil for the region's rich dishes. In Romagna, robust red Sangiovese is a favorite with meat while dry, white Trebbiano or Albana is preferred with fish dishes.

Being one of Italy's most productive agricultural areas, it follows that Emilia-Romagna is also a center for food processing and packaging. The nation's largest cattle market is in Modena and the fishing industry accounts for one quarter of Italy's production. Other industries include automotive, chemical and clothing manufacturing. Tourism also ranks high in the economy. The region is the most popular vacation spot for Italians with Bologna and Romagna's coastal beach resorts the preferred destinations. Bologna's art and monument treasures are located in its many piazzas with the historic center revolving around Piazza Maggiore in the heart of the city. The Pinacoteca Nazionale gallery houses some of Bologna's most important artworks.

Lasagna Florentine

2 tablespoons BERTOLLI® Olive Oil
3 medium carrots, finely chopped
1 package (8 to 10 ounces) sliced mushrooms
1 medium onion, finely chopped
2 cloves garlic, finely chopped
1 jar (1 pound 10 ounces) RAGÚ® Robusto! Pasta Sauce
1 container (15 ounces) ricotta cheese
2 cups shredded mozzarella cheese, divided
1 box (10 ounces) frozen chopped spinach, thawed and squeezed dry
¼ cup grated Parmesan cheese
2 eggs
1 teaspoon salt
1 teaspoon dried Italian seasoning
16 lasagna noodles, cooked and drained

Preheat oven to 375°F. In 12-inch skillet, heat oil over medium heat and cook carrots, mushrooms, onion and garlic until carrots are almost tender, about 5 minutes. Stir in Ragú® Robusto! Pasta Sauce; heat through.

Meanwhile, in medium bowl, combine ricotta cheese, 1½ cups mozzarella cheese, spinach, Parmesan cheese, eggs, salt and Italian seasoning; set aside.

In 13×9-inch baking dish, evenly spread ½ cup sauce mixture. Arrange 4 lasagna noodles, lengthwise over sauce, overlapping edges slightly. Spread ⅓ of the ricotta mixture over noodles; repeat layers, ending with noodles. Top with remaining sauce and ½ cup mozzarella cheese. Cover with foil and bake 40 minutes. Remove foil and continue baking 10 minutes or until bubbling. *Makes 8 servings*

Lasagna Florentine

Angel Hair Al Fresco

³/₄ cup skim milk
1 tablespoon margarine or butter
1 package (4.8 ounces) PASTA RONI® Angel Hair Pasta with Herbs
1 can (6¹/₈ ounces) white tuna in water, drained, flaked *or* 1¹/₂ cups
   chopped cooked chicken
2 medium tomatoes, chopped
¹/₃ cup sliced green onions
¹/₄ cup dry white wine or water
¹/₄ cup slivered almonds, toasted (optional)
1 tablespoon chopped fresh basil *or* 1 teaspoon dried basil

1. In 3-quart saucepan, combine 1¹/₃ cups water, skim milk and margarine. Bring just to a boil.

2. Stir in pasta, Special Seasonings, tuna, tomatoes, onions, wine, almonds and basil. Return to a boil; reduce heat to medium.

3. Boil, uncovered, stirring frequently, 6 to 8 minutes. Sauce will be thin, but will thicken upon standing.

4. Let stand 3 minutes or until desired consistency. Stir before serving.

Makes 4 servings

Lasagna Verdi

SAUCE

- 1/4 cup (1/2 stick) butter *or* margarine
- 3 tablespoons flour
- 1 (14 1/2-ounce) can chicken broth
- 1 cup milk
- 2 tablespoons TABASCO® brand Green Pepper Sauce

FILLING

- 2 tablespoons vegetable oil
- 1 pound ground turkey
- 1 medium onion, diced
- 1 tablespoon TABASCO® brand Green Pepper Sauce
- 1 teaspoon salt
- 1 (15-ounce) container ricotta cheese
- 1 egg
- 2 tablespoons chopped fresh parsley
- 12 no-boil lasagna noodles
- 1 (8-ounce) package mozzarella cheese, shredded
- 1/4 cup grated Parmesan cheese

For sauce, melt butter in 2-quart saucepan over medium heat; stir in flour until well blended and smooth. Gradually add chicken broth, milk and 2 tablespoons TABASCO® Green Pepper Sauce; cook over high heat until mixture boils and thickens, stirring frequently.

Preheat oven to 375°F. For filling, heat oil in 12-inch skillet over medium-high heat. Add turkey and onion; cook until meat is well browned, stirring frequently. Stir in 1 tablespoon TABASCO® Green Pepper Sauce and salt. Mix ricotta cheese, egg and parsley in small bowl.

Grease 12×8-inch baking dish. Spread 1 cup sauce on bottom of baking dish. Layer 3 lasagna noodles in baking dish. Spread 1/3 of turkey mixture, 1/3 of ricotta mixture, 1/4 of mozzarella cheese and 1/4 of remaining sauce over noodles. Repeat layers two more times. Top with remaining 3 lasagna noodles. Spread remaining sauce over noodles; sprinkle with remaining mozzarella cheese and Parmesan cheese.

Cover with foil and bake 30 minutes. Uncover and bake 10 minutes or until lasagna is hot and bubbly. Let stand 5 minutes before serving.   *Makes 8 servings*

Fusilli with Fresh Red & Yellow Tomato Sauce

- ½ cup (1 stick) I CAN'T BELIEVE IT'S NOT BUTTER!® Spread
- 1 medium onion, chopped
- 2 cloves garlic, finely chopped (optional)
- 1½ pounds red and/or yellow cherry tomatoes, halved
- ⅓ cup chopped fresh basil leaves
- 1 box (16 ounces) fusilli (long curly pasta) or linguine, cooked and drained
  Grated Parmesan cheese

In 12-inch nonstick skillet, melt I Can't Believe It's Not Butter! Spread over medium heat and cook onion, stirring occasionally, 2 minutes or until softened. Stir in garlic and tomatoes and cook, stirring occasionally, 5 minutes or until tomatoes soften but do not lose their shape and sauce thickens slightly. Stir in basil and season, if desired, with salt and ground black pepper. In large serving bowl, toss sauce with hot fusilli and sprinkle with cheese. *Makes 4 servings*

Penne Puttanesca

- 3 tablespoons olive or vegetable oil
- 2 cloves garlic, finely chopped
- 1 jar (26 to 28 ounces) RAGÚ® Old World Style® Pasta Sauce
- ¼ cup chopped pitted oil-cured olives
- 1 tablespoon capers, rinsed
- ½ teaspoon dried oregano leaves, crushed
- ¼ teaspoon crushed red pepper flakes
- 1 box (16 ounces) penne pasta, cooked, drained

In 12-inch skillet, heat oil over low heat and cook garlic 30 seconds. Stir in remaining ingredients except pasta. Simmer uncovered, stirring occasionally, 15 minutes. Serve sauce over hot pasta. *Makes 8 servings*

Fusilli with Fresh Red & Yellow Tomato Sauce

Manicotti Marinara

1 package (8 ounces) BARILLA® Manicotti *or* ½ package (8 ounces)
   BARILLA® Jumbo Shells
2 jars (26 ounces each) BARILLA® Marinara Pasta Sauce, divided
2 eggs
1 container (15 ounces) ricotta cheese
4 cups (16 ounces) shredded mozzarella cheese, divided
1 cup (4 ounces) grated Parmesan cheese, divided
¼ cup chopped fresh parsley *or* 1 tablespoon dried parsley

1. Cook manicotti shells according to package directions; drain. Preheat oven to
350°F. Spray bottom of 15×10×2-inch glass baking dish with nonstick cooking
spray. Spread 1 jar marinara sauce over bottom of baking dish.

2. Beat eggs in large bowl. Stir in ricotta, 3 cups mozzarella, ¾ cup Parmesan and
parsley. Fill each cooked shell with ricotta mixture. Arrange filled shells in baking
dish over sauce. Top with second jar of marinara sauce, remaining 1 cup mozzarella
and ¼ cup Parmesan.

3. Cover with foil and bake about 45 minutes or until bubbly. Uncover and
continue baking about 5 minutes or until cheese is melted. Let stand 5 minutes
before serving. *Makes 6 servings*

Note: One package (10 ounces) frozen chopped spinach, thawed and well drained,
may be added to the ricotta mixture.

Manicotti Marinara

Portofino Primavera

1 pound dry pasta
2 tablespoons olive oil
1 small onion, chopped
1 large clove garlic, minced
1 can (14.5 ounces) CONTADINA® Recipe Ready Diced Tomatoes,
    undrained
1 can (6 ounces) CONTADINA® Tomato Paste
1 cup chicken broth or water
1 cup quartered sliced zucchini
½ cup sliced pitted ripe olives, drained
2 tablespoons capers
½ teaspoon salt

1. Cook pasta according to package directions; drain and keep warm.

2. Heat oil in medium saucepan. Add onion and garlic; sauté for 1 minute.

3. Add undrained tomatoes, tomato paste, broth, zucchini, olives, capers and salt.

4. Bring to a boil. Reduce heat to low; simmer, uncovered, for 15 to 20 minutes or until heated through. Serve over pasta. *Makes 8 servings*

Prep Time: 6 minutes
Cook Time: 22 minutes

Primavera can be loosely translated as "spring-like." In food terms it typically refers to the use of fresh vegetables.

Portofino Primavera

Pasta with Spinach and Ricotta

8 ounces uncooked tri-colored rotini
1 box (10 ounces) frozen chopped spinach, thawed and drained
2 teaspoons bottled minced garlic
1 cup fat-free or part-skim ricotta cheese
3 tablespoons grated Parmesan cheese, divided

1. Cook pasta according to package directions; drain.

2. While pasta is cooking, coat skillet with nonstick cooking spray; heat over medium-low heat. Add spinach and garlic; cook and stir 5 minutes. Stir in ricotta cheese, half of Parmesan cheese and 1/2 cup water; season with salt and pepper to taste.

3. Add pasta to skillet; stir until well blended. Sprinkle with remaining Parmesan cheese.

Makes 4 servings

Note: For a special touch, garnish with fresh basil leaves.

Prep and Cook Time: 24 minutes

Fettuccine alla Carbonara

3/4 pound uncooked fettuccine or spaghetti

4 ounces pancetta (Italian bacon) or lean American bacon, cut into 1/2-inch-wide strips

3 cloves garlic, cut into halves

1/4 cup dry white wine

1/3 cup heavy or whipping cream

1 egg

1 egg yolk

2/3 cup freshly grated Parmesan cheese, divided

Generous dash white pepper

Fresh oregano leaves for garnish

1. Cook fettuccine according to package directions just until al dente; remove from heat. Drain well; return to dry pot.

2. Cook and stir pancetta and garlic in large skillet over medium-low heat 4 minutes or until pancetta is light brown. Reserve 2 tablespoons drippings in skillet with pancetta. Discard garlic and remaining drippings.

3. Add wine to pancetta mixture; cook over medium heat 3 minutes or until wine is almost evaporated. Stir in cream; cook and stir 2 minutes. Remove from heat.

4. Whisk egg and egg yolk in top of double boiler. Place top of double boiler over simmering water, adjusting heat to maintain simmer. Whisk 1/3 cup cheese and pepper into egg mixture; cook and stir until sauce thickens slightly.

5. Pour pancetta mixture over fettuccine in pot; toss to coat. Heat over medium-low heat until heated through. Stir in egg mixture. Toss to coat evenly. Remove from heat. Serve with remaining 1/3 cup cheese. Garnish, if desired.　　*Makes 4 servings*

Rigatoni Con Ricotta

1 package (16 ounces) BARILLA® Rigatoni
2 eggs
1 container (15 ounces) ricotta cheese
¾ cup (3 ounces) grated Parmesan cheese
1 tablespoon dried parsley
2 jars (26 ounces each) BARILLA® Lasagna & Casserole Sauce or
    Marinara Pasta Sauce, divided
3 cups (12 ounces) shredded mozzarella cheese, divided

1. Preheat oven to 375°F. Spray 13×9×2-inch baking pan with nonstick cooking spray. Cook rigatoni according to package directions; drain.

2. Beat eggs in small bowl. Stir in ricotta, Parmesan and parsley.

3. To assemble casserole, spread 2 cups lasagna sauce to cover bottom of pan. Place half of cooked rigatoni over sauce; top with half of ricotta mixture, dropped by spoonfuls. Layer with 1 cup mozzarella, 2 cups lasagna sauce, remaining rigatoni and ricotta mixture. Top with 1 cup mozzarella, remaining lasagna sauce and remaining 1 cup mozzarella.

4. Cover with foil and bake 60 to 70 minutes or until bubbly. Uncover and continue cooking about 5 minutes or until cheese is melted. Let stand 15 minutes before serving. *Makes 12 servings*

Rigatoni Con Ricotta

Caponata-Style Fettuccine

  1 medium eggplant (about 1 pound), cut into $^1/_4$-inch slices
1$^1/_4$ teaspoons salt, divided
  $^1/_3$ cup olive oil, divided
  1 small green bell pepper, cored, membrane removed and sliced
  1 medium onion, coarsely chopped
  2 cloves garlic, minced
  3 medium tomatoes (about 1 pound), seeded and coarsely chopped
  $^1/_3$ cup *each* raisins and halved pitted green olives
  $^1/_4$ cup balsamic or red wine vinegar
  2 tablespoons capers (optional)
  $^1/_4$ teaspoon *each* ground cinnamon and black pepper
 10 ounces fresh spinach fettuccine, cooked, drained and kept warm
    Fresh basil leaves for garnish

1. Place eggplant slices in a single layer on baking sheet or jelly-roll pan; brush both sides lightly with some of oil. Bake 10 minutes or until lightly browned on bottoms. Turn slices over; bake about 5 minutes more or until tops are lightly browned and slices are softened; set aside.

2. Place oven rack at lowest position. Preheat oven to 450°F. Place eggplant slices in large colander over bowl; sprinkle with 1 teaspoon salt. Drain 1 hour.

3. Heat remaining oil in large skillet over medium-high heat. Add bell pepper to skillet; cook and stir 5 minutes or until pepper turns bright green. Remove pepper; set aside.

4. Add onion and garlic to same skillet; cook and stir 5 minutes or until onion is soft. Add tomatoes, raisins, olives, vinegar, capers, cinnamon, black pepper and remaining $^1/_4$ teaspoon salt. Cook until most of the liquid has evaporated.

5. Cut roasted eggplant slices into quarters; add to tomato mixture. Add bell pepper; cook until heated through. Serve over fettuccine. Garnish, if desired.

Makes 4 main-dish or 8 appetizer servings

Note: Caponata is a Sicilian eggplant dish that may be served cold as an appetizer or on lettuce as a salad. Here it is made into a vegetarian sauce for pasta.

Caponata-Style Fettuccine

Greens and Gemelli

8 ounces BARILLA® Gemelli
1 tablespoon olive oil
1 bag (10 ounces) spinach, washed and trimmed
1 jar (26 ounces) BARILLA® Green & Black Olive Pasta Sauce
8 ounces Italian sausage, cooked and crumbled
¼ cup crumbled feta cheese

1. Cook gemelli according to package directions; drain.

2. Meanwhile, add olive oil to large skillet. Add spinach; cook and stir 1 minute over medium-high heat.

3. Reduce heat; stir in pasta sauce and cooked sausage. Cook 5 minutes.

4. Pour sauce over hot drained gemelli; sprinkle with cheese.

Makes 4 to 6 servings

Tagliatelle with Creamy Sauce

7 to 8 ounces tagliatelle pasta, cooked, drained
1 cup GALBANI® Mascarpone cheese
1 package (10 ounces) frozen peas, cooked, drained
2 ounces (½ cup) finely chopped GALBANI® Prosciutto di Parma
1½ cups (6 ounces) shredded mozzarella cheese
Butter or margarine

Layer ½ of the tagliatelle in buttered 9×9-inch baking dish. Spoon ½ of the Mascarpone onto tagliatelle. Sprinkle with ½ of the peas and ½ of the prosciutto. Top with ½ of the mozzarella. Repeat layers. Dot with butter. Bake in preheated 350°F oven 20 minutes or until heated through. *Makes 4 to 6 servings*

Greens and Gemelli

Il Prima

The Italian art of eating represents a focus on family that no other culinary tradition can match. A typical Italian lunch splits the day with a two- to four-hour break. This midday meal is the largest of the day, featuring Il Primo, or the main course, and is frequently followed by a brief nap, or siesta. People come home from work and children from school for this important daily event. No fine china or silverware for this occasion, just the joy of one's family. In this fast-paced day and age, we should all try having a long lunch with friends and family, and of course a little siesta.

Chicken Cacciatore (page 154)

Steak San Marino

- ¼ cup all-purpose flour
- 1 teaspoon salt
- ½ teaspoon black pepper
- 4 beef round steaks, about 1 inch thick
- 1 can (8 ounces) tomato sauce
- 2 carrots, chopped
- ½ onion, chopped
- 1 rib celery, chopped
- 1 teaspoon dried Italian seasoning
- ½ teaspoon Worcestershire sauce
- 1 bay leaf
- Hot cooked rice

SLOW COOKER DIRECTIONS

Combine flour, salt and pepper in small bowl. Dredge each steak in flour mixture. Place in slow cooker. Combine tomato sauce, carrots, onion, celery, Italian seasoning, Worcestershire sauce and bay leaf in small bowl; pour into slow cooker. Cover and cook on LOW 8 to 10 hours or on HIGH 4 to 5 hours.

Remove and discard bay leaf. Serve steaks and sauce over rice. *Makes 4 servings*

Steak San Marino

Peasant Risotto

1 teaspoon olive oil
3 ounces chopped low fat turkey-ham
2 cloves garlic, minced
1 cup arborio or white short-grain rice
1 can (15 ounces) Great Northern beans, rinsed and drained
$^1/_4$ cup chopped green onions with tops
$^1/_2$ teaspoon dried sage leaves
2 cans (14 ounces each) $^1/_3$-less-salt chicken broth, heated
1$^1/_2$ cups Swiss chard, rinsed, stems removed and shredded
$^1/_4$ cup freshly grated Parmesan cheese

1. Heat oil in large saucepan over medium heat. Add turkey-ham and garlic. Cook and stir until garlic is browned. Add rice, beans, green onions and sage; blend well. Add warm broth; bring to a boil. Reduce heat to low. Cook about 25 minutes or until rice is creamy, stirring frequently.

2. Add Swiss chard and Parmesan; mix well. Cover; remove from heat. Let stand covered 2 minutes or until Swiss chard is wilted. Serve immediately.

Makes 4 servings

Peasant Risotto

Orzo Risotto with Shrimp and Vegetables

   Nonstick cooking spray
1 zucchini, sliced and halved
2 teaspoons grated lemon peel
1 cup sliced mushrooms
1/2 cup chopped onion
2 cloves garlic
3/4 teaspoon dried sage leaves
1/4 to 1/2 teaspoon dried thyme leaves
1 1/4 cups uncooked orzo
2 cans (14 1/2 ounces each) fat-free reduced-sodium chicken broth
8 ounces shrimp, peeled and deveined
3/4 cup frozen peas, thawed
1/4 cup grated Parmesan cheese
   Salt and black pepper

1. Spray large saucepan with cooking spray. Heat over medium heat until hot. Add zucchini and lemon peel; cook and stir 2 to 3 minutes or until zucchini is tender. Remove from saucepan; set aside.

2. Add mushrooms, onion, garlic, sage and thyme to saucepan; cook and stir 2 to 3 minutes or until onion is tender. Stir in orzo; cook and stir until browned.

3. Bring chicken broth to a boil in medium saucepan. Add broth to orzo mixture, 1/2 cup at a time, stirring constantly until broth is absorbed before adding next 1/2 cup. Continue cooking 10 to 15 minutes or until orzo is tender.

4. Stir shrimp and peas into orzo mixture during last half of cooking time; stir in zucchini mixture last 2 to 3 minutes of cooking time. Stir in cheese; season to taste with salt and pepper.   *Makes 4 main-dish servings*

*Orzo Risotto
with Shrimp and Vegetables*

Como
• Milan
LOMBARDY

Lombardy

FROM THE SNOWY ALPS BORDERING SWITZERLAND TO THE LUSH PLAINS OF THE PO VALLEY, LOMBARDY'S DIVERSE GEOGRAPHY IS REFLECTED IN A VARIED CUISINE.

Named after the Lombards, a barbaric German tribe that invaded northern Italy in the sixth century, Lombardy is the richest and most densely populated region in Italy. From the snowy Alps bordering Switzerland to the lush plains of the Po Valley, Lombardy's diverse geography is reflected in a varied cuisine. A history of wars and revolutions with the French, Spanish and Austrians resulted in a culinary heritage that ranges from sophisticated dishes fit for royalty (veal with tuna sauce) to simple peasant dishes relying on the daily harvest (polenta and minestrone).

While Lombardian specialties vary from province to province, there are recurring food themes that unite the region: risotto's popularity over pasta and polenta; the use of butter, cream and lard over olive oil; a steady consumption of meats (beef, veal, pork) and poultry (duck, goose and turkey); and notable cheeses from every province. Every area has its own rendition of risotto, flavored with local ingredients. The most famous, risotto alla milanese from Milan, is tinted golden with saffron. In Monza the dish is made with sausage, in Lomellina with frogs' legs and in Como perch is used.

Cheese-making is a highly organized industry in Lombardy that was started in the twelfth century by French monks who raised dairy and beef cattle. Made mainly from cows' milk, the list reads like a who's who of cheeses. There are blue-veined Gorgonzola, buttery Bel Paese, creamy mascarpone and Parmesan-like grana padano to name just a few.

Lombardy is not a major wine region, but several areas do produce fine local varieties. South of the Po River hearty reds, such as Barbacarlo and Buttafuoco, as well as traditional whites, Pinot Grigio and Riesling, are produced. Further north near Lake Como, red Valtellina Superiore wines are made from the Nebbiolo grape and aged for at least two years. And the widely acclaimed Franciacorta spumante, both white and rosé, are from the Brescia area.

Milan is the capital of Lombardy and Italy's most important industrial, commercial and financial center. Generating sixty percent of the national income, it is headquarters to the advertising, banking, publishing, design and fashion industries. Thousands of factories in the area produce chemicals, appliances, textiles and transportation equipment. Today most Milanese are not native to the region as jobs attract laborers from throughout Italy. As a result, Milan has become a cultural mosaic, fusing a new collective identity. Since the city is also Italy's gastronomic capital, this fusion is sure to affect culinary traditions over time. In addition to risotto, classic Milanese dishes include ossobuco (braised veal shanks) served with gremolada (minced parsley, lemon and garlic); costoletta alla milanese (breaded, butter-fried veal chops); busecca (tripe, vegetable and salami soup); and panettone (sweet, fruit-studded Christmas yeast bread).

The artistic treasures of Milan along with the alpine lake and mountain resorts draw tourists to Lombardy year-round. The famous gilt statue of the "Madonnina" stands as the symbol of Milan. Leonardo da Vinci's "The Last Supper" hangs in the monastery adjoining the fifteenth century church of Santa Maria delle Grazie, and performances are still held at the neoclassic La Scala Theater. In the north, Lake Como offers spectacular alpine views, beautiful gardens and the picturesque villages of Bellagio and Tremezzo.

Polenta with Pasta Sauce & Vegetables

  1 can (about 14 ounces) reduced-sodium chicken broth
1 1/2 cups water
  1 cup yellow cornmeal
  2 teaspoons olive oil
 12 ounces assorted cut vegetables, such as broccoli florets, bell peppers, red
       onions, zucchini squash and julienned carrots
  2 teaspoons fresh or bottled minced garlic
  2 cups prepared tomato-basil pasta sauce
 1/2 cup grated Asiago cheese
 1/4 cup chopped fresh basil (optional)

1. To prepare polenta, whisk together chicken broth, water and cornmeal in large microwavable bowl. Cover with waxed paper; microwave at HIGH 5 minutes. Whisk well and microwave at HIGH 4 to 5 minutes more or until polenta is very thick. Whisk again; cover and keep warm.

2. Meanwhile, heat oil in a large deep nonstick skillet over medium heat. Add vegetables and garlic; cook and stir 5 minutes. Add pasta sauce; reduce heat, cover and simmer 5 to 8 minutes or until vegetables are tender.

3. Spoon polenta onto serving plates; top with pasta sauce mixture. Sprinkle with cheese and basil, if desired.   *Makes 4 servings*

Prep Time: 5 minutes
Cook Time: 15 minutes

Polenta with Pasta Sauce & Vegetables

Chicken Breasts with Polenta

4 cups defatted low-sodium chicken broth
1 cup yellow cornmeal
$^1/_2$ teaspoon garlic powder
$^1/_2$ teaspoon dried Italian seasoning
$^1/_4$ teaspoon salt
$^1/_4$ teaspoon black pepper
8 skinless chicken breast halves (3 pounds)
  Nonstick cooking spray
  Fresh spinach leaves, steamed (optional)
  Tuscan Tomato Sauce (recipe page 146)

1. In large nonstick saucepan, heat chicken broth to a boil; slowly stir in cornmeal. Reduce heat to low; cook, stirring frequently, 15 to 20 minutes or until mixture is very thick and pulls away from side of pan. (Mixture may be lumpy.) Pour polenta into greased 9×5-inch loaf pan. Cool; refrigerate 2 to 3 hours or until firm.

2. Heat oven to 350°F. Combine garlic powder, Italian seasoning, salt and pepper in small bowl; rub on chicken. Arrange chicken in single layer in 13×9-inch baking pan. Bake, uncovered, about 45 minutes or until chicken is no longer pink in center and juices run clear.

3. Remove polenta from pan; transfer to cutting board. Cut polenta crosswise into 16 slices. Cut slices into triangles, if desired. Spray large nonstick skillet with cooking spray; heat over medium heat until hot. Cook polenta about 4 minutes per side or until lightly browned.

4. Place spinach leaves, if desired, on serving plates. Arrange polenta slices and chicken over spinach; top with Tuscan Tomato Sauce.   *Makes 8 servings*

Chicken Breast with Polenta

Tuscan Tomato Sauce

    Nonstick cooking spray
1/2 cup chopped onion
  2 cloves garlic, minced
  8 plum tomatoes, coarsely chopped
  1 can (8 ounces) tomato sauce
  2 teaspoons dried basil leaves
  2 teaspoons dried oregano leaves
  2 teaspoons dried rosemary
1/2 teaspoon black pepper

1. Spray medium nonstick saucepan with cooking spray; heat over medium heat until hot. Add onion and garlic; cook and stir about 5 minutes or until tender.

2. Stir in tomatoes, tomato sauce, basil, oregano, rosemary and pepper; heat to a boil. Reduce heat to low and simmer, uncovered, about 6 minutes or until desired consistency, stirring occasionally.

Makes about 3 cups

*R*ice Napoli

  2 bags SUCCESS® Brown Rice
  1 tablespoon reduced-calorie margarine
  1 large green bell pepper, chopped
  1 clove garlic, minced
  1 can (14 1/2 ounces) Italian-style tomatoes, drained
  1 envelope (.7 ounce) Italian dressing mix
  1 cup (4 ounces) shredded Mozzarella cheese
1/2 cup sliced pitted ripe olives (optional)

Prepare rice according to package directions.

Melt margarine in large skillet over medium-high heat. Add green pepper and garlic; cook and stir until pepper is crisp-tender. Add tomatoes and dressing. Bring to a boil. Reduce heat to low; simmer 10 minutes, stirring occasionally. Stir in rice. Top with cheese. Sprinkle with olives, if desired.

Makes 8 servings

Grilled Pork and Potatoes Vesuvio

1 center-cut boneless pork loin roast (1 1/2 pounds), well trimmed and cut into 1-inch cubes
1/2 cup dry white wine
2 tablespoons olive oil
4 cloves garlic, minced and divided
1 1/2 to 2 pounds small red potatoes (about 1 1/2 inches in diameter), scrubbed
6 lemon wedges
Salt (optional)
Pepper (optional)
1/4 cup chopped fresh Italian or curly leaf parsley
1 teaspoon finely grated lemon peel

1. Place pork in large resealable plastic food storage bag. Combine wine, oil and 3 cloves garlic in small bowl; pour over pork.

2. Place potatoes in single layer in microwavable dish. Pierce each potato with tip of sharp knife. Microwave at HIGH (100% power) 6 to 7 minutes or until almost tender when pierced with fork. (Or, place potatoes in large saucepan. Cover with cold water. Bring to a boil over high heat. Simmer about 12 minutes or until almost tender when pierced with fork.) Immediately rinse with cold water; drain. Add to pork in bag. Seal bag tightly, turning to coat. Marinate in refrigerator at least 2 hours or up to 8 hours, turning occasionally.

3. Prepare barbecue grill for direct cooking.

4. Meanwhile, drain pork mixture; discard marinade. Alternately thread about 3 pork cubes and 2 potatoes onto each of 6 skewers. Place 1 lemon wedge on end of each skewer. Season pork and potaotes to taste with salt and pepper.

5. Place skewers on grid. Grill skewers, on covered grill, over medium coals 14 to 16 minutes or until pork is juicy and no longer pink in center and potatoes are tender, turning halfway through grilling time.

6. Remove skewers from grill. Combine parsley, lemon peel and remaining minced clove garlic in small bowl. Sprinkle over pork and potatoes. To serve, squeeze lemon wedges over pork and potatoes. *Makes 6 servings*

Sicilian Caponata

5 tablespoons olive or vegetable oil, divided
8 cups (1 1/2 pounds) cubed unpeeled eggplant
2 1/2 cups onion slices
1 cup chopped celery
1 can (14.5 ounces) CONTADINA® Recipe Ready Diced Tomatoes with
  Roasted Garlic, undrained
1/3 cup chopped pitted ripe olives, drained
1/4 cup balsamic or red wine vinegar
2 tablespoons capers
2 teaspoons granulated sugar
1/2 teaspoon salt
  Dash of ground black pepper

1. Heat 3 tablespoons oil in medium skillet. Add eggplant; sauté 6 minutes. Remove eggplant from skillet.

2. Heat remaining oil in same skillet. Add onion and celery; sauté 5 minutes or until vegetables are tender.

3. Stir in undrained tomatoes and eggplant; cover. Simmer 15 minutes or until eggplant is tender.

4. Stir in olives, vinegar, capers, sugar, salt and pepper; simmer, uncovered, 5 minutes, stirring occasionally. Serve with toasted bread slices, if desired.

Makes 4 1/2 cups

Choose firm, smooth-skinned eggplants that feel heavy for their size. Avoid those with blemishes or soft spots. The stems should be bright green and look fresh. Usually the smaller the eggplants the sweeter and more tender it is.

Sicilian Caponata

Pork Medallions with Marsala

1 pound pork tenderloin, cut into ½-inch slices
  All-purpose flour
2 tablespoons olive oil
1 clove garlic, minced
½ cup sweet Marsala wine
2 tablespoons chopped fresh parsley

1. Lightly dust pork with flour. Heat oil in large skillet over medium-high heat until hot. Add pork slices; cook 3 minutes per side or until browned. Remove from pan. Reduce heat to medium.

2. Add garlic to skillet; cook and stir 1 minute. Add wine and pork; cook 3 minutes or until pork is barely pink in center. Remove pork from skillet. Stir in parsley. Simmer wine mixture until slightly thickened, 2 to 3 minutes. Serve over pork.

Makes 4 servings

Tip: For a special touch, sprinkle with chopped red onion just before serving.

Note: Marsala is rich smoky-flavored wine imported from the Mediterranean island of Sicily. This sweet varietal is served with dessert or used for cooking. Dry Marsala is served as a before-dinner drink.

Prep and Cook Time: 20 minutes

Pork Medallions with Marsala

Roasted Herb & Garlic Tenderloin

1   well-trimmed beef tenderloin roast (3 to 4 pounds)
1   tablespoon black peppercorns
2   tablespoons chopped fresh basil *or* 2 teaspoons dried basil leaves
4½   teaspoons chopped fresh thyme *or* 1½ teaspoons dried thyme leaves
1   tablespoon chopped fresh rosemary *or* 1 teaspoon dried rosemary
1   tablespoon minced garlic
    Salt and black pepper (optional)

1. Preheat oven to 425°F. To hold shape of roast, tie roast with cotton string at 1½-inch intervals. Place roast on meat rack in shallow roasting pan.

2. Place peppercorns in small heavy resealable plastic food storage bag. Squeeze out excess air; seal bag tightly. Pound peppercorns with flat side of meat mallet or rolling pin until peppercorns are cracked.

3. Combine cracked peppercorns, basil, thyme, rosemary and garlic in small bowl; rub over top surface of roast.

4. Roast 40 to 50 minutes for medium or until internal temperatures reaches 145°F when tested with meat thermometer inserted into the thickest part of roast.

5. Transfer roast to cutting board; cover with foil. Let stand 10 to 15 minutes before carving. Internal temperature will continue to rise 5 to 10°F during stand time. Remove and discard string. To serve, carve crosswise into ½-inch-thick slices with large carving knife. Season with salt and pepper.   *Makes 10 to 12 servings*

Roasted Herb & Garlic Tenderloin

Chicken Cacciatore

8 ounces dry noodles
1 can (15 ounces) chunky Italian-style tomato sauce
1 cup chopped green bell pepper
1 cup sliced onion
1 cup sliced mushrooms
4 boneless skinless chicken breast halves (1 pound)

1. Cook noodles according to package directions; drain.

2. While noodles are cooking, combine tomato sauce, bell pepper, onion and mushrooms in microwavable dish. Cover loosely with plastic wrap or waxed paper; microwave at HIGH 6 to 8 minutes, stirring halfway through cooking time.

3. While sauce mixture is cooking, coat large skillet with nonstick cooking spray and heat over medium-high heat. Cook chicken breasts 3 to 4 minutes per side or until lightly browned.

4. Add sauce mixture to skillet with salt and pepper to taste. Reduce heat to medium and simmer 12 to 15 minutes. Serve over noodles.   *Makes 4 servings*

Prep and Cook Time: 30 minutes

Gnocchi with BelGioioso Gorgonzola

2 pounds potatoes
2⅓ cups flour
1 egg
  Salt to taste
1 cup BELGIOIOSO® Gorgonzola
1 tablespoon water
  Black pepper to taste

Boil and peel potatoes; mash. Coat potatoes with flour, egg and salt; mix by hand until dough is soft and compact. With floured hands, make small potato rolls (almost like dumplings). Drop into boiling water to cook. Meanwhile, cut BelGioioso Gorgonzola into cubes; melt in pan over low heat. Add water and pepper. Toss cooked gnocchi with Gorgonzola sauce; serve.   *Makes 6 servings*

Leek Frittata

3 leeks
4 eggs
1 large potato, cooked and mashed (about $^1/_2$ cup)
$^1/_2$ cup grated Romano cheese
1 tablespoon FILIPPO BERIO® Olive Oil
$^1/_2$ teaspoon salt
$^1/_2$ teaspoon dried Italian herb seasoning

Preheat oven to 375°F. Grease bottom and side of 1-quart casserole dish or 8-inch round cake pan with olive oil. Cut off root ends and tops of leeks. Split leeks; wash thoroughly and drain. Thinly slice white and pale green parts to measure 2 cups. Steam leeks 8 to 10 minutes or until tender. In large bowl, beat eggs with electric mixer at medium speed until foamy. Stir in leeks, potato, Romano cheese, olive oil, salt and Italian seasoning. Pour into prepared dish. Bake 30 to 40 minutes or until top is golden brown.   *Makes 8 servings*

Fresco Marinated Chicken

1 envelope LIPTON® RECIPE SECRETS® Savory Herb with Garlic
   Soup Mix*
$^1/_3$ cup water
$^1/_4$ cup olive or vegetable oil
1 teaspoon lemon juice or vinegar
4 boneless, skinless chicken breast halves (about $1^1/_4$ pounds)

Also terrific with LIPTON® RECIPE SECRETS® Golden Onion Soup Mix.

1. For marinade, blend all ingredients except chicken.

2. In shallow baking dish or plastic bag, pour $^1/_2$ cup of the marinade over chicken. Cover, or close bag, and marinate in refrigerator, turning occasionally, up to 3 hours. Refrigerate remaining marinade.

3. Remove chicken, discarding marinade. Grill or broil chicken, turning once and brushing with refrigerated marinade until chicken is no longer pink in center.
                      Makes 4 servings

Zucchini Mushroom Frittata

1½ cups EGG BEATERS® Healthy Real Egg Product
½ cup (2 ounces) shredded reduced-fat Swiss cheese
¼ cup fat-free (skim) milk
½ teaspoon garlic powder
¼ teaspoon seasoned pepper
    Nonstick cooking spray
1 medium zucchini, shredded (1 cup)
1 medium tomato, chopped
1 (4-ounce) can sliced mushrooms, drained
    Tomato slices and fresh basil leaves, for garnish

In medium bowl, combine Egg Beaters®, cheese, milk, garlic powder and seasoned pepper; set aside.

Spray 10-inch ovenproof nonstick skillet lightly with nonstick cooking spray. Over medium-high heat, sauté zucchini, tomato and mushrooms in skillet until tender. Pour egg mixture into skillet, stirring well. Cover; cook over low heat for 15 minutes or until cooked on bottom and almost set on top. Remove lid and place skillet under broiler for 2 to 3 minutes or until desired doneness. Slide onto serving platter; cut into wedges to serve. Garnish with tomato slices and basil.

Makes 6 servings

Prep Time: 20 minutes
Cook Time: 20 minutes

Zucchini Mushroom Frittata

Turkey Scaloppine

1 pound turkey cutlets or 4 boneless, skinless chicken breast halves (about
    1 pound), pounded to $^1/_8$-inch thick
2 tablespoons all-purpose flour
1$^1/_2$ teaspoons LAWRY'S® Seasoned Salt, divided
1 teaspoon LAWRY'S® Lemon Pepper
3 tablespoons olive oil, divided
1 medium-sized green bell pepper, cut into strips
1 cup sliced butternut squash or zucchini
$^1/_2$ cup sliced fresh mushrooms
1 teaspoon cornstarch
$^1/_2$ teaspoon LAWRY'S® Garlic Powder with Parsley
$^1/_4$ cup dry white wine
$^1/_3$ cup chicken broth
1 tablespoon plus 1$^1/_2$ teaspoons lemon juice

In large resealable plastic food storage bag, combine flour, $^3/_4$ teaspoon Seasoned
Salt and Lemon Pepper. Add turkey, a few pieces at a time, to plastic bag; seal bag.
Shake until well coated. In large skillet, heat 2 tablespoons oil. Add turkey and
cook over medium-high heat about 5 minutes on each side or until no longer pink
in center. Remove from skillet; keep warm. In same skillet, heat remaining
1 tablespoon oil. Add bell pepper, squash and mushrooms and cook over medium-
high heat until bell peppers are crisp-tender. Reduce heat to low. In small bowl,
combine cornstarch, Garlic Powder with Parsley and remaining $^3/_4$ teaspoon
Seasoned Salt; mix well. Stir in combined wine, broth and lemon juice. Add to
skillet. Bring just to a boil over medium-high heat, stirring constantly. Simmer
1 minute. Garnish, if desired. *Makes 4 servings*

Serving Suggestion: On platter, layer vegetables, turkey or chicken and top
with sauce.

Turkey Scaloppine

Florentine Strata

8 ounces BARILLA® Spaghetti or Linguine

1 jar (26 ounces) BARILLA® Roasted Garlic and Onion Pasta Sauce, divided

1 package (12 ounces) frozen spinach soufflé, thawed

2 cups (8 ounces) shredded mozzarella cheese, divided

¼ cup (1 ounce) grated Parmesan cheese, divided

1. Cook spaghetti according to package directions until partially done but still firm, 5 to 8 minutes. Drain.

2. Meanwhile, coat microwave-safe 13×9×2-inch baking dish with nonstick cooking spray. Pour 1½ cups pasta sauce into baking dish; top with half of drained spaghetti, half of spinach soufflé, 1 cup mozzarella cheese and 2 tablespoons Parmesan. Repeat layers of spaghetti, pasta sauce, spinach soufflé and cheeses.

3. Cover with plastic wrap and microwave on HIGH, turning every 4 minutes, until strata is bubbly and cheese is melted, 8 to 10 minutes. Let stand 3 minutes before serving.

Makes 8 servings

Tip: When preparing pasta that will be used in a casserole, it's important to reduce the suggested cooking time on the package by about one third. The pasta will continue to cook and absorb liquid while the casserole is cooking.

Florentine Strata

Classic Veal Florentine

6 ounces fresh spinach, chopped
6 tablespoons butter or margarine, divided
2 cloves garlic, minced
1 can (14½ ounces) whole peeled tomatoes, undrained
¼ cup dry white wine
¼ cup water
1 tablespoon tomato paste
½ teaspoon sugar
¾ teaspoon salt, divided
¼ teaspoon black pepper, divided
¼ cup all-purpose flour
4 veal cutlets, cut ⅜ inch thick (about 4 ounces each)
1 tablespoon olive oil
1 cup (4 ounces) mozzarella cheese, shredded
Homemade Angel Hair Pasta (recipe page 163, optional)

1. Place spinach in large saucepan over medium heat. Cover and steam 4 minutes or until tender, stirring occasionally. Add 2 tablespoons butter; cook and stir until butter is absorbed. Remove from pan; set aside.

2. To make tomato sauce, heat 2 tablespoons butter in medium saucepan over medium heat until melted and bubbly. Add garlic; cook and stir 30 seconds. Press tomatoes with juice through sieve into garlic mixture; discard seeds. Add wine, water, tomato paste, sugar, ½ teaspoon salt and ⅛ teaspoon pepper to tomato mixture. Bring to a boil; reduce heat to low. Simmer, uncovered, 10 minutes, stirring occasionally. Remove from heat; set aside.

3. Mix flour, remaining ¼ teaspoon salt and ⅛ teaspoon pepper in small resealable plastic food storage bag. Pound veal with meat mallet to ¼-inch thickness. Pat dry with paper towels. Shake veal, 1 cutlet at a time, in seasoned flour to coat evenly.

4. Heat oil and remaining 2 tablespoons butter in large skillet over medium heat until bubbly. Add veal to skillet; cook 2 to 3 minutes per side until light brown. Remove from heat. Spoon off excess fat. Top veal with reserved spinach, then cheese.

5. Pour reserved tomato mixture into skillet, lifting edges of veal to let sauce flow under. Cook over low heat until bubbly. Cover and simmer 8 minutes or until heated through. Serve with pasta. Garnish as desired. *Makes 4 servings*

Homemade Angel Hair Pasta

  2 cups plus 2 tablespoons all-purpose flour
$^1/_4$ teaspoon salt
  3 eggs
  1 tablespoon milk
  1 teaspoon olive oil
$^1/_2$ cup freshly grated Parmesan cheese (optional)
    Fresh marjoram sprigs for garnish

1. Place flour, salt, eggs, milk and oil in food processor; process until dough forms. Shape into ball.

2. Place dough on lightly floured surface; flatten slightly. Cut dough into 4 pieces. Wrap 3 dough pieces in plastic wrap; set aside.

3. To knead dough by pasta machine,* set rollers of pasta machine at widest setting (position 1). Feed unwrapped dough piece through flat rollers by turning handle. (Dough may crumble slightly at first but will hold together after two to three rollings.)

4. Lightly flour dough strip; fold strip into thirds. Feed through rollers again. Continue process 7 to 10 times until dough is smooth and elastic.

5. To roll out dough by machine, reduce setting to position 3. Feed dough strip through rollers. Without folding strip into thirds, repeat on positions 5 and 6. Let dough stand 5 to 10 minutes until slightly dry.

6. Attach handle to angel hair pasta roller and feed dough through, catching angel hair pasta with free hand as it emerges.** Repeat kneading and rolling with reserved dough pieces.

7. Cook angel hair pasta in large pot of boiling salted water 1 to 2 minutes just until al dente; remove from heat. Drain well; divide angel hair pasta into 2 large bowls.   *Makes 4 to 6 servings*

*Follow manufacturer's directions for appropriate method of rolling pasta if position settings are different.

**Angel hair pasta can be dried and stored at this point. Hang pasta strips over pasta rack or clean broom handle covered with plastic wrap and propped between two chairs. (Or, twirl pasta into nests and place on clean kitchen towel.) Dry at least 3 hours; store in airtight container at room temperature up to 4 days. To serve, cook angel hair pasta in large pot of boiling salted water 3 to 4 minutes just until al dente. Drain well; proceed as directed in step 8.

Beefy Calzones

  1 pound ground beef
¼ cup finely chopped onion
¼ cup finely chopped green bell pepper
  2 cloves garlic, minced
  1 (15-ounce) can tomato sauce
½ cup A.1.® THICK & HEARTY Steak Sauce
  1 teaspoon Italian seasoning
  2 (11-ounce) packages refrigerated pizza crust dough
  2 cups shredded mozzarella cheese (8 ounces)

In large skillet, over medium-high heat, cook beef, onion, pepper and garlic until beef is no longer pink, stirring to break up meat; drain. Keep warm.

In small skillet, over medium-high heat, heat tomato sauce, steak sauce and Italian seasoning to a boil. Reduce heat to low; simmer 5 minutes or until slightly thickened. Stir 1 cup tomato sauce mixture into beef mixture; set aside. Keep remaining tomato sauce mixture warm.

Unroll pizza dough from 1 package; divide into 4 equal pieces. Roll each piece into 6-inch square; spoon ⅓ cup reserved beef mixture onto center of each square. Top with ¼ cup cheese. Fold dough over to form triangle. Press edges together, sealing well with tines of fork. Place on lightly greased baking sheets. Repeat with remaining dough, filling and cheese to make a total of 8 calzones. Bake at 400°F 20 minutes or until golden brown. Serve with warm sauce. Garnish as desired.

Makes 8 servings

Beefy Calzones

Chicken Vesuvio

1 whole chicken (about 3¾ pounds)
¼ cup olive oil
3 tablespoons lemon juice
4 cloves garlic, minced
3 large baking potatoes
    Salt and lemon pepper

Preheat oven to 375°F. Place chicken, breast side down, on rack in large shallow roasting pan. Combine olive oil, lemon juice and garlic; brush half of oil mixture over chicken. Set aside remaining oil mixture. Roast chicken, uncovered, 30 minutes.

Meanwhile, peel potatoes; cut lengthwise into quarters. Turn chicken, breast side up. Arrange potatoes around chicken in roasting pan. Brush chicken and potatoes with remaining oil mixture; sprinkle with salt and lemon pepper seasoning to taste. Roast chicken and potatoes, basting occasionally with pan juices, 50 minutes or until meat thermometer inserted into thickest part of chicken thigh, not touching bone, registers 180°F and potatoes are tender.   *Makes 4 to 6 servings*

When thawing a whole frozen chicken, transfer it from the freezer to the refrigerator and allow three to four hours per pound to defrost. Or, for quicker thawing, chicken can be immersed (wrapped in water-tight packaging) in cold water, changing the water frequently so the chicken remains cold. Frozen chicken should be cooked as soon as fully thawed. Chicken can also be thawed in the microwave, following manufacturer's directions; be careful that edges do not begin to cook before chicken is completely thawed. Never thaw chicken at rooom temperature.

Chicken Vesuvio

Saltimbocca

4 boneless thin veal slices cut from the leg, or thinly sliced veal cutlets
    (about 1 ¼ pounds)
1 tablespoon FILIPPO BERIO® Olive Oil
1 clove garlic, cut into halves
4 slices prosciutto, cut into halves
8 fresh sage leaves*
½ cup beef broth
5 tablespoons Marsala wine or medium sherry
¼ cup half-and-half
    Freshly ground black pepper

*Omit sage if fresh is unavailable. Do not substitute dried sage leaves.

Pound veal between 2 pieces waxed paper with flat side of meat mallet or rolling pin until very thin. Cut each piece in half to make 8 small pieces. In large skillet, heat olive oil with garlic over medium heat until hot. Add veal; cook until brown, turning occasionally. Top each piece with slice of prosciutto and sage leaf. Add beef broth and Marsala. Cover; reduce heat to low and simmer 5 minutes or until veal is cooked through and tender. Transfer veal to warm serving platter; keep warm. Add half-and-half to mixture in skillet; simmer 5 to 8 minutes, stirring occasionally, until liquid is reduced and thickened, scraping bottom of skillet to loosen browned bits. Remove garlic. Spoon sauce over veal. Season to taste with pepper.

Makes 4 servings

Saltimbocca

Osso Buco

    3 pounds veal shanks (about 4 shanks)
$^3/_4$ teaspoon salt, divided
$^1/_2$ teaspoon black pepper
$^1/_2$ cup all-purpose flour
    2 tablespoons olive oil
    1 cup finely chopped carrot
    1 cup chopped onion
    1 cup finely chopped celery
    2 cloves garlic, minced
$^1/_2$ cup dry white wine
    1 can ($14^1/_2$ ounces) diced tomatoes, undrained
    1 cup beef broth
    1 tablespoon chopped fresh basil or rosemary leaves
    1 bay leaf
       Parmesan Gremolata (recipe follows)
    1 package (about $5^1/_2$ ounces) risotto (optional)

1. Season veal shanks with $^1/_2$ teaspoon salt and pepper. Place flour in shallow bowl; dredge veal shanks, one at a time, in flour, shaking off excess.

2. Heat oil in large ovenproof Dutch oven over medium-high heat until hot. Brown veal shanks 20 minutes, turning $^1/_4$ turn every 5 minutes and holding with tongs to brown all edges. Remove to plate.

3. Preheat oven to 350°F. Add carrot, onion, celery and garlic to Dutch oven; cook 5 minutes or until vegetables are soft. To deglaze Dutch oven, pour wine over carrot mixture. Cook over medium-high heat 2 to 3 minutes, stirring to scrape up any browned bits. Add tomatoes with juice, broth, basil, bay leaf and remaining $^1/_4$ teaspoon salt to Dutch oven; bring to boil. Return veal shanks to Dutch oven. Cover; bake 2 hours.

4. Prepare Parmesan Gremolata and risotto. Remove bay leaf; discard. Remove veal shanks to individual serving bowls; spoon vegetable mixture over each serving. Sprinkle with Parmesan Gremolata. Serve with risotto.   *Makes 4 to 6 servings*

Parmesan Gremolata: Finely grate peel of 1 lemon removing only yellow portion, not white pith. Combine peel, $^1/_3$ cup freshly grated Parmesan cheese, $^1/_4$ cup chopped fresh parsley and 1 clove garlic in small bowl. Cover; refrigerate. Makes about $^1/_3$ cup.

Osso Buco

— 170 —

Tuscan Turkey Cutlets

1 pound turkey cutlets
³/₄ teaspoon salt, divided
³/₄ teaspoon black pepper, divided
1 tablespoon olive oil, divided
2 cups coarsely chopped onion
1 cup coarsely chopped carrot
3 to 4 cloves garlic, minced
¹/₂ teaspoon dried oregano
¹/₂ teaspoon dried thyme
1 (10-ounce) bag fresh spinach leaves, stems removed
1 (14¹/₂-ounce) can diced tomatoes, undrained
1 (19-ounce) can cannellini beans, drained and rinsed
¹/₄ cup Parmesan cheese, divided

1. Place cutlets on cutting board and sprinkle with ¹/₄ teaspoon salt and ¹/₄ teaspoon pepper. Slice cutlets into ¹/₂-inch strips.

2. In 12-inch or larger non-stick skillet over medium-high heat, sauté turkey strips in 1¹/₂ teaspoons oil, 4 to 5 minutes or until no longer pink (165°F). Remove from skillet; set aside.

3. Add remaining 1¹/₂ teaspoons oil to skillet. Sauté onion, carrot, garlic, oregano and thyme 5 minutes or until vegetables are tender. Gradually add spinach and stir an additional 2 minutes or until spinach is wilted, but not quite done. Add tomatoes and remaining ¹/₂ teaspoon salt and ¹/₂ teaspoon pepper; cook 2 minutes.

4. Stir in turkey strips and beans. Cook until heated through.

5. Serve topped with Parmesan cheese.   *Makes 4 servings*

Serving Suggestion: Serve over orzo, noodles or a whole grain such as quinoa.

Favorite recipe from *National Turkey Federation*

Asiago and Spinach Rigatoni

    3   cups boiling water
    4   ounces sun-dried tomatoes, not packed in oil (about 2 cups)
   12   ounces rigatoni pasta, uncooked
    2   tablespoons extra-virgin olive oil
    2   cloves garlic, crushed
        Salt and black pepper to taste
    1   10-ounce bag fresh spinach, rinsed, spun dry and torn
   3/4 cup BELGIOIOSO® Asiago, grated
   1/2 cup BELGIOIOSO® Parmesan, grated

Combine boiling water and sun-dried tomatoes in medium bowl; let stand
30 minutes. Drain, reserving water. Chop tomatoes and set aside.

Return water to large pot, adding additional 3 cups water; Bring to a boil. Add pasta
and cook until al dente. Drain and set aside. Meanwhile, combine tomatoes, oil,
garlic, salt and pepper in large bowl. Add pasta and spinach; toss gently. Sprinkle
with BelGioioso Asiago and BelGioioso Parmesan; serve.   *Makes 8 servings*

Chicken di Napolitano

    1   tablespoon olive oil
    2   boneless, skinless chicken breasts (about 8 ounces)
    1   can (14 1/2 ounces) diced tomatoes, undrained
 1 1/4 cups water
    1   box UNCLE BEN'S® COUNTRY INN® Rice Pilaf
   1/4 cup chopped fresh basil *or* 1 1/2 teaspoons dried basil leaves

1. Heat oil in large skillet. Add chicken; cook over medium-high heat 8 to
10 minutes or until lightly browned on both sides.

2. Add tomatoes, water, rice and contents of seasoning packet. Bring to a boil.
Cover; reduce heat and simmer 15 to 18 minutes or until chicken is no longer pink
in center and liquid is absorbed.

3. Stir in basil. Slice chicken and serve over rice.   *Makes 2 servings*

La Casseruola

With dishes like lasagna, baked ziti, strata, manicotti and stuffed shells, it might seem that Italians invented casserole cooking. However, no one actually knows for sure where the first casseroles were prepared. The first known publication of a casserole recipe was in England, circa 1705. The word "casserole" has origins in the ancient Greek and Roman languages and refers to both the finished dish as well as the vessel in which it was cooked. Regardless, one thing is certain: Casseroles are popular in America us well as in Italy because they make meal preparation easier, can often utilize leftover foods, and, of course, they taste delicious.

Ravioli with Homemade Tomato Sauce (page 188)

Artichoke-Olive Chicken Bake

1½ cups uncooked rotini
1 tablespoon olive oil
1 medium onion, chopped
½ green bell pepper, chopped
2 cups shredded cooked chicken
1 can (14½ ounces) diced tomatoes with Italian-style herbs, undrained
1 can (14 ounces) artichoke hearts, drained and quartered
1 can (6 ounces) sliced black olives, drained
1 teaspoon dried Italian seasoning
2 cups (8 ounces) shredded mozzarella cheese

Preheat oven to 350°F. Spray 2-quart casserole with nonstick cooking spray.

Cook pasta according to package directions until al dente. Drain and set aside.

Meanwhile, heat oil in large deep skillet over medium heat until hot. Add onion and pepper; cook and stir 1 minute. Add chicken, tomatoes with juice, pasta, artichokes, olives and Italian seasoning; mix until combined.

Place half of chicken mixture in prepared dish; sprinkle with half of cheese. Top with remaining chicken mixture and cheese.

Bake, covered, 35 minutes or until hot and bubbly. *Makes 8 servings*

The artichoke, specifically the globe artichoke, is actually the unopened flower bud of a thistle-like plant. A passion of Catherine de Médici in fifteenth-century Florence, Italy, the artichoke was brought to the United States in the nineteenth century, first to Louisiana and later to California. Today, California, especially the area around Castroville, produces virtually the entire domestic crop. Artichokes are also grown in abundance in the Mediterranean region where they are a very popular vegetable.

Artichoke-Olive Chicken Bake

Baked Cut Ziti

1 package (16 ounces) BARILLA® Cut Ziti
3 tablespoons butter
3 tablespoons all-purpose flour
$^1/_2$ teaspoon *each* salt, pepper and dried oregano
$1^1/_2$ cups milk
4 ripe tomatoes (about 2 pounds), divided
$^1/_4$ cup Italian-flavored bread crumbs
1 tablespoon olive oil
$^1/_2$ cup grated Parmesan cheese
$^1/_4$ cup fresh basil, chopped

1. Cook ziti according to package directions; drain and set aside.

2. To prepare white sauce, melt butter in small saucepan over medium heat. Add flour, salt, pepper and oregano; cook and stir 1 minute or until bubbly. Gradually stir in milk; cook 2 to 3 minutes or until thickened, stirring constantly. Remove from heat.

3. Preheat oven to 350°F. Peel, seed and chop 3 tomatoes. Slice remaining tomato. Combine bread crumbs and olive oil in small cup.

4. Combine cooked ziti, white sauce, chopped tomatoes, cheese and basil in large bowl. Transfer to 2-quart baking dish; arrange tomato slices on top and sprinkle with bread crumbs. Bake 30 minutes. Cool slightly before serving.

Makes 6 to 8 servings

Baked Cut Ziti

Eggplant Squash Bake

  1/2 cup chopped onion
   1 clove garlic, minced
     Nonstick olive oil cooking spray
   1 cup part-skim ricotta cheese
   1 jar (4 ounces) diced pimiento, drained
  1/4 cup grated Parmesan cheese
   2 tablespoons fat-free (skim) milk
1 1/2 teaspoons dried marjoram
  3/4 teaspoon dried tarragon
  1/4 teaspoon salt
  1/4 teaspoon ground nutmeg
  1/4 teaspoon black pepper
   1 cup no-sugar-added meatless spaghetti sauce, divided
  1/2 pound eggplant, peeled and cut into thin crosswise slices
   6 ounces zucchini, cut in half then lengthwise into thin slices
   6 ounces yellow summer squash, cut in half then lengthwise into thin slices
   2 tablespoons shredded part-skim mozzarella cheese

1. Combine onion and garlic in medium microwavable bowl. Spray lightly with cooking spray. Microwave at HIGH (100%) 1 minute.

2. Add ricotta, pimiento, Parmesan, milk, marjoram, tarragon, salt, nutmeg and pepper. Spray 9- or 10-inch round microwavable baking dish with cooking spray. Spread 1/3 cup spaghetti sauce in bottom of dish.

3. Layer half of eggplant, zucchini and squash in dish; top with ricotta mixture. Layer remaining eggplant, zucchini and summer squash over ricotta mixture. Top with remaining 2/3 cup spaghetti sauce.

4. Cover with vented plastic wrap. Microwave at HIGH (100%) 17 to 19 minutes or until vegetables are tender, rotating dish every 6 minutes. Top with mozzarella cheese. Let stand 10 minutes before serving. *Makes 4 servings*

Eggplant Squash Bake

Palermo

SICILY

Sicily

IN A CUISINE THAT MINGLES ARAB AND GREEK SPICES WITH SPANISH AND FRENCH SAUCES, IT'S EVIDENT THAT EVERY DISH IS A LIVING ARTIFACT OF THE REGION'S HISTORY.

Separated from continental Italy by the Strait of Messina, Sicily is Italy's largest region and the largest and most populous Mediterranean island. Surrounded by the Ionian, Tyrrhenian and Mediterranean Seas, it's two miles from Calabria at the Strait's narrowest point and about 100 miles from Tunisia on the north African coast. Northern Sicily is mountainous and home to Europe's greatest active volcano, Mt. Etna. Hills and plains lie to the south. Once heavily forested, the hills are mostly barren due to irresponsible logging by the ancient Romans. Sicily's location in the Mediterranean made it a natural target for many invaders. It's rich history began with Paleolithic peoples followed by the Neolithic settlers called the Sicels. The Greeks, Carthaginians, Romans, Bzyantines, Arabs, Normans, French and Spanish each took turns conquering the island, which has been part of Italy for less than 150 years. Each foreign invader added to Sicily's culture and culinary tradition, forming a unique melting pot that amazingly created harmony out of diversity. In a cuisine that mingles Arab and Greek spices with Spanish and French sauces, it's evident that every dish is a living artifact of the region's history.

Sicily's culinary influx began with fifth century Greeks who brought olives and grapes to the island. Ancient Romans are responsible for some of today's best Italian breads with their gifts of wheat and corn. The Arabs' rich contributions included rice, citrus fruits, dates, spices, pistachios, chickpeas and couscous. And tomatoes, so prized throughout southern Italy, were bestowed by the Spanish. All these imported ingredients have been fused over centuries with Sicily's fruits of the seas—swordfish, tuna, sardines, anchovies—and, of course, with pasta. Spaghetti, macaroni, ziti and gnocchi are all popular, but the most famous Sicilian pasta dish is pasta con le sarde made with sweet-sour sardines, wild fennel, raisins and pine nuts in a tomato sauce. Along the coasts irrigated fields grow fruits and vegetables. Tomatoes, peppers and eggplants are the most abundantly produced and appear in such classic dishes as caponata (eggplant, tomato, olive and caper stew) and peperonata (bell pepper, tomato and olive stew). In the central hills, lamb, goat and pork replace seafood. Sicilians supposedly invented polpetti (meatballs), which are eaten as a main course with tomato sauce but no pasta. Many sweets are of Arab origin, including the elaborate cassata (sponge cake layered with ricotta, chocolate, candied fruit and nuts). Creamy ricotta also fills crisp, fried cannoli tubes. Other regional specialties include blood oranges, prickly pears, almonds, prized olive oils, and pungent pecornio cheese known as tuma.

Sicily is Italy's second largest producer of wine. Marsala is the region's premier wine, developed by English merchant traders in the eighteenth century. Red wines from the Mt. Etna area are made from Nerello grapes, such as the premium dry, red Faro. About 75 percent of Sicily's wine is produced by cooperatives. Some high-quality table wines produced in Regaleali vineyards are preferred by many Sicilians, such as Rosso del Conte.

While Sicily has often prospered throughout history, its economy has been underdeveloped since the fifteenth century with a high rate of unemployment. Sulfur mining, an industry since ancient times, was weakened by foreign competition around 1900. The discovery of oil in the 1950's and recent land reform programs have slightly improved the economic situation. Food processing, fishing, shipbuilding, asphalt production and salt mining are all thriving industries. Tourism is also a major source of income as Sicily offers world famous coastal resorts and an inland enriched by every great ancient civilization.

Spinach Stuffed Manicotti

  1 package (10 ounces) frozen spinach
  8 uncooked manicotti shells
1 1/2 teaspoons olive oil
  1 teaspoon dried rosemary
  1 teaspoon dried sage leaves
  1 teaspoon dried oregano leaves
  1 teaspoon dried thyme leaves
  1 teaspoon chopped garlic
1 1/2 cups chopped fresh tomatoes
  1/2 cup ricotta cheese
  1/2 cup fresh whole wheat bread crumbs
  2 egg whites, lightly beaten
    Yellow pepper rings and sage sprig for garnish

1. Cook spinach according to package directions. Place in colander to drain. Let stand until cool enough to handle. Squeeze spinach with hands to remove excess moisture. Set aside.

2. Cook pasta according to package directions, drain. Rinse under cold running water until cool enough to handle; drain.

3. Preheat oven to 350°F. Heat oil in small saucepan over medium heat. Cook and stir rosemary, sage, oregano, thyme and garlic in hot oil about 1 minute. *Do not let herbs turn brown.* Add tomatoes; reduce heat to low. Simmer, uncovered, 10 minutes, stirring occasionally.

4. Combine spinach, cheese and crumbs in bowl. Fold in egg whites. Fill shells with spinach mixture using spoon.

5. Place one third of tomato mixture on bottom of 13×9-inch baking pan. Arrange manicotti in pan. Pour tomato mixture over top. Cover with foil.

6. Bake 30 minutes or until bubbly. Garnish, if desired.   *Makes 4 servings*

Spinach Stuffed Manicotti

Parmesan and Roasted Red Pepper Strata

1 loaf (16 ounces) French bread, cut into ½-inch-thick slices
2 jars (7½ ounces each) roasted red peppers, drained and cut into
   ½-inch pieces
1 cup grated Parmesan cheese
1 cup sliced green onions
3 cups (12 ounces) shredded mozzarella cheese
8 eggs
¾ cup reduced-fat (2%) milk
1 container (7 ounces) prepared pesto
2 teaspoons minced garlic
¾ teaspoon salt

1. Grease 13×9-inch baking dish. Arrange half of bread slices in single layer on bottom of prepared baking dish. Top bread with half of red peppers, ½ cup Parmesan, ½ cup green onions and 1½ cups mozzarella. Repeat layers with remaining bread, red peppers, Parmesan, green onions and mozzarella.

2. Combine eggs, milk, pesto, garlic and salt in medium bowl; whisk to combine. Pour egg mixture evenly over strata. Cover and refrigerate overnight.

3. Preheat oven to 375°F. Bake, uncovered, 30 minutes or until hot and bubbly.

Makes 6 servings

If time allows, you may want to let the strata stand at room temperature about 15 minutes before baking.

*Parmesan and Roasted
Red Pepper Strata*

Ravioli with Homemade Tomato Sauce

3 cloves garlic, peeled
1/2 cup fresh basil leaves
3 cups seeded, peeled tomatoes, cut into quarters
2 tablespoons tomato paste
2 tablespoons fat-free Italian salad dressing
1 tablespoon balsamic vinegar
1/4 teaspoon black pepper
1 package (9 ounces) refrigerated reduced-fat cheese ravioli
2 cups shredded spinach leaves
1 cup (4 ounces) shredded part-skim mozzarella cheese

1. To prepare tomato sauce, process garlic in food processor until coarsely chopped. Add basil; process until coarsely chopped. Add tomatoes, tomato paste, salad dressing, vinegar and pepper; process using on/off pulsing action until tomatoes are chopped.

2. Spray 9-inch square microwavable dish with nonstick cooking spray. Spread 1 cup tomato sauce in dish. Layer half of ravioli and spinach over tomato sauce. Repeat layers with 1 cup tomato sauce and remaining ravioli and spinach. Top with remaining 1 cup of tomato sauce.

3. Cover with plastic wrap; refrigerate 1 to 8 hours. Vent plastic wrap. Microwave at MEDIUM (50%) 20 minutes or until pasta is tender and hot. Sprinkle with cheese. Microwave at HIGH (100%) 3 minutes or just until cheese melts. Let stand, covered, 5 minutes before serving. *Makes 6 servings*

Macaroni Italiano

1 tablespoon salt
8 ounces elbow macaroni
2 cups (16 ounces) canned tomatoes, undrained
$^1/_2$ teaspoon low-sodium baking soda
1 cup (8 ounces) tomato sauce
$1^1/_4$ cups low-fat cottage cheese, at room temperature
$^1/_4$ cup grated Parmesan cheese
1 package (10 ounces) frozen chopped spinach, thawed and squeezed dry
$1^1/_2$ cups frozen peas, thawed
1 teaspoon dried basil leaves
$^1/_2$ teaspoon black pepper
$^3/_4$ cup chopped toasted* California walnuts
2 tablespoons chopped fresh parsley
Salt to taste

*Toasting is optional.

Bring about 6 quarts of water to a boil with 1 tablespoon salt. Add macaroni and cook, stirring occasionally, about 8 minutes or until done.

While macaroni is cooking, place tomatoes and juice into large bowl. Add baking soda; with fork or fingers, break tomatoes into small chunks. Stir in tomato sauce. Add cottage cheese, Parmesan cheese, spinach, peas, basil and pepper. Toss to combine; set aside. When macaroni is done, drain well. Add to cheese mixture; toss to mix thoroughly. Pour mixture into oiled $2^1/_2$-quart baking dish.

Preheat oven to 350°F. Cover baking dish with foil and bake casserole 20 minutes; uncover and bake 10 minutes more. Stir in walnuts and sprinkle with parsley.

Makes 6 servings

Favorite recipe from **Walnut Marketing Board**

Penne, Sausage & Ham Casserole

1 pound HILLSHIRE FARM® Smoked Sausage, cut into ½-inch slices
4 ounces HILLSHIRE FARM® Ham, cubed
2 cups milk
2 tablespoons all-purpose flour
8 ounces uncooked penne pasta, cooked and drained
2½ cups (10 ounces) shredded mozzarella cheese
⅓ cup grated Parmesan cheese
1 jar (16 ounces) prepared pasta sauce
⅓ cup bread crumbs

Preheat oven to 350°F.

Lightly brown Smoked Sausage and Ham in large skillet over medium heat. Stir in milk and flour; bring to a boil, stirring constantly. Stir in pasta and cheeses. Pour sausage mixture into small casserole; pour pasta sauce over top. Bake, covered, 25 minutes. Uncover and sprinkle with bread crumbs; place under broiler to brown topping.

Makes 4 servings

Penne, Sausage & Ham Casserole

$\mathcal{T}$orta Rustica

1 package active dry yeast
1 teaspoon sugar
1 cup warm water (105° to 115°F)
3 cups plus 2 tablespoons all-purpose flour, divided
1½ teaspoons salt, divided
3 tablespoons vegetable oil, divided
1½ teaspoons dried basil leaves, divided
1½ cups chopped onions
1 cup chopped carrots
2 cloves garlic, minced
2 medium zucchini, cubed
½ pound button mushrooms, sliced
1 can (16 ounces) whole tomatoes, undrained, chopped
1 can (15 ounces) artichoke hearts, drained, cut into halves
1 medium red bell pepper, seeded and cut into 1-inch squares
½ teaspoon dried oregano leaves
¼ teaspoon black pepper
2 cups (8 ounces) shredded provolone or mozzarella cheese

1. To proof yeast, sprinkle yeast and sugar over warm water in small bowl; stir until yeast is dissolved. Let stand 5 minutes or until mixture is bubbly.*

2. Combine 3 cups flour and 1 teaspoon salt in food processor. With food processor running, add yeast mixture, 2 tablespoons oil and ½ teaspoon basil.

3. Process until mixture forms dough that leaves side of bowl. If dough is too dry, add 1 to 2 tablespoons water. If dough is too wet, add remaining 1 to 2 tablespoons flour until dough leaves side of bowl. Dough will be sticky.

4. Place dough in large greased bowl. Turn dough over so that top is greased. Cover with towel; let rise in warm place about 1 hour or until doubled in bulk. To test if dough has risen enough, lightly press two fingertips about ½ inch into dough. Dough is ready if indentations remain when fingertips are removed.

If yeast mixture does not bubble, it is no longer active. This may be the result of water that is too hot or yeast that is too old. (Always check expiration date on yeast package.) Discard yeast mixture and start again with new ingredients.

continued on page 194

Torta Rustica

5. Heat remaining 1 tablespoon oil in large saucepan over medium heat until hot. Add onions, carrots and garlic; cook and stir 5 minutes or until onions are tender. Stir in zucchini, mushrooms, tomatoes, artichoke hearts, bell pepper, remaining 1 teaspoon basil, remaining ½ teaspoon salt, oregano and black pepper. Bring to boil over high heat. Reduce heat to low. Cover and simmer 10 minutes.

6. Meanwhile, to punch down dough, push down on center of dough with your fist. Push edges of dough into center. Knead dough on lightly floured surface 1 minute. Cover with towel; let rest 10 minutes.

7. Preheat oven to 400°F. Grease 2-quart casserole or soufflé dish. Roll ⅔ of dough on lightly floured surface to ½-inch thickness. Ease dough into casserole, allowing dough to extend 1 inch over edge of casserole.

8. Spoon half the vegetable mixture into casserole. Sprinkle with 1 cup cheese. Repeat layers.

9. Roll remaining dough on lightly floured surface into circle 2 inches larger than top of casserole; cut decorative designs in top of dough with paring knife. Place dough over filling. Fold edges of top dough over bottom dough; pinch with fingertips to seal edges.

10. Bake 30 to 35 minutes or until crust is golden brown, covering edge of dough with foil if necessary to prevent overbrowning. *Makes 6 servings*

The word "rustic" is frequently associated with a style of cooking that is simpler, less refined than a more professional approach. Rustic cooking typically refers to regional fare that has its roots in peasant dishes.

Four-Cheese Lasagna

$\frac{1}{2}$	pound ground beef
$\frac{1}{2}$	cup chopped onion
$\frac{1}{3}$	cup chopped celery
1	clove garlic, minced
$1\frac{1}{2}$	teaspoons dried basil leaves
$\frac{1}{4}$	teaspoon dried oregano leaves
$\frac{1}{4}$	teaspoon salt
$\frac{1}{8}$	teaspoon ground black pepper
1	package (3 ounces) cream cheese, cubed
$\frac{1}{3}$	cup light cream or milk
$\frac{1}{2}$	cup dry white wine
$\frac{1}{2}$	cup (2 ounces) shredded Wisconsin Cheddar or Gouda cheese
1	egg, slightly beaten
1	cup cream-style cottage cheese
6	ounces lasagna noodles, cooked and drained
6	ounces sliced Wisconsin Mozzarella cheese

In large skillet, brown meat with onion, celery and garlic; drain. Stir in basil, oregano, salt and pepper. Reduce heat to low. Add cream cheese and cream. Cook, stirring frequently, until cream cheese is melted. Stir in wine. Gradually add Cheddar cheese, stirring until Cheddar cheese is almost melted. Remove from heat. In small bowl, combine egg and cottage cheese.

Into greased 10×6-inch baking dish, layer $\frac{1}{2}$ each of the noodles, meat sauce, cottage cheese mixture and Mozzarella cheese; repeat layers. Bake, uncovered, at 375°F, 30 to 35 minutes or until hot and bubbly. Let stand 10 minutes before cutting to serve.

Makes 6 servings

Prep Time: $1\frac{1}{2}$ hours

Favorite recipe from *Wisconsin Milk Marketing Board*

paghetti Bake

1 pound BOB EVANS® Dinner Link Sausage (regular or Italian)
1 (8-ounce) can tomato sauce
1 (6-ounce) can tomato paste
1 (4-ounce) can sliced mushrooms, drained
$^1\!/_2$ teaspoon salt
$^1\!/_2$ teaspoon dried basil leaves
$^1\!/_2$ teaspoon dried oregano leaves
6 ounces spaghetti, cooked according to package directions and drained
$^1\!/_3$ cup shredded mozzarella cheese
2 tablespoons grated Parmesan cheese
Fresh basil leaves and tomato slices (optional)

Preheat oven to 375°F. Cut sausage links into bite-size pieces. Cook in medium skillet over medium heat until browned, stirring occasionally. Drain off any drippings; set aside. Combine tomato sauce, tomato paste, mushrooms, salt, basil and oregano in large bowl. Add spaghetti and reserved sausage; mix well. Spoon into lightly greased 1$^1\!/_2$-quart casserole dish; sprinkle with cheeses. Bake 20 to 30 minutes or until heated through. Garnish with fresh basil and tomato slices, if desired. Serve hot. Refrigerate leftovers. *Makes 4 servings*

Spaghetti Bake

Cannellini Parmesan Casserole

2 tablespoons olive oil
1 cup chopped onion
2 teaspoons minced garlic
1 teaspoon dried oregano leaves
$^{1}/_{4}$ teaspoon black pepper
2 cans ($14^{1}/_{2}$ ounces each) onion- and garlic-flavored diced tomatoes, undrained
1 jar (14 ounces) roasted red peppers, drained and cut into $^{1}/_{2}$-inch squares
2 cans (19 ounces each) white cannellini beans or Great Northern beans, rinsed and drained
1 teaspoon dried basil leaves *or* 1 tablespoon chopped fresh basil
$^{3}/_{4}$ cup (3 ounces) grated Parmesan cheese

1. Heat oil in Dutch oven over medium heat until hot. Add onion, garlic, oregano and pepper; cook and stir 5 minutes or until onion is tender.

2. Increase heat to high. Add tomatoes with juice and red peppers; cover and bring to a boil.

3. Reduce heat to medium. Stir in beans; cover and simmer 5 minutes, stirring occasionally. Stir in basil and sprinkle with cheese.   *Makes 6 servings*

Prep and Cook Time: 20 minutes

Cannellini Parmesan Casserole

Johnnie Marzetti

1 tablespoon CRISCO® Oil*
1 cup chopped celery
1 cup chopped onion
1 medium green bell pepper, chopped
1 pound ground beef round
1 can (14¹/₂ ounces) Italian-style stewed tomatoes, undrained
1 can (8 ounces) tomato sauce
1 can (6 ounces) tomato paste
1 cup water
1 bay leaf
1¹/₂ teaspoons dried basil leaves
1¹/₄ teaspoons salt
¹/₄ teaspoon black pepper
1 package (12 ounces) egg noodles, cooked and well drained
¹/₂ cup plain dry bread crumbs
1 cup (4 ounces) shredded sharp Cheddar cheese

*Use your favorite Crisco Oil product.

1. Heat oven to 375°F. Oil 12¹/₂×8¹/₂×2-inch baking dish lightly. Place cooling rack on countertop.

2. Heat one tablespoon oil in large skillet on medium heat. Add celery, onion and green pepper. Cook and stir until tender. Remove vegetables from skillet. Set aside. Add meat to skillet. Cook until browned, stirring occasionally. Return vegetables to skillet. Add tomatoes, tomato sauce, tomato paste, water, bay leaf, basil, salt and black pepper. Reduce heat to low. Simmer 5 minutes, stirring occasionally. Remove bay leaf.

3. Place noodles in baking dish. Spoon meat mixture over noodles. Sprinkle with bread crumbs and cheese.

4. Bake at 375°F for 15 to 20 minutes or until cheese melts. *Do not overbake.* Remove baking dish to cooling rack. Garnish, if desired.   *Makes 8 servings*

Johnnie Marzetti

Sausage Tetrazzini

1 pound BOB EVANS® Italian Roll Sausage
1 medium onion, chopped
1 red or green bell pepper, chopped
½ pound spaghetti, cooked according to package directions and drained
1 (10½-ounce) can condensed cream of mushroom soup
1 (10-ounce) can condensed tomato soup
1 (16-ounce) can stewed tomatoes, undrained
½ pound fresh mushrooms, chopped
1 teaspoon minced garlic
½ teaspoon black pepper
Salt to taste
1½ cups (6 ounces) shredded Cheddar cheese

Preheat oven to 350°F. Crumble sausage into large skillet. Cook over medium heat until lightly browned, stirring occasionally. Remove sausage. Add onion and bell pepper to drippings in skillet; cook and stir until tender. Place in large bowl. Stir in spaghetti, soups, tomatoes with juice, mushrooms, garlic, black pepper, salt and reserved sausage; place in 3-quart casserole dish. Sprinkle with cheese; bake, uncovered, 30 to 35 minutes or until heated through. Serve hot. *Makes 6 to 8 servings*

Easy Baked Ravioli

½ pound ground beef, cooked, drained
1 package (15 ounces) DI GIORNO® Marinara Sauce
1 package (9 ounces) DI GIORNO® Four Cheese Ravioli, cooked, drained
1 cup KRAFT® Shredded Low-Moisture Part-Skim Mozzarella Cheese, divided
¼ cup DI GIORNO® 100% Grated Parmesan Cheese

MIX cooked meat and sauce together. Stir in pasta and ½ cup Mozzarella cheese.

POUR into a 2-quart casserole. Top with remaining Mozzarella and Parmesan cheese.

BAKE at 375°F, uncovered, for 20 minutes. *Makes 4 servings*

Stuffed Shells Florentine

18 jumbo pasta shells
1 package (10 ounces) frozen chopped spinach, thawed and drained
1$^1/_3$ cups *French's*® French Fried Onions, divided
2 eggs, beaten
$^3/_4$ cup (4 ounces) chopped boiled ham
$^1/_2$ cup ricotta cheese
$^1/_2$ teaspoon Italian seasoning
$^1/_2$ teaspoon garlic powder
1 can (10$^3/_4$ ounces) condensed cream of chicken soup
1 cup milk
$^1/_2$ cup grated Parmesan cheese

Preheat oven to 350°F. Cook pasta according to package directions using shortest cooking time. Drain; cool in single layer.

Combine spinach, *$^2/_3$ cup* French Fried Onions, eggs, ham, ricotta cheese, Italian seasoning and garlic powder in large bowl; mix well. Spoon about 2 tablespoons mixture into each shell.

Combine soup, milk and Parmesan cheese in medium bowl. Pour half of the soup mixture into bottom of 2-quart shallow baking dish. Arrange shells in dish. Pour remaining soup mixture over shells.

Bake, uncovered, 30 minutes or until hot and bubbly. Sprinkle with remaining *$^2/_3$ cup* onions. Bake 5 minutes or until onions are golden.   *Makes 6 servings*

Prep Time: 20 minutes
Cook Time: 45 minutes

Rice Lasagna

1 bag SUCCESS® Rice
   Vegetable cooking spray
2 tablespoons reduced-calorie margarine
1 pound ground turkey
1 cup chopped onion
1 cup sliced fresh mushrooms
1 clove garlic, minced
2 cans (8 ounces each) no-salt-added tomato sauce
1 can (6 ounces) no-salt-added tomato paste
1 teaspoon dried oregano leaves, crushed
1 carton (15 ounces) lowfat cottage cheese
1/2 cup (2 ounces) grated Parmesan cheese
2 cups (8 ounces) shredded mozzarella cheese
1 tablespoon dried parsley flakes

Prepare rice according to package directions.

Preheat oven to 350°F.

Spray 13×9-inch baking dish with cooking spray; set aside. Melt margarine in large skillet over medium heat. Add ground turkey, onion, mushrooms and garlic; cook until turkey is no longer pink and vegetables are tender, stirring occasionally to separate turkey. Drain. Stir in tomato sauce, tomato paste and oregano; simmer 15 minutes, stirring occasionally. Layer half each of rice, turkey mixture, cottage cheese, Parmesan cheese and mozzarella cheese in prepared baking dish; repeat layers. Sprinkle with parsley; cover. Bake 30 minutes. Uncover; continue baking 15 minutes.

Makes 8 servings

Rice Lasagna

Broccoli Lasagna

- 1 tablespoon CRISCO® Oil* plus additional for oiling
- 1 cup chopped onion
- 3 cloves garlic, minced
- 1 can (14½ ounces) no salt added tomatoes, undrained and chopped
- 1 can (8 ounces) no salt added tomato sauce
- 1 can (6 ounces) no salt added tomato paste
- 1 cup thinly sliced fresh mushrooms
- ¼ cup chopped fresh parsley
- 1 tablespoon red wine vinegar
- 1 teaspoon dried oregano leaves
- 1 teaspoon dried basil leaves
- 1 bay leaf
- ½ teaspoon salt
- ¼ teaspoon crushed red pepper
- 1½ cups lowfat cottage cheese
- 1 cup (4 ounces) shredded low moisture part-skim mozzarella cheese, divided
- 6 lasagna noodles, cooked (without salt or fat) and well drained
- 3 cups chopped broccoli, cooked and well drained
- 1 tablespoon grated Parmesan cheese

Use your favorite Crisco Oil product.

1. Heat oven to 350°F. Oil 11¾×7½×2-inch baking dish lightly.

2. Heat 1 tablespoon oil in large saucepan on medium heat. Add onion and garlic. Cook and stir until tender. Stir in tomatoes, tomato sauce, tomato paste, mushrooms, parsley, vinegar, oregano, basil, bay leaf, salt and crushed red pepper. Bring to boil. Reduce heat to low. Cover. Simmer 30 minutes, stirring occasionally. Remove bay leaf. Combine cottage cheese and ½ cup mozzarella cheese in small bowl. Stir well.

3. Place 2 lasagna noodles in bottom of baking dish. Layer with one cup broccoli, one-third of the tomato sauce and one-third of the cottage cheese mixture. Repeat layers. Cover with foil.

4. Bake at 350°F for 25 minutes. Uncover. Sprinkle with remaining ½ cup mozzarella cheese and Parmesan cheese. Bake, uncovered, 10 minutes or until cheese melts. *Do not overbake.* Let stand 10 minutes before serving.

Makes 8 servings

Broccoli Lasagna

Dal Mare

Since Italy is a peninsula, with the Adriatic Sea on its eastern coast and the Mediterranean Sea on the west, seafood has always played a prominent role in the cuisine of many of the country's regions. But for the handful of landlocked regions (Lombardy, Umbria, Valle d'Aosta, Piedmont and Trentino Alto Adige), i frutti di mare or "fruits of the sea" as seafood is called, can also be found in regional fare. From squid, clams and scallops to snapper, tuna and salmon, every offering from Italy's coastal waters has at some time found its way to the Italian kitchen.

Baked Snapper with Artichokes
(page 233)

Red Snapper Scampi

1/4 cup margarine or butter, softened
1 tablespoon white wine
1 1/2 teaspoons minced garlic
1/2 teaspoon grated lemon peel
1/8 teaspoon black pepper
1 1/2 pounds red snapper, orange roughy or grouper fillets (about 4 to 5 ounces each)

1. Preheat oven to 450°F. Combine margarine, wine, garlic, lemon peel and pepper in small bowl; stir to blend.

2. Place fish on foil-lined shallow baking pan. Top with seasoned margarine. Bake 10 to 12 minutes or until fish begins to flake easily when tested with fork.

Makes 4 servings

Tip: Serve fish over mixed salad greens, if desired. Or, add sliced carrots, zucchini and bell pepper, cut into matchstick-size strips, to the fish in the baking pan for an easy vegetable side dish.

Prep and Cook Time: 12 minutes

Red Snapper Scampi

Tortellini with Three-Cheese Tuna Sauce

1 pound uncooked spinach or egg, cheese-filled tortellini
2 green onions, thinly sliced
1 clove garlic, minced
1 tablespoon butter or margarine
1 cup low-fat ricotta cheese
1/2 cup low-fat milk
1 (7-ounce) pouch of STARKIST® Premium Albacore or Chunk Light Tuna
1/2 cup (2 ounces) shredded low-fat mozzarella cheese
1/4 cup grated Parmesan or Romano cheese
2 tablespoons chopped fresh basil *or* 2 teaspoons dried basil leaves, crushed
1 teaspoon grated lemon peel
Fresh tomato wedges, red peppers and basil leaves for garnish (optional)

In large saucepan, cook tortellini in boiling salted water according to package directions. When tortellini are almost done, in separate large saucepan, cook and stir onions and garlic in butter 2 minutes. Whisk in ricotta cheese and milk. Add tuna, cheeses, basil and lemon peel. Cook over medium-low heat until mixture is heated through and cheeses are melted.

Drain pasta; add to sauce. Toss well to coat; garnish if desired. Serve immediately.

Makes 4 to 5 servings

Prep Time: 25 minutes

Tortellini with
Three-Cheese Tuna Sauce

Poached Seafood Italiano

1 tablespoon olive or vegetable oil
1 large clove garlic, minced
$^1/_4$ cup dry white wine or chicken broth
4 (6-ounce) salmon steaks or fillets
1 can (14.5 ounces) CONTADINA® Recipe Ready Diced Tomatoes with Italian Herbs, undrained
2 tablespoons chopped fresh basil (optional)

1. Heat oil in large skillet. Add garlic; sauté 30 seconds. Add wine. Bring to boil.

2. Add salmon; cover. Reduce heat to medium; simmer 6 minutes.

3. Add undrained tomatoes; simmer 2 minutes or until salmon flakes easily when tested with fork. Sprinkle with basil just before serving, if desired.

Makes 4 servings

Pasta with Tuna Sauce

3 cups bow tie pasta, uncooked
1 box (9 ounces) BIRDS EYE® frozen Italian Green Beans
1 jar (15 ounces) prepared spaghetti sauce
1 can ($6^1/_8$ ounces) tuna packed in water, drained
Chopped Italian parsley (optional)

Cook pasta according to package directions; drain.

Cook green beans according to package directions; drain.

Combine pasta, beans, spaghetti sauce, tuna and parsley. Cook and stir over medium-high heat 5 minutes or until heated through. *Makes about 2 servings*

Prep Time: 5 minutes
Cook Time: 20 minutes

Poached Seafood Italiano

Grilled Squid with Pasta and Mushrooms

2 pounds (about 20) frozen squid, thawed
1/3 cup prepared pesto
1 pound pasta, such as bow ties, radiatore or rotini
3 to 4 tablespoons olive oil, divided
1/2 pound wild mushrooms, such as shiitake, cremini, oyster or morel, sliced
2 cloves garlic, minced
1/2 teaspoon salt
1/2 teaspoon black pepper
1/2 cup fresh basil leaves, cut into narrow strips
1/2 cup grated Parmesan cheese

Cut off tentacles of squid just above eyes; reserve tentacles. Cut back side of body lengthwise with kitchen shears. Remove and discard entrails. Remove and discard transparent quill. With a knife, score the inside (dull side) of body lengthwise to a depth of about 1/16-inch at 1/4-inch intervals. Repeat with remaining squid. Brush each side of bodies and tentacles liberally with pesto.

Prepare grill for direct cooking.

Cook pasta al dente according to package directions in large saucepan; drain. Set aside and keep warm.

Place 2 tablespoons oil in medium skillet over medium heat. Add mushrooms and garlic; cook and stir 2 to 3 minutes or until tender. Add salt and pepper; stir. Cover; set aside.

Place squid on grid. Grill over high heat 3 minutes or until tender, turning halfway through grilling time. Cut squid bodies into strips through score lines; cover with foil and set aside.

Combine pasta, mushroom mixture, basil, cheese and 1 to 2 tablespoons remaining oil in large serving bowl. (Add just enough oil to moisten.) Top with squid.

Makes 5 to 6 servings

Spaghetti with Puttanesca Sauce

    1 box (8 ounces) spaghetti or linguine
    1 box (9 ounces) BIRDS EYE® frozen Deluxe Italian Green Beans
    1 jar (15 ounces) spaghetti sauce
 ½ cup sliced, pitted ripe olives
    1 can (2 ounces) anchovies, drained and mashed
    1 teaspoon crushed red pepper flakes

In large saucepan, cook spaghetti according to package directions. Add beans during last 5 minutes; drain and keep warm.

Meanwhile, in medium saucepan, combine spaghetti sauce, olives and anchovies.

Bring to boil over high heat; reduce heat to medium and simmer 5 minutes. Season with pepper flakes.

Serve over spaghetti and beans.   *Makes 4 servings*

Variation: Add 1 tablespoon drained capers to sauce with olives.

Prep Time: 5 minutes
Cook Time: 15 minutes

If you find anchovies to be too salty, try soaking them for up to 30 minutes in cold water. Once drained and patted dry in paper towels, much of the salt will have been removed. If you do drain the salt off, remember to store any unused filets in vegetable oil.

Seafood Lasagna

1 package (16 ounces) lasagna noodles
2 tablespoons margarine or butter
1 large onion, finely chopped
1 package (8 ounces) cream cheese, cut into $^1/_2$-inch pieces, at room temperature
1$^1/_2$ cups cream-style cottage cheese
2 teaspoons dried basil leaves
$^1/_2$ teaspoon salt
$^1/_8$ teaspoon black pepper
1 egg, lightly beaten
2 cans (10$^3/_4$ ounces each) cream of mushroom soup
$^1/_3$ cup milk
1 clove garlic, minced
$^1/_2$ pound bay scallops, rinsed and patted dry
$^1/_2$ pound flounder fillets, rinsed, patted dry and cut into $^1/_2$-inch cubes
$^1/_2$ pound medium raw shrimp, peeled and deveined
$^1/_2$ cup dry white wine
1 cup (4 ounces) shredded mozzarella cheese
2 tablespoons grated Parmesan cheese

1. Cook lasagna noodles according to package directions; drain.

2. Melt margarine in large skillet over medium heat. Cook onion in hot margarine until tender, stirring frequently. Stir in cream cheese, cottage cheese, basil, salt and pepper; mix well. Stir in egg; set aside.

3. Combine soup, milk and garlic in large bowl until well blended. Stir in scallops, fillets, shrimp and wine.

4. Preheat oven to 350°F. Grease 13×9-inch baking pan.

5. Place a layer of noodles in prepared pan, overlapping the noodles. Spread half the cheese mixture over noodles. Place a layer of noodles over cheese mixture and top with half the seafood mixture. Repeat layers. Sprinkle with mozzarella and Parmesan cheeses. Bake 45 minutes or until bubbly. Let stand 10 minutes before cutting.

Makes 8 to 10 servings

Seafood Lasagna

Angel Hair Pasta with Seafood Sauce

½ pound firm whitefish, such as sea bass, monkfish or grouper
2 teaspoons olive oil
½ cup chopped onion
2 cloves garlic, minced
3 pounds fresh plum tomatoes, seeded and chopped
¼ cup chopped fresh basil
2 tablespoons chopped fresh oregano
1 teaspoon red pepper flakes
½ teaspoon sugar
2 bay leaves
½ pound fresh bay scallops or shucked oysters
8 ounces uncooked angel hair pasta
2 tablespoons chopped fresh parsley

1. Cut whitefish into ¾-inch pieces. Set aside.

2. Heat oil in large nonstick skillet over medium heat; add onion and garlic. Cook and stir 3 minutes or until onion is tender. Reduce heat to low; add tomatoes, basil, oregano, red pepper flakes, sugar and bay leaves. Cook, uncovered, 15 minutes, stirring occasionally.

3. Add whitefish and scallops. Cook, uncovered, 3 to 4 minutes or until fish flakes easily when tested with fork and scallops are opaque. Remove bay leaves; discard. Set seafood sauce aside.

4. Cook pasta according to package directions, omitting salt. Drain well.

5. Combine pasta with seafood sauce in large serving bowl. Mix well. Sprinkle with parsley. Serve immediately. *Makes 6 servings*

Angel Hair Pasta with Seafood Sauce

Easy Calzone

1 can (10 ounces) refrigerated ready-to-use pizza dough
1 package (10 ounces) frozen chopped spinach, thawed
1 (7-ounce) pouch of STARKIST® Premium Albacore or Chunk Light Tuna
1 cup chopped tomatoes
2 cans (4 ounces each) sliced mushrooms, drained
1 cup shredded low-fat Cheddar or mozzarella cheese
1 teaspoon Italian seasoning or dried oregano, crushed
1 teaspoon dried basil, crushed
¼ teaspoon garlic powder
    Vegetable oil
    Cornmeal (optional)
1 can (8 ounces) pizza sauce

Preheat oven to 425°F. Unroll pizza dough onto a lightly floured board; cut crosswise into 2 equal pieces. Roll each piece of dough into a 12-inch circle.

Squeeze all liquid from spinach; chop fine. Over the bottom half of each circle of dough, sprinkle spinach, tuna, tomatoes, mushrooms, cheese and seasonings to within 1 inch of bottom edge. Fold top half of dough over filling, leaving bottom edge uncovered. Moisten bottom edge of dough with a little water, then fold bottom edge of dough over top edge, sealing with fingers or crimping with fork. Brush top of dough lightly with oil; sprinkle with cornmeal if desired. Place 2 filled calzones on ungreased baking sheet; bake for 25 to 30 minutes, or until deep golden brown.

Meanwhile, in saucepan, heat pizza sauce. Cut each calzone in half crosswise to serve. Pass sauce to spoon over. *Makes 4 servings*

Prep Time: 25 minutes

Easy Calzones

— 222 —

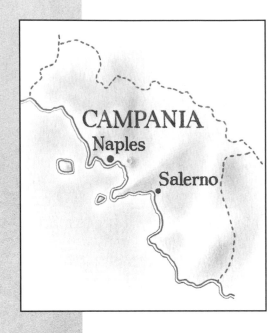

CAMPANIA
Naples
Salerno

Campania

THE SIMPLE, NATURAL CUISINE OF THE REGION HAS SO INFLUENCED THE REST OF THE COUNTRY THAT IT HAS BECOME THE DOMINANT FEATURE OF ITALY'S CULINARY CULTURE.

Located south of Lazio with the Tyrrhenian Sea on its west coast, Campania was named by the Romans after the Latin word campus (field) even though only a small percentage of its terrain is plains. It was first inhabited in Paleolithic times followed by Etruscan, Greek and Roman settlements. Some of the highest Apennine peaks are in Campania as is Italy's most famous mountain—the volcano Vesuvius. The rich volcanic coastal soils, mild Mediterranean climate and access to the sea attracted both the ancient Greeks and Romans to the area. Today, these same natural resources continue to make Campania the leading agricultural and industrial territory in southern Italy. The simple, natural cuisine of the region—headed by pasta with tomato sauce—has so influenced the rest of the country that it has become the dominant feature of Italy's culinary culture.

It is Campania's cuisine that comes to mind when one thinks of classic Italian food—spaghetti with meat sauce, mozzarella, ripe plum tomatoes, pizzas, stuffed eggplants and hearty wines. The fertile volcanic soils coveted by earlier civilizations make this a land of agricultural bounty with tomatoes, eggplants, cherries, potatoes, chestnuts, hazelnuts, peppers, lemons, figs, wheat and grapes.

The prosperity of the region lies primarily in the coastal provinces, which include the capital of Naples and Salerno. Historically, Naples reigned as a center for haute cuisine. Yet despite its resources, the province became a mecca for street food. The famous Neapolitan pizzas and calzoni (pizza dough folded over a filling) are still cooked street side by the pizzaioli, who masterfully work the dough so that it bakes in moments to a soft, slightly crunchy crust.

Authentic toppings are simply tomato sauce, basil, olive oil and mozzarella. Devoted to pasta, Campanians cook macaroni and spaghetti with reverence. A plate of overcooked spaghetti with an inferior sauce is a cook's disgrace, whether served at a special occasion or everyday meal. The sauces that top the pizzas and pastas—such as the well-known spaghetti alla puttanesca—are made with no ordinary tomatoes. The prized, tiny San Marzano plum tomatoes grown in the fertile valley southeast of Vesuvius are preferred. Water buffalo graze in the lowlands near Salerno and provide milk for tender, fresh mozzarella, as well as ricotta, provolone, mascarpone and scamorza cheeses. Seafood is a mainstay of the urban Neapolitan diet, while rural hill dwellers prefer lamb, pork, poultry and rabbit.

> *The ancient Greeks are attributed with introducing the first grapevines to Campania, which still stand out to this day.*

A majority of wine producers in the region are striving to make the most of native vines, including "archaeological" varieties that date back to antiquity. The noblest red variety is the Aglianico that produces earthy aged Taurasi wines. From provinces east of Naples come outstanding dry white wines, namely Greco di Tufo and Fiano di Avellino.

With the second highest number of residents after Lombardy and the highest population density in all of Italy, it follows that Campania is the most industrialized region in southern Italy. The heaviest concentrations of industry are around the coastal provinces of Naples and Salerno with the inland and mountain areas relatively unpopulated in comparison. Major industries include engineering and metalworking, chemicals, construction materials, food processing and textiles. Artisan industries and tourism are also important in some areas. In addition to the historical attractions in Naples, the islands of Capri and Ischia, and the provinces of Amalfi, Sorrento, Pompeii and Salerno also draw many tourists.

Quick Pasta Puttanesca

1 package (16 ounces) spaghetti or linguine, uncooked
3 tablespoons plus 1 teaspoon olive oil, divided
1/4 to 1 teaspoon red pepper flakes*
2 cans (6 ounces each) chunk light tuna packed in water, drained
1 tablespoon dried minced onion
1 teaspoon minced garlic
1 can (28 ounces) diced tomatoes, undrained
1 can (8 ounces) tomato sauce
24 pitted Kalamata or ripe olives
2 tablespoons capers, drained

*For a mildly spicy dish, use 1/4 teaspoon red pepper. For a very spicy dish, use 1 teaspoon red pepper.

1. Cook spaghetti according to package directions. Drain pasta; do not rinse. Return pasta to pan; add 1 teaspoon oil and toss to coat.

2. While pasta is cooking, heat remaining 3 tablespoons oil in large skillet over medium-high heat. Add red pepper flakes; cook and stir 1 to 2 minutes or until they sizzle. Add tuna; cook and stir 2 to 3 minutes. Add onion and garlic; cook and stir 1 minute. Add tomatoes with juice, tomato sauce, olives and capers. Cook over medium-high heat stirring frequently or until sauce is heated through.

3. Add sauce to pasta; mix well. Divide pasta among individual bowls or plates.

Makes 6 to 8 servings

Pasta should be cooked at a fast boil. This circulates the pasta during cooking so that the cooking results will be more consistent. Leftover pasta can be frozen and reheated or microwaved. Refrigerated pasta can be freshened by rinsing with hot or cold water, depending on how you plan to use it.

Quick Pasta Puttanesca

Shrimp Scampi

2 tablespoons olive or vegetable oil

½ cup diced onion

1 large clove garlic, minced

1 small green bell pepper, cut into strips

1 small yellow bell pepper, cut into strips

8 ounces medium shrimp, peeled, deveined

1 can (14.5 ounces) CONTADINA® Recipe Ready Diced Tomatoes with Italian Herbs, undrained

2 tablespoons chopped fresh parsley *or* 2 teaspoons dried parsley flakes

1 tablespoon lemon juice

½ teaspoon salt

Hot cooked orzo pasta

1. Heat oil in large skillet over medium-high heat. Add onion and garlic; sauté 1 minute.

2. Add bell peppers; sauté 2 minutes. Add shrimp; cook 2 minutes or until shrimp turn pink.

3. Add undrained tomatoes, parsley, lemon juice and salt; cook 2 to 3 minutes or until heated through. Serve over hot cooked orzo pasta, if desired.

Makes 4 servings

Shrimp Scampi

Chilled Seafood Lasagna with Herbed Cheese

    8   (2-inch wide) uncooked lasagna noodles
    2   cups ricotta cheese
 1 1/2 cups mascarpone cheese
    2   tablespoons lemon juice
    1   tablespoon minced fresh basil leaves
    1   tablespoon minced dill
    1   tablespoon minced fresh tarragon leaves
  1/4   teaspoon white pepper
    1   pound lox, divided
    4   ounces Whitefish caviar, gently rinsed
        Lox and fresh tarragon sprigs for garnish

1. Cook lasagna noodles according to package directions until tender but still firm. Drain and set aside.

2. Process the ricotta cheese, mascarpone cheese, lemon juice, basil, dill, tarragon and pepper in food processor or blender until well combined.

3. Line terrine mold* with plastic wrap, allowing wrap to extend 5 inches over sides of mold.

4. Place 1 noodle in bottom of mold. Spread 1/2 cup cheese mixture over noodle. Cover cheese mixture with 2 ounces lox; spread 2 rounded teaspoons caviar over lox. Repeat layers with remaining ingredients, ending with noodle. Set aside remaining 2 ounces lox for garnish.

5. Cover; refrigerate several hours or until firm. Carefully lift lasagna from mold and remove plastic wrap.

6. Garnish with remaining strips of lox rolled to look like roses and fresh tarragon sprigs, if desired. Slice with warm knife.   *Makes 24 first-course servings*

Can be prepared without terrine mold. Layer lasagna on plastic wrap. Cover and wrap with foil.

*Chilled Seafood Lasagna
with Herbed Cheese*

Mini Rigatoni with Grilled Salmon and Caramelized Onions

2 salmon steaks (8 ounces each), about 1 inch thick
   Salt and pepper
¼ cup fresh lemon juice, divided
¼ cup fresh dill, divided
4 cups thin onion wedges
3 tablespoons extra-virgin olive oil
1 package (16 ounces) BARILLA® Mini Rigatoni

1. Preheat broiler. Sprinkle salmon steaks generously with salt and pepper. Sprinkle with 1 tablespoon lemon juice and 1 tablespoon fresh dill. Broil about 8 minutes or until browned. Carefully turn and broil about 2 minutes until cooked through. Cool slightly. Remove skin and bones. Break salmon into 1-inch chunks.

2. Meanwhile, cook onions in olive oil in large deep covered skillet over medium-low heat about 15 minutes or until golden (caramelized).

3. Cook rigatoni according to package directions, reserving 1 cup pasta-cooking water before draining. Add rigatoni to onions in skillet; stir in as much cooking water as needed to keep mixture moist. Gently stir in salmon and remaining 3 tablespoons lemon juice and dill.
Makes 8 servings

Baked Snapper with Artichokes

    Juice of 2 lemons
3 large artichokes
8 tablespoons olive oil, divided
2 cloves garlic, minced
1 whole red snapper or sea bass (about 2 pounds), gutted and scaled with
      head and tail intact
    Salt and black pepper to taste
3 small sprigs fresh rosemary, divided
1 tablespoon finely chopped fresh parsley

1. Pour half the lemon juice and squeezed lemon halves in large bowl. Fill bowl half full with cold water; set aside. Reserve remaining lemon juice.

2. To prepare artichokes, bend back dark outer leaves and snap off at base. Continue snapping off leaves until bottom halves are yellow. Cut $1\frac{1}{2}$ inches off tops of artichokes; trim stems to 1 inch. Peel tough green layer from stem and base. Cut artichokes lengthwise (from tops) into quarters; place quarters in lemon water to help prevent discoloration.

3. Working with 1 artichoke quarter at a time, remove small-shaped heart leaves from center by grasping with fingers, then pulling and twisting. Scoop out fuzzy choke with spoon. Cut artichoke quarters lengthwise into thin slices. Quickly return slices to lemon water. Repeat step 3 with remaining artichoke quarters.

4. Drain artichoke slices. Heat 6 tablespoons oil in large skillet over medium heat until hot. Add artichokes and garlic. Cover; cook 5 minutes until tender, stirring occasionally.

5. Preheat oven to 425°F. Rinse fish; pat dry with paper towels. Season fish inside and out with salt and pepper. Place in baking pan. Stuff fish cavity with as many artichoke slices as will fit and 1 sprig rosemary. Arrange remaining artichoke slices and 2 sprigs rosemary around fish.

6. Combine reserved lemon juice, remaining 2 tablespoons oil and parsley; drizzle over fish. Bake 30 minutes or until fish flakes when tested with fork, basting occasionally with pan juices. *Makes 4 servings*

Seafood Primavera

1/3 cup olive oil
1 medium onion, chopped
4 green onions with tops, chopped
3 cloves garlic, minced
3 carrots, cut into julienne strips
1 zucchini, cut into julienne strips
1 each small red and yellow bell pepper, cut into strips
3 ounces snow peas
1/3 cup sliced mushrooms
1/2 pound peeled and deveined medium shrimp
1/2 pound scallops
2/3 cup bottled clam juice
1/3 cup dry white wine
1 cup heavy cream
1/2 cup freshly grated Parmesan cheese
2/3 cup flaked crabmeat
2 tablespoons chopped fresh parsley
2 tablespoons lemon juice
1/4 teaspoon dried basil leaves
1/4 teaspoon dried oregano leaves
Black pepper to taste
1 package (8 ounces) linguine, cooked and drained

Heat oil in large skillet over medium-high heat. Add onions and garlic; cook and stir until tender. Add remaining vegetables. Reduce heat to medium-low; cover. Simmer until tender, stirring occasionally. Remove vegetable mixture from skillet; set aside. Add shrimp and scallops to skillet; cook and stir until shrimp turn pink and scallops are opaque. Remove from skillet, reserving liquid in skillet. Add clam juice and wine to skillet; bring to a boil. Stir in cream and Parmesan. Reduce heat; simmer 3 minutes until thickened, stirring constantly. Return vegetables and seafood to skillet. Heat thoroughly, stirring occasionally. Stir in all remaining ingredients except linguine. Pour over hot linguine in large bowl; toss gently to coat.

Makes 6 servings

Seafood Primavera

Salmon Linguini Supper

   8 ounces linguini, cooked in unsalted water and drained
   1 package (10 ounces) frozen peas
   1 cup milk
   1 can (10¾ ounces) condensed cream of celery soup
   ¼ cup (1 ounce) grated Parmesan cheese
   ⅛ teaspoon dried tarragon, crumbled (optional)
   1 can (15½ ounces) salmon, drained and flaked
   1 egg, slightly beaten
   ¼ teaspoon salt
   ¼ teaspoon pepper
   1⅓ cups *French's*® French Fried Onions, divided

Preheat oven to 375°F. Return hot pasta to saucepan; stir in peas, milk, soup, cheese and tarragon. Spoon into 12×8-inch baking dish. In medium bowl, using fork, combine salmon, egg, salt, pepper and *⅔ cup* French Fried Onions. Shape salmon mixture into 4 oval patties. Place patties on pasta mixture. Bake, covered, at 375°F for 40 minutes or until patties are done. Top patties with remaining *⅔ cup* onions; bake, uncovered, 3 minutes or until onions are golden brown.

Makes 4 servings

Microwave Directions: Prepare pasta mixture as above, except increase milk to 1¼ cups; spoon into 12×8-inch microwave-safe dish. Cook, covered, on HIGH (100%) 3 minutes; stir. Prepare salmon patties as above using 2 eggs. Place patties on pasta mixture. Cook, covered, 10 to 12 minutes or until patties are done. Rotate dish halfway through cooking time. Top patties with remaining onions; cook, uncovered, 1 minute. Let stand 5 minutes.

Salmon Linguini Supper

Tuna & Zucchini-Stuffed Manicotti

1 cup diced zucchini
1/2 cup chopped onion
1 clove garlic, minced
1 tablespoon vegetable oil
1 (3-ounce) pouch of STARKIST® Premium Albacore or Chunk Light Tuna
1 cup low-fat ricotta cheese
1/2 cup shredded mozzarella cheese
1/4 cup grated Parmesan or Romano cheese
1 extra-large egg, lightly beaten
2 teaspoons dried basil, crushed
8 manicotti shells, cooked and drained

MARINARA SAUCE

1 1/2 cups chopped fresh tomatoes
1 1/4 cups tomato sauce
2 tablespoons minced parsley
1 teaspoon dried basil, crushed
1 teaspoon dried oregano or marjoram, crushed
Salt and pepper to taste

In a medium skillet sauté zucchini, onion and garlic in oil for 3 minutes; remove from heat. Stir in tuna. In a medium bowl stir together ricotta, mozzarella, Parmesan, egg and basil until blended. Stir cheese mixture into tuna mixture; set aside.

Preheat oven to 350°F. Place drained manicotti shells in a bowl of cold water. Set aside. For Marinara Sauce, in a medium saucepan stir together tomatoes, tomato sauce and herbs. Heat to a boil; remove from heat. Season to taste with salt and pepper. Transfer mixture to blender container or food processor bowl. Cover and process in 2 batches until nearly smooth. Spray a 13×9×2-inch baking dish with aerosol shortening.

Spread 1/2 cup of the Marinara Sauce over bottom of baking dish. Blot manicotti shells carefully with paper towels. Generously pipe filling into shells. In baking dish arrange manicotti in a row. Pour remaining sauce over manicotti; cover with foil. Bake for 30 minutes; uncover and bake for 5 to 10 minutes more, or until sauce is bubbly. Let stand for 5 minutes before serving. *Makes 4 servings*

Prep Time: 30 minutes

Tuna & Zucchini-Stuffed Manicotti

Scallops with Vermicelli

1 pound bay scallops
2 tablespoons fresh lemon juice
2 tablespoons chopped fresh parsley
1 onion, chopped
1 clove garlic, minced
2 tablespoons olive oil
2 tablespoons butter, divided
1 1/2 cups canned Italian tomatoes, undrained and chopped
2 tablespoons chopped fresh basil *or* 1/2 teaspoon dried basil leaves
1/4 teaspoon dried oregano leaves
1/4 teaspoon dried thyme leaves
2 tablespoons heavy cream
Dash ground nutmeg
12 ounces uncooked vermicelli, hot cooked and drained

Rinse scallops. Combine scallops, juice and parsley in glass dish. Cover; marinate in refrigerator while preparing sauce.

Cook and stir onion and garlic in oil and 1 tablespoon butter in large skillet over medium-high heat until onion is tender. Add tomatoes with juice, basil, oregano and thyme. Reduce heat to low. Cover; simmer 30 minutes, stirring occasionally.

Drain scallops; cook and stir in remaining 1 tablespoon butter in another large skillet over medium heat until scallops are opaque, about 2 minutes. Add cream, nutmeg and tomato sauce mixture.

Pour sauce over vermicelli in large bowl; toss gently to coat. Garnish as desired.

Makes 4 servings

Favorite recipe from *New Jersey Department of Agriculture*

Orzo Pasta with Shrimp

  8 ounces uncooked orzo pasta
  3 tablespoons plus $^1/_2$ teaspoon FILIPPO BERIO® Olive Oil, divided
  3 cloves garlic, minced
$1^1/_4$ pounds raw small shrimp, shelled and deveined
$1^1/_2$ medium tomatoes, chopped
  2 tablespoons chopped fresh cilantro
  2 tablespoons chopped fresh Italian parsley
     Juice of 1 lemon
  2 ounces feta cheese, crumbled
     Salt and freshly ground black pepper

Cook pasta according to package directions until al dente (tender but still firm). Drain. Toss with $^1/_2$ teaspoon olive oil; set aside. Heat remaining 3 tablespoons olive oil in large skillet over medium heat until hot. Add garlic; cook and stir 2 to 3 minutes or until golden. Add shrimp; cook and stir 3 to 5 minutes or until shrimp are opaque *(do not overcook)*. Stir in pasta. Add tomatoes, cilantro, parsley and lemon juice. Sprinkle with feta cheese. Season to taste with salt and pepper.

Makes 4 servings

Fish alla Milanese

1/3 cup plus 2 tablespoons olive oil, divided
2 tablespoons lemon juice
1/2 teaspoon salt
Dash pepper
1 small onion, finely chopped
1 pound flounder or haddock fillets (4 to 8 pieces)
2 eggs
1 tablespoon milk
1/2 cup all-purpose flour
3/4 cup fine dry unseasoned bread crumbs
1/4 cup plus 2 tablespoons butter or margarine, divided
1 clove garlic, minced
1 tablespoon chopped fresh parsley
Fresh thyme sprig for garnish
Lemon slices (optional)

1. For marinade, whisk 1/3 cup oil, lemon juice, salt and pepper in small bowl; stir in onion. Pour marinade into 13×9-inch glass baking dish.

2. Rinse fish; pat dry with paper towels. Place fish in baking dish; spoon marinade over fish to coat thoroughly. Marinate, covered, in refrigerator 1 hour, turning fish over occasionally.

3. Combine eggs and milk in shallow bowl; mix well. Spread flour and bread crumbs on separate plates. Remove fish from marinade; pat dry with paper towels. Discard marinade.

4. Dip fish to coat both sides evenly, first in flour, then in egg mixture, then in bread crumbs. Press crumb coating firmly onto fish. Place on waxed paper; refrigerate 15 minutes.

5. Heat remaining 2 tablespoons oil and 2 tablespoons butter in large nonstick skillet over medium heat until melted and bubbly; add fish. Cook 2 to 3 minutes per side until fish flakes easily with a fork and topping is light brown. Remove to heated serving plate.

6. Melt remaining 1/4 cup butter in medium skillet over medium heat. Add garlic. Cook 1 to 2 minutes until butter turns light brown; stir in parsley. Pour browned butter mixture over fish. Garnish, if desired. Serve immediately with lemon slices.

Makes 4 servings

Fish alla Milanese

Squid Mediterranean

2 pounds cleaned, whole squid (body and tentacles)
1 tablespoon olive oil
3/4 cup finely chopped onion
1 clove garlic, minced
2 (16-ounce) cans Italian-style tomatoes, drained and chopped
3 tablespoons sliced black olives
1 tablespoon capers
1/2 teaspoon dried oregano
1/4 teaspoon dried marjoram
1/8 teaspoon crushed red pepper

Cut body of squid into 1/2-inch slices; set aside. Heat olive oil in a large skillet; add onion and garlic. Cook until onion is tender. Add squid and remaining ingredients. Bring to a boil. Cover, reduce heat and simmer 30 minutes or until squid is tender.

Makes 4 servings

Prep Time: about 45 minutes

Favorite recipe from *National Fisheries Institute*

To clean a squid's edible parts (the tubular body sac, tentacles and fins), carefully pull the head from the body sac. Pull off and discard the purplish outer skin covering the sac and fins. Pull off the fins and reserve. Cut the tentacles from the head; discard head. Remove and discard the hard beak from the tentacles.

Squid Mediterranean

Swordfish Messina Style

2 tablespoons olive or vegetable oil

¹/₂ cup chopped fresh parsley

2 tablespoons chopped fresh basil *or* 2 teaspoons dried basil leaves, crushed

2 cloves garlic, minced

1 can (8 ounces) CONTADINA® Tomato Sauce

³/₄ cup sliced fresh mushrooms

1 tablespoon capers

1 tablespoon lemon juice

¹/₈ teaspoon ground black pepper

3 pounds swordfish or halibut steaks

1. Heat oil in small saucepan. Add parsley, basil and garlic; sauté for 1 minute. Reduce heat to low. Add tomato sauce, mushrooms and capers; simmer, uncovered, for 5 minutes.

2. Stir in lemon juice and pepper. Place swordfish in single layer in greased 13×9-inch baking dish; cover with sauce.

3. Bake in preheated 400°F oven for 20 minutes or until fish flakes easily when tested with fork. *Makes 8 servings*

Prep Time: 5 minutes
Cook Time: 26 minutes

Swordfish Messina Style

I Pane

Bread, the staff of life, is one of the most revered foods in Italian cuisine. Italians often use bread as a medium for other foods, to accomodate pizza and focaccia toppings as well as for dipping into extra-virgin olive oil. Italians are so connected with their bread that they've been known to go to great lengths to continue to prepare it, even in the face of taxation. Legend has it that in the 13th or 14th century when salt was heavily taxed, Tuscan bakers created Pane Toscano, a saltless bread which today remains quite popular despite a somewhat bland taste.

Pizza Breadsticks (page 259)

Whole-Wheat Focaccia

1 teaspoon olive oil
1 cup chopped onion
3 cloves garlic, chopped
$^1/_4$ cup chopped red bell pepper
$^1/_2$ teaspoon paprika
2 teaspoons canola *or* vegetable oil
2 cups whole-wheat flour
$^1/_2$ cup all-purpose flour, divided
1 package ($^1/_4$ ounce) quick-rising yeast
$^1/_2$ teaspoon sugar
$^1/_4$ teaspoon salt
1 cup warm water (105° to 115°F)
2 teaspoons dried oregano leaves, crushed
$^1/_4$ to $^1/_2$ teaspoon black pepper

For topping, heat olive oil in large nonstick skillet over medium-low heat. Cook and stir onion, garlic, bell pepper and paprika 5 minutes or until tender. Set aside.

Brush 12-inch pizza pan with canola oil; set aside. Combine whole-wheat flour, 2 tablespoons all-purpose flour, yeast, sugar and salt in large bowl. Stir in warm water until well mixed.

Sprinkle kneading surface with 1 tablespoon all-purpose flour. Turn out dough onto surface; knead 3 minutes or until smooth, adding up to 2 tablespoons all-purpose flour to prevent sticking if necessary. Cover with inverted bowl or clean towel; let stand 10 minutes. Place oven rack in lowest position; preheat oven to 425°F.

Knead dough on lightly floured surface about 3 minutes or until smooth and elastic, adding remaining 3 tablespoons all-purpose flour to prevent sticking if necessary. Roll out dough into 13-inch round; transfer to prepared pan. Crimp edge of dough to form rim.

Spread topping on dough; sprinkle with oregano and black pepper. Bake 15 to 20 minutes or until rim of crust is lightly browned. Remove from pan; let cool on wire rack 5 minutes before cutting into wedges. *Makes 8 servings*

Last Minute Tomato Swirl Bread

2 loaves (16 ounces each) frozen bread dough, thawed according to
    package directions
2 large cloves garlic, pressed
1 jar (8 ounces) SONOMA® Marinated Tomatoes, drained and blotted
    with paper towels
3 tablespoons grated Parmesan cheese
2 tablespoons dried basil leaves
    Cornmeal for baking sheets
1 egg, beaten

Preheat oven to 400°F. On lightly floured surface, roll and pat one loaf of dough
into 12×7-inch rectangle. Gently sprinkle half of garlic over dough. Distribute
half of tomatoes evenly over dough, leaving ½-inch border. Sprinkle with half of
cheese and basil. Starting from one long edge, roll dough up tightly, jelly-roll style.
Carefully pinch seam to seal. Repeat procedure with second loaf. Sprinkle baking
sheets with cornmeal. Place loaves on baking sheets, seam sides down. Brush with
egg. *Do not let rise.* Bake immediately 25 to 30 minutes or until loaves are browned
and sound hollow when tapped. Remove to racks to cool before slicing. If desired,
loaves can be wrapped well and frozen up to 1 month.   *Makes 2 loaves (24 slices)*

*The flavorful oil from Marinated Tomatoes
can be used for sautéing or for vinaigrettes.*

Festive Focaccia Pizza Bread

1 pound frozen bread dough, thawed
1½ teaspoons dried Italian herbs
¾ cup (3 ounces) pitted California ripe olives, sliced in thirds (rinse and pat dry before slicing)
¾ cup coarsely chopped California walnuts
1 cup (1 medium) thinly sliced onion
1½ cups (6 ounces) shredded JARLSBERG Cheese
1 tablespoon Lucini Premium Select Extra Virgin Olive Oil
Freshly ground pepper

Pat and stretch dough to fit 12-inch round baking pan. Cover with oiled waxed paper; let rise in warm place about 1 hour or until doubled in bulk.

Preheat oven to 375°F. Dimple dough with fingertips, making deep indentations. Sprinkle with herbs, then with olives, walnuts, onion and cheese. Drizzle with oil and sprinkle with pepper to taste.

Bake focaccia in lower third of oven 30 minutes or until golden brown. Serve warm or cool completely, wrap and refrigerate. Reheat before serving.

Makes 10 to 12 servings

Festive Focaccia Pizza Bread

CALABRIA
Catanzaro

Calabria

SHAPED BY A LEGACY OF POVERTY, CALABRIA'S CUISINE IS SIMPLE, ANCIENT FARE FILLED WITH INTENSE FLAVORS AND AROMAS THAT ECHO GREEK AND ARAB INFLUENCES.

The long peninsula of Calabria forms the toe of Italy's boot. With the Ionian and Tyrrhenian Seas running along its east and west coasts respectively, this region possesses the longest beaches in Italy. At the southern tip is the Strait of Messina, which separates Calabria from Sicily. First settled by the ancient Greeks, the region suffered successive invasions by the Arabs, Romans, Byzantines, Normans, Spanish, Austrians and French. This long, violent history of oppressive foreign rule—along with periodic devastating earthquakes—prevented arid, mountainous and desolate Calabria from developing its full potential. Today, despite recent spurts of intense economic growth, it has the lowest per capita income in Italy. Yet it is this very legacy of poverty that has shaped its inventive and vibrant culinary heritage.

Calabria's cuisine is simple, ancient fare filled with intense flavors and aromas that echo Greek and Arab influences. Pork, pasta and vegetables are the trilogy upon which much of the Calabrian diet is based, with seafood added in coastal areas. Most of the region's agriculture is located on two large, fertile plains on the northeast and west coasts. During the twentieth century, the agricultural industry was revived by consolidating land and assigning it to high technology methods. Wheat, the main grain crop, is transformed into a variety of pasta shapes, including lágane (wide fettuccine of Greek origin), and breads, such as focaccia and the local pizza (pitte) topped with native ingredients. Peppers, beans, tomatoes, potatoes and sugar

beets are among the many vegetables grown, but eggplant reigns as number one. Calabria's dry, calcium-deficient soil imbues the eggplants' flesh with unparalleled flavor, and it is used extensively and creatively: sautéed with garlic, stuffed, cooked with sugar and vinegar, and baked with pecorino (not Parmesan) for the original version of eggplant parmigiana. Tender red onions from Tropea, famous for their sweet taste, are also popular and often served raw with a simple dressing and bits of cheese.

Olives and citrus fruits are widely cultivated in Calabria. The region produces about 25% of Italy's olive oil and is known for clementines and the unique bergamots (small acidic oranges) whose peels contain essential oils that are used to flavor Earl Grey tea. In the highlands, a string of heavily forested plateaus, called the sile, are abundant with chestnuts and woodland mushrooms, including the prized porcino silano. Calabrian dishes also reflect the food preservation necessary to sustain life on the edge of survival. The milk of sheep and goats are made into cheeses. Tomatoes are dried by the sun. Vegetables and fish are preserved in the ubiquitous olive oil and pork is cured or dried for ham, salame and other sausages.

Most of Calabria's wines are not well known in other parts of Italy. Despite a long tradition of Greek wine making, the region's hot climate is believed to work against vine cultivation. Red wines dominate, led by the famous Cirò Rosso made from the ancient Greek Gaglioppo grape. Crisp, dry and fruity Cirò Bianco is the leading white wine.

Industrially underdeveloped, Calabria has a small number of manufacturing companies. The region's most important industries include construction, food processing, chemicals (located in the capital of Catanzaro), textiles, metalworking and wood processing. Craft industries, such as fabric, ceramics and woodworking, are economically significant. Calabria, like many southern regions, has enormous tourist potential. Due to the lack of industry and population, it's home to some of the cleanest water on the entire Italian coastline. Seaside resorts, splendid scenery, tiny picturesque villages and historic treasures are just some of the region's attractions.

Red wines dominate, led by the famous Cirò Rosso made from the ancient Greek Gaglioppo grape. Crisp, dry and fruity Cirò Blanc is the leading white.

ocaccia

1 cup water
1 tablespoon olive oil, plus additional for brushing
1 teaspoon salt
1 tablespoon sugar
3 cups bread flour
2¼ teaspoons RED STAR® Active Dry Yeast
    Suggested toppings: sun-dried tomatoes, grilled bell pepper slices,
        sautéed onion rings, fresh and dried herbs of any combination, grated
        hard cheese, sliced red onions

BREAD MACHINE METHOD

Place room temperature ingredients, except toppings, in pan in order listed. Select dough cycle. Check dough consistency after 5 minutes of kneading, making adjustments if necessary.

HAND-HELD MIXER METHOD

Combine yeast, 1 cup flour, sugar and salt. Combine water and 1 tablespoon oil; heat mixture to 120° to 130°F. Combine dry mixture and liquid mixture in mixing bowl on low speed. Beat 2 to 3 minutes on medium speed. By hand, stir in enough remaining flour to make firm dough. Knead on floured surface 5 to 7 minutes or until smooth and elastic. Add additional flour, if necessary.

STAND MIXER METHOD

Combine yeast, 1 cup flour, sugar and salt. Combine water and 1 tablespoon oil; heat mixture to 120° to 130°F. Combine dry mixture and liquid mixture in mixing bowl with paddle or beaters 4 minutes on medium speed. Gradually add remaining flour and knead with dough hook 5 to 7 minutes or until smooth and elastic. Add additional flour, if necessary.

FOOD PROCESSOR METHOD

Combine yeast, 1 cup flour, sugar and salt. Combine water and 1 tablespoon oil. Put dry mixture in processing bowl with steel blade. While motor is running, add liquid mixture. Process until mixed. Continue processing, adding remaining flour until dough forms a ball. Add additional flour, if necessary.

continued on page 258

Focaccia

RISING, SHAPING, AND BAKING

Place dough in lightly oiled bowl and turn to grease top. Cover; let rise until dough tests ripe.* Turn dough onto lightly floured surface; punch down to remove air bubbles. On lightly floured surface, shape dough into a ball. Place on greased cookie sheet. Flatten to 14-inch circle. With knife, cut circle in dough about 1 inch from edge, cutting almost through to cookie sheet. Pierce center with fork. Cover; let rise about 15 minutes. Brush with oil and sprinkle with desired toppings. Bake in preheated 375°F oven 25 to 30 minutes or until golden brown. Remove from cookie sheet to cool. Serve warm or cold.   *Makes 1 (14-inch) loaf*

Place two fingers into the dough and them remove them. If the holes remain the dough is ripe and ready to punch down.

ℛepperoni-Oregano Focaccia

  1 tablespoon cornmeal
  1 package (10 ounces) refrigerated pizza crust dough
  ½ cup finely chopped pepperoni (3 to 3½ ounces)
1½ teaspoons finely chopped fresh oregano leaves *or* ½ teaspoon dried
       oregano leaves, crushed
  2 teaspoons olive oil

Preheat oven to 425°F. Grease large baking sheet, then sprinkle sheet with cornmeal; set aside.

Unroll dough onto lightly floured surface. Pat dough into 12×9-inch rectangle. Sprinkle half the pepperoni and half the oregano over one side of dough. Fold over dough making 6×4½-inch rectangle.

Roll dough into 12×9-inch rectangle. Place on prepared baking sheet. Prick dough with fork at 2-inch intervals, about 30 times. Brush with oil; sprinkle with remaining pepperoni and oregano.

Bake 12 to 15 minutes until golden brown. (Prick dough several more times if dough puffs as it bakes.) Cut into squares.   *Makes 12 servings*

Pizza Breadsticks

1 package (¹/₄ ounce) active dry yeast
³/₄ cup warm water (105° to 115°F)
2¹/₂ cups all-purpose flour
¹/₂ cup (2 ounces) shredded part-skim mozzarella cheese
¹/₄ cup (1 ounce) shredded Parmesan cheese
¹/₄ cup chopped red bell pepper
1 green onion with top, sliced
1 medium clove garlic, minced
¹/₂ teaspoon dried basil leaves, crushed
¹/₂ teaspoon dried oregano leaves,
¹/₄ teaspoon red pepper flakes (optional)
¹/₄ teaspoon salt
1 tablespoon olive oil

1. Preheat oven to 400°F. Spray 2 large nonstick baking sheets with nonstick cooking spray; set aside.

2. Sprinkle yeast over warm water in small bowl; stir until yeast dissolves. Let stand 5 minutes or until bubbly.

3. Meanwhile, place all remaining ingredients except olive oil in food processor; process a few seconds to combine. With food processor running, gradually add yeast mixture and olive oil. Process just until mixture forms a ball. (Add an additional 2 tablespoons flour if dough is too sticky.)

4. Transfer dough to lightly floured surface; knead 1 minute. Let dough rest 5 minutes. Roll out dough with lightly floured rolling pin to form 14×8-inch rectangle; cut dough crosswise into ¹/₂-inch-wide strips. Twist dough strips; place on prepared baking sheets.

5. Bake 14 to 16 minutes or until lightly browned.   *Makes 14 servings*

Santa Lucia Bread Wreath

INGREDIENTS

 1 to 1 1/2 teaspoons ground cardamom
 1 package (16 ounces) hot roll mix plus ingredients to prepare mix
 1/2 recipe Cookie Glaze (recipe follows)
   Red and green candied cherries

SUPPLIES

   Small custard cup
   Artificial holly leaves* (optional)
 5 (7- or 8-inch) candles

Real holly leaves are toxic; do not use on food.

1. Stir cardamom into hot roll mix. Prepare mix according to package directions. Knead dough on lightly floured surface until smooth, about 5 minutes. Cover loosely; let stand in bowl about 15 minutes.

2. Grease large baking sheet and outside of custard cup. Place inverted custard cup in center of prepared baking sheet; set aside. Punch down dough; divide into 3 equal pieces. On floured surface, roll and stretch 2 pieces of dough into 20-inch ropes. Braid ropes together; shape into 7-inch circle around custard cup.

3. Divide remaining dough piece in half. Place dough on floured surface; roll and stretch each piece into 12-inch rope. Braid 2 ropes together; shape into 5-inch circle. Place around custard cup, overlapping top of larger braid already on baking sheet.

4. To make holes for candles, shape small sheets of foil into 5 balls, each 1 inch in diameter. Insert balls between 2 braids, evenly spacing them around wreath. Cover dough loosely; let rise in warm place until doubled in size, 20 to 30 minutes.

5. Preheat oven to 375°F. Uncover dough. Bake 25 to 30 minutes or until golden brown. Remove custard cup. Cool wreath on wire rack. Drizzle Cookie Glaze over wreath; decorate with cherries and artificial holly leaves, if desired. Before serving, remove balls of foil. Wrap bottoms of candles with small pieces of additional foil; insert candles into holes. *Makes 8 to 10 servings*

Cookie Glaze: Combine 4 cups powdered sugar and 4 tablespoons milk in small bowl. Stir; add 1 to 2 tablespoons more milk as needed to make medium-thick, pourable glaze.

Santa Lucia Bread Wreath

Tomato and Cheese Focaccia

1 package active dry yeast
3/4 cup warm water, 105° to 115°F
2 cups all-purpose flour
1/2 teaspoon salt
4 tablespoons olive oil, divided
1 teaspoon dried Italian seasoning
8 oil-packed sun-dried tomatoes, well drained
1/2 cup (2 ounces) shredded provolone cheese
1/4 cup (1 ounce) freshly grated Parmesan cheese

Dissolve yeast in warm water; let stand 5 minutes. Combine flour and salt in work bowl of food processor. Stir in yeast mixture and 3 tablespoons oil. Process until ingredients form a ball. Process 1 minute more. Turn out onto lightly floured surface. Knead about 2 minutes or until smooth and elastic. Place dough in oiled bowl; turn once to oil dough surface. Cover with clean kitchen towel. Let rise in warm place about 30 minutes or until doubled in bulk.

Punch dough down. Let rest 5 minutes. Press dough into oiled 10-inch cake pan, deep-dish pizza pan or springform pan. Brush with remaining 1 tablespoon oil. Sprinkle with Italian seasoning. Press sun-dried tomatoes around dough, about 1 inch from edge. Sprinkle with cheeses. Cover and let rise in warm place 15 minutes.

Preheat oven to 425°F. Bake 20 to 25 minutes or until golden brown. Cool completely in pan on wire rack.   *Makes 1 (10-inch) bread*

Note: If mixing dough by hand, combine flour and salt in large bowl. Stir in yeast mixture and 3 tablespoons oil until ball forms. Turn out onto lightly floured surface and knead about 10 minutes or until smooth and elastic. Proceed as directed.

One-Bowl Focaccia

1¼ cups warm water (110°F)
  1 package (1½ teaspoons) active dry yeast
 ¼ cup plus 2 tablespoons extra virgin olive oil
  3 cups unbleached all-purpose flour
1½ teaspoons salt
    Additional flour for kneading
    Toppings of your choice*

Suggested toppings: ½ teaspoon black pepper and ½ teaspoon red pepper flakes; 1 tablespoon mixed Italian seasoning; 1 tablespoon dried minced onion and 1 tablespoon dried basil; 1½ tablespoons chopped mixed fresh herbs (basil, rosemary, sage, parsley); 1 can (8 ounces) prepared pizza sauce

1. Combine water and yeast in a large bowl. Stir to dissolve yeast. Stir in ¼ cup olive oil.

2. In a separate bowl, mix flour and salt. Add all at once to yeast mixture. Stir with a large spoon until dough forms and leaves side of bowl.

3. Dip hands lightly in flour and knead dough in the bowl, flouring hands as needed, until dough is smooth and springy, 3 to 5 minutes. Lift dough from bowl with one hand and spray bowl lightly with olive oil spray. Return dough to bowl, then turn so oiled side is up.

4. Cover with plastic wrap and let rise in a warm (85°F) place about 1 hour, until doubled in bulk.

5. Oil 15½×10½ inch baking pan with 1 tablespoon of the olive oil. Uncover dough and, without kneading or punching down, place into prepared pan. Spread and stretch dough over bottom of pan with hands.

6. Cover crust with waxed paper that has been sprayed with nonstick olive oil spray. Let rise in a warm place 45 minutes to 1 hour, until doubled in bulk.

7. Preheat oven to 400°F. Uncover dough, spread with remaining 1 tablespoon olive oil and sprinkle with your choice of toppings. Make indentations in the dough with your fingertips. Bake about 25 minutes, until edges are golden brown. Serve warm or at room temperature.   *Makes 12 servings*

Italian Bread

1 cup plus 2 tablespoons water, divided
3 to 3½ cups all-purpose flour, divided
1 package active dry yeast
1 teaspoon sugar
¾ teaspoon salt
1 teaspoon cornmeal
1 egg

Heat 1 cup water in small saucepan over low heat until temperature reaches 120° to 130°F. Combine 2 cups flour, yeast, sugar and salt in large bowl. Stir heated water into flour mixture with rubber spatula to form soft dough. Gradually add about 1 cup flour, stirring 2 minutes or until dough begins to lose its stickiness.

Turn out dough onto lightly floured surface. Knead 5 to 8 minutes or until smooth and elastic, gradually adding remaining flour to prevent sticking, if necessary. Shape dough into ball; place in lightly greased bowl. Turn dough over so top is greased. Cover loosely with plastic wrap; let rise in warm place 1 hour or until doubled in bulk.

Punch down dough. Gently flatten into 10-inch circle. Starting with one side, roll up tightly, jelly-roll style. Pinch seams and ends to seal. Taper ends gently by rolling back and forth. (Finished loaf should be about 12 inches long.) Grease large cookie sheet; sprinkle lightly with cornmeal. Place loaf on cookie sheet, seam side down. Loosely cover with lightly greased piece of plastic wrap. Let rise in warm place 30 to 40 minutes or until almost doubled in bulk.

Preheat oven to 350°F. Beat egg and remaining 2 tablespoons water in small bowl. Uncover loaf. Cut 4 or 5 diagonal slashes, each about 3 inches long, in top of loaf using sharp knife. Gently brush egg mixture evenly over loaf. Bake 30 to 35 minutes or until loaf sounds hollow when tapped. Remove immediately from cookie sheet. Cool completely on wire rack.   *Makes 12 servings*

Italian Bread

Italian Herbed Oatmeal Focaccia

2 tablespoons cornmeal

1½ to 2¼ cups all-purpose flour, divided

1 cup QUAKER® Oats (quick or old fashioned, uncooked)

2 tablespoons dried Italian seasoning, divided

1 package (¼ ounce, about 2¼ teaspoons) quick-rising yeast

2 teaspoons granulated sugar

1½ teaspoons garlic salt, divided

1 cup water

¼ cup plus 2 tablespoons olive oil, divided

4 to 6 sun-dried tomatoes packed in oil, drained and chopped

¼ cup grated Parmesan cheese

Lightly spray 13×9-inch baking pan with no-stick cooking spray; dust with cornmeal. In large bowl, combine 1 cup flour, oats, 1 tablespoon Italian seasoning, yeast, sugar and 1 teaspoon garlic salt; mix well. In small saucepan, heat water and ¼ cup olive oil until very warm (120°F to 130°F); stir into flour mixture. Gradually stir in enough remaining flour to make a soft dough. Turn dough out onto lightly floured surface. Knead 8 to 10 minutes or until smooth and elastic. Cover and let rest 10 minutes.

Pat dough into prepared pan, pressing dough out to edges of pan. Using fingertips, poke indentations over surface of dough. Brush remaining 2 tablespoons oil over dough. Sprinkle with remaining 1 tablespoon Italian seasoning and ½ teaspoon garlic salt. Arrange sun-dried tomatoes across top; sprinkle with cheese. Cover; let rise in warm place until doubled, about 30 minutes. Heat oven to 400°F. Bake 25 to 30 minutes or until golden brown. Cut into strips or squares. Serve warm.

Makes 12 servings

Onion Focaccia

2 tablespoons olive oil, divided
1 medium red onion, thinly sliced
3 green onions, cut into $1^1/_2$-inch pieces, cut lengthwise in half
1 teaspoon dried rosemary, crushed
$2^1/_4$ to $2^3/_4$ cups all-purpose flour, divided
3 tablespoons wheat germ
2 tablespoons sugar
1 package ($^1/_4$ ounce) quick-rising dry yeast
$^3/_4$ teaspoon salt
$^3/_4$ cup water
$^1/_3$ cup 1% low fat milk

Heat 1 tablespoon olive oil in large nonstick skillet over low heat. Add red onion; cook and stir 10 minutes until transparent. Remove pan from heat; stir in green onions and rosemary. Set aside to cool.

Combine $1^1/_4$ cups flour, wheat germ, sugar, yeast and salt in large bowl. Heat water and milk in small saucepan until very warm (120° to 130°F). Add liquid to flour mixture with remaining 1 tablespoon olive oil; beat with electric mixer on low speed until combined. Increase speed to medium; continue beating 3 minutes, scraping bowl occasionally. Stir in 1 cup flour with wooden spoon. Add as much remaining flour as necessary to make soft dough.

Turn out dough onto lightly floured surface. Knead about 8 minutes or until dough is smooth and elastic. Shape into a ball; cover with towel and let rest 10 minutes. Coat 15×10-inch pan with nonstick cooking spray.

Roll out dough to fit pan; place in prepared pan. Cover with towel; let rise in warm place 30 minutes or until slightly risen. Place oven rack in lowest position; preheat oven to 400°F.

Make indentations in dough 2 inches apart with end of wooden spoon. Spread onion mixture over top of dough; smooth out evenly with spatula, pressing in gently.

Bake 18 to 20 minutes or until golden brown. Cut into 9 pieces with serrated knife or kitchen shears. Serve warm. *Makes 9 servings*

Almond Amaretto Loaf

1 cup milk
1 large egg
2 tablespoons butter or margarine
¼ cup amaretto liqueur
1 teaspoon lemon juice
¾ teaspoon salt
3 cups bread flour
½ cup chopped almonds, toasted
¼ cup sugar
2 teaspoons FLEISCHMANN'S® Bread Machine Yeast
Amaretto Glaze (recipe follows)
¼ cup sliced almonds, toasted

Add all ingredients except glaze and sliced almonds to bread machine pan in the order suggested by manufacturer, adding chopped almonds with flour. (If dough is too dry or stiff, or too soft or slack, adjust dough consistency.) Recommended cycle: Basic/white bread cycle; light or medium/normal crust color setting.

Remove bread from pan; cool on wire rack. Drizzle with Amaretto Glaze and sprinkle with sliced almonds.   *Makes 1 (½-pound) loaf*

Amaretto Glaze: Combine 1 cup powdered sugar, sifted, 2 tablespoons amaretto liqueur and enough milk (1 to 2 teaspoons) to make glaze of drizzling consistency.

Almond Amaretto Loaf

Smoked Focaccia

2 teaspoons sugar
1½ teaspoons active dry yeast
¾ cup warm water (110° to 115°F)
2 tablespoons finely chopped sun-dried tomatoes
1 tablespoon minced basil *or* 1 teaspoon dried basil
1 tablespoon olive oil
½ teaspoon minced garlic
¼ teaspoon salt
1¾ cups bread flour
¼ cup cornmeal
   Nonstick cooking spray
1 Grilled Bell Pepper (recipe page 272)
¼ teaspoon coarse salt

1. Sprinkle sugar and yeast over warm water; stir until yeast is dissolved. Let stand 5 to 10 minutes or until bubbly. Stir in tomatoes, basil, oil, garlic and salt. Add flour, about ½ cup at a time, stirring until dough begins to pull away from side of bowl and forms a ball; stir in cornmeal.

2. Turn out dough onto lightly floured surface; flatten slightly. Knead gently about 5 minutes or until smooth and elastic, adding additional flour to prevent sticking, if necessary. Place dough in large bowl sprayed with nonstick cooking spray and turn dough so all sides are coated. Let rise, covered, in warm place about 1 hour or until doubled in bulk. (Dough may be refrigerated overnight.) Prepare Grilled Bell Pepper.

3. Punch down dough; turn onto lightly floured surface and knead 1 minute. Divide dough in half; press each half into a 9×7-inch rectangle on large sheet of foil sprayed with cooking spray. Fold edges of foil to form "pan." Dimple surfaces of dough using fingertips; spray tops with cooking spray. Cut bell pepper into strips and arrange on focaccia; sprinkle with coarse salt. Let rise, covered, 30 minutes.

4. Grill focaccia on covered grill over medium coals 8 to 12 minutes or until they sound hollow when tapped, keeping on foil "pans." Check bottoms of focaccia after about 6 minutes; move to upper grill rack or over indirect heat to finish if browning too quickly.

Makes 6 servings

Smoked Focaccia

Grilled Bell Pepper

1 bell pepper (any color), stemmed, seeded and halved

Grill bell pepper halves skin-side down on covered grill over medium to hot coals 15 to 25 minutes or until skin is charred, without turning. Remove from grill and place in plastic bag until cool enough to handle, about 10 minutes. Remove skin with paring knife and discard.

Italian Pan Rolls

$^3/_4$ cup warm water
1 teaspoon garlic salt
1 tablespoon cold butter or margarine
$2^3/_4$ cups all-purpose flour
1 tablespoon sugar
$^1/_2$ teaspoon dried Italian seasoning *or* $^1/_4$ teaspoon *each* dried oregano and basil leaves
2 teaspoons active dry yeast
2 tablespoons olive oil, vegetable oil or melted butter
$^1/_4$ cup grated Parmesan cheese

1. Measuring carefully, place all ingredients except olive oil and cheese in bread machine pan in order specified by owner's manual. Program dough cycle setting; press start.

2. Divide dough into quarters, then divide again into quarters, making 16 pieces. Shape each piece into smooth ball. Dip each ball in oil; coat with cheese and arrange in greased 8- or 9-inch round or square cake pan. Cover loosely with plastic wrap and let rise in warm place 1 to $1^1/_2$ hours or until doubled.

3. Preheat oven to 375°F. Uncover rolls and bake 25 minutes or until golden. Remove immediately from pan; cool on wire rack. *Makes 16 rolls*

Focaccia with Dried Tomatoes and Fontina

1 tablespoon olive oil
1 loaf (1 pound) frozen bread dough, thawed according to package
   directions
1 jar (8 ounces) SONOMA® Marinated Dried Tomatoes, drained,
   2 tablespoons oil reserved
4 cloves garlic, minced
2/3 cup sliced black olives
1 tablespoon dried basil
1 teaspoon dried oregano
1 teaspoon dried rosemary
2 cups grated fontina cheese

Preheat oven to 425°F. Oil a 13×9×2-inch baking pan. Roll and stretch dough on lightly floured surface; fit dough into pan.

Combine reserved tomato oil with garlic; brush over dough. Sprinkle olives, basil, oregano and rosemary evenly over dough. Arrange tomatoes on top; cover with cheese.

Bake for 35 to 40 minutes until bread is springy to the touch and golden brown around the edges. (Cover loosely with foil during the last 10 minutes if becoming too brown.) Cut into squares while still warm. *Makes 16 squares*

Focaccia has been around for nearly 2000 years. Originally from the Latin word focacia, *meaning hearth or fireside, focaccia is a cross between pizza bread and traditional bread. In fact, focaccia was a precursor to what we now know as pizza. Toppings were added to the slightly chewy, flat bread and it was served as an appetizer. Eventually cheese and sauce were added, and pizza was born. But the classic focaccia lives on.*

Garlic and Herb Parmesan Buns

8 BUNS

1¼ cups water

1 tablespoon sugar

1½ teaspoons salt

1 teaspoon garlic powder

2 teaspoons dried Italian herbs

⅓ cup grated Parmesan cheese

3 cups bread flour

1 tablespoon rapid-rise yeast

12 BUNS

1½ cups water

2 tablespoons sugar

2 teaspoons salt

1½ teaspoons garlic powder

1 tablespoon dried Italian herbs

½ cup grated Parmesan cheese

4 cups bread flour

1 tablespoon rapid-rise yeast

TOPPING

1 to 2 tablespoons grated Parmesan cheese

1. Measuring carefully, place all ingredients except topping in bread machine pan in order specified by owner's manual. Program dough cycle setting; press start.

2. Turn out dough onto lightly oiled surface. Cut dough into 8 pieces for small batch or 12 pieces for large batch. Shape into smooth balls. Place on greased baking sheet; flatten slightly. Let rise in warm place 45 minutes or until doubled.

3. Preheat oven to 400°F. Brush buns with water; sprinkle tops with pinch of cheese. Bake 15 minutes or until lightly browned. Serve warm or transfer to wire racks to cool completely. *Makes 8 or 12 buns*

Garlic and Herb Parmesan Buns

Cheesy Onion Focaccia

  $^1/_2$ cup plus 3 tablespoons honey, divided
 $2^1/_3$ cups warm water, 105° to 115°F, divided
 $1^1/_2$ packages active dry yeast
    6 tablespoons olive oil, divided
  $^1/_3$ cup cornmeal
    3 cups whole wheat flour
 $4^1/_2$ teaspoons coarse salt
    3 to 4 cups all-purpose flour, divided
    1 large red onion, thinly sliced
    1 cup red wine vinegar
       Additional cornmeal
    1 cup grated Parmesan cheese
  $^1/_2$ teaspoon onion salt
       Black pepper to taste

1. To proof yeast, place 3 tablespoons honey in large bowl. Pour $^1/_3$ cup water over honey. Do not stir. Sprinkle yeast over water. Let stand at room temperature about 15 minutes or until bubbly. Add remaining 2 cups water, 3 tablespoons olive oil, $^1/_3$ cup cornmeal and whole wheat flour to yeast mixture; mix until well blended. Stir in salt and 2 cups all-purpose flour. Gradually stir in enough remaining all-purpose flour until mixture clings to sides of bowl.

2. Turn dough out onto lightly floured surface. To knead in remaining flour, fold the dough in half toward you and press dough away from you with heels of hands. Give dough a quarter turn and continue folding, pushing and turning until the dough is smooth and satiny, about 10 minutes. Halve the dough. Place each half in a large, lightly greased bowl; turn each dough half over to grease surface. Cover each with clean kitchen towel and let dough rise in warm place (85°F) until doubled in bulk. Meanwhile, combine onion, vinegar and remaining $^1/_2$ cup honey. Marinate at room temperature at least 1 hour.

3. Grease 2 (12-inch) pizza pans and sprinkle with additional cornmeal. Stretch dough and pat into pans; create valleys with fingertips. Cover dough with greased plastic wrap; let rise for 1 hour. Dough will double in size. Preheat oven to 400°F. Drain onions and scatter them over dough. Sprinkle with remaining 3 tablespoons olive oil, Parmesan cheese and onion salt; season with pepper. Bake 25 to 30 minutes until crusty and golden. Cut into wedges to serve. Serve warm.

Makes 2 breads (6 to 8 servings each)

Cheesy Onion Focaccia

Le Pizze

The flat crust so common to modern pizza has its roots in the flat breads of early Israel, Egypt and other Middle Eastern cultures. Despite its ancient origins, pizza was first created in the 1800's by Raffaele Esposito to impress a visiting Italian monarch, King Umberto. Esposito topped flat bread with ingredients that represented the color of the Italian flag, red tomatoes, white mozzarella and green basil. The creation was such a success that pizza became popular throughout the country. Although Italians immigrating to America brought their pizza recipes with them, it wasn't until American GI's returned from World War II Italy that the dish began to be served in American cities like New York and Chicago.

Three Pepper Pizza (page 287)

Calzone Italiano

Pizza dough for one 14-inch pizza
1 can (15 ounces) CONTADINA® Pizza Sauce, divided
3 ounces sliced pepperoni *or* ¹/₂ pound crumbled Italian sausage, cooked, drained
2 tablespoons chopped green bell pepper
1 cup (4 ounces) shredded mozzarella cheese
1 cup (8 ounces) ricotta cheese

1. Divide dough into 4 equal portions. Place on lightly floured, large, rimless cookie sheet. Press or roll out dough to 7-inch circles.

2. Spread 2 tablespoons pizza sauce onto half of each circle to within ¹/₂ inch of edge; top with ¹/₄ each pepperoni, bell pepper and mozzarella cheese.

3. Spoon ¹/₄ cup ricotta cheese onto remaining half of each circle; fold dough over. Press edges together tightly to seal. Cut slits into top of dough to allow steam to escape.

4. Bake in preheated 350°F oven for 20 to 25 minutes or until crusts are golden brown. Meanwhile, heat remaining pizza sauce; serve over calzones.

Makes 4 servings

Note: If desired, 1 large calzone may be made instead of 4 individual calzones. To prepare, shape dough into 1 (13-inch) circle. Spread ¹/₂ cup pizza sauce onto half of dough; proceed as above. Bake for 25 minutes.

Prep Time: 15 minutes
Cook Time: 25 minutes

Calzone Italiano

Herbed Mushroom Pizza

2 tablespoons olive oil

8 ounces sliced button or wild mushrooms, such as portobello or shiitake

1½ teaspoons bottled minced garlic

½ teaspoon dried basil leaves

½ teaspoon dried thyme leaves

¼ teaspoon salt

¼ teaspoon black pepper

⅓ cup pizza or marinara sauce

1 (12-inch) bread-style pizza crust

1½ cups (6 ounces) shredded Mozzarella cheese

1. Preheat oven to 450°F. Heat oil in large skillet over medium-high heat until hot. Add mushrooms and garlic; cook 4 minutes, stirring occasionally. Stir in basil, thyme, salt and pepper.

2. Spread pizza sauce evenly over crust. Top with mushroom mixture; sprinkle with cheese. Bake directly on oven rack 8 minutes or until crust is golden brown and cheese is melted. Slide cookie sheet under pizza to remove from oven.

Makes 4 servings

Prep and Cook Time: 15 minutes

Herbed Mushroom Pizza

Roasted Red Pepper, Eggplant, Goat Cheese and Olive Pizza

Nonstick cooking spray
1 small eggplant, cut into ¼-inch-thick slices
1 tablespoon olive oil
¼ cup finely chopped onion
1 tablespoon minced fresh rosemary *or* 2 teaspoons dried rosemary
3 cloves garlic, minced
½ cup roasted red pepper strips
1 (12-inch) round prepared Italian bread shell or New York-Style Pizza Crust (recipe page 286)
2 ounces goat cheese, crumbled
6 kalamata olives, pitted and halved
Black pepper

1. Preheat oven to 500°F. Spray baking sheet with cooking spray. Place eggplant slices on pan; spray with cooking spray. Bake 8 to 10 minutes or until light golden. Turn slices over and bake 6 to 8 minutes or until slices are golden and very tender. Set aside.

2. Meanwhile, heat oil, onion, rosemary and garlic in small skillet over medium heat. Cook and stir 3 to 4 minutes or until onion is translucent. Set aside.

3. Place red peppers in food processor or blender; process until smooth. Set aside.

4. Bake bread shell 3 to 4 minutes or until top is crisp and beginning to brown. Spread puréed red peppers evenly over pizza, leaving 1-inch border. Arrange eggplant over top, slightly overlapping slices. Spoon or brush onion mixture over eggplant. Top with cheese, olives and black pepper. Bake 3 to 5 minutes or until crust is deep golden.

Makes 4 servings

Roasted Red Pepper, Eggplant,
Goat Cheese and Olive Pizza

New York-Style Pizza Crust

$^2/_3$ cup warm water (110° to 115°F)
1 teaspoon sugar
$^1/_2$ ($^1/_4$-ounce) package rapid-rise or active dry yeast
1$^3/_4$ cups all-purpose or bread flour
$^1/_2$ teaspoon salt
1 tablespoon cornmeal (optional)

1. Combine water and sugar in small bowl; stir to dissolve sugar. Sprinkle yeast on top; stir to combine. Let stand 5 to 10 minutes or until foamy.

2. Combine flour and salt in medium bowl. Add yeast mixture. Stir until soft dough forms. Remove dough to lightly floured surface. Knead 5 minutes or until dough is smooth and elastic, adding additional flour, 1 tablespoon at a time, as needed. Place dough in medium bowl coated with nonstick cooking spray. Turn dough in bowl so top is coated with cooking spray; cover with towel or plastic wrap. Let rise in warm place 30 minutes or until doubled in bulk.

3. Punch dough down; place on lightly floured surface and knead about 2 minutes or until smooth. Pat dough into flat disc about 7 inches in diameter. Let rest 2 to 3 minutes. Pat and gently stretch dough from edges until dough seems to not stretch anymore. Let rest 2 to 3 minutes. Continue patting and stretching until dough is 12 to 14 inches in diameter.

4. Spray 12- to 14-inch pizza pan with nonstick spray; sprinkle with cornmeal, if desired. Press dough into pan.

5. Preheat oven to 500°F. Follow directions for individual recipes, baking pizza on bottom rack of oven.

*Makes 1 medium-thin 12-inch crust, 1 very thin 14-inch crust,
2 (8- to 9-inch) crusts, 4 (6- to 7- inch) crusts or 20 (2$^1/_2$-inch) mini pizza crusts*

Three-Pepper Pizza

    1   cup (½ of 15 ounce can) CONTADINA® Four Cheese Pizza Sauce
    1   (12-inch) prepared pre-baked pizza crust
1½ cups (6 ounces) shredded mozzarella cheese, divided
    ½   cup each: red, green and yellow bell peppers, sliced into thin rings
    2   tablespoons shredded Parmesan cheese
    1   tablespoon chopped fresh basil *or* 1 teaspoon dried basil leaves, crushed

1. Spread pizza sauce onto crust to within 1 inch of edge.

2. Sprinkle with 1 cup mozzarella cheese, bell peppers, remaining mozzarella cheese and Parmesan cheese.

3. Bake according to pizza crust package directions or until crust is crisp and cheese is melted. Sprinkle with basil.   *Makes 8 servings*

Cheesy Beef Stromboli

    ¾   pound lean ground beef
    1   jar (1 pound) RAGÚ® Cheese Creations!® Double Cheddar Sauce
    1   teaspoon chili powder
    1   pound frozen pizza or bread dough, thawed
    1   egg yolk

1. Preheat oven to 375°F. In 10-inch skillet, brown ground beef over medium-high heat; drain. Remove from heat. Stir in ½ cup Ragú Cheese Creations! Sauce and chili powder and set aside.

2. Meanwhile, on greased jelly-roll pan, press dough to form 11×8-inch rectangle. Arrange beef mixture over dough, leaving 1-inch border around edges. Roll, starting at longest side, jelly-roll style. Fold in ends and pinch to seal. Arrange on pan, seam-side down.

3. Brush with egg yolk. Bake 40 minutes or until bread is golden. Let stand 10 minutes before slicing. Serve with remaining sauce, heated.   *Makes 6 servings*

Prep Time: 10 minutes
Cook Time: 40 minutes

Cheese-Tomato Pizza

DOUGH:

3¼ cups all-purpose flour
1 tablespoon sugar
1 envelope FLEISCHMANN'S® RapidRise™ Yeast
1½ teaspoons salt
1 cup water
2 tablespoons peanut oil

TOPPING:

Quick Tomato Sauce (recipe follows)
1½ cups mozzarella and provolone cheese blend
½ cup grated Cheddar cheese
½ cup grated fresh Parmesan cheese

In large bowl, combine 2 cups flour, sugar, undissolved yeast and salt. Heat water and peanut oil until very warm (120° to 130°F). Gradually stir into dry ingredients. Stir in enough remaining flour to make stiff dough. Turn out onto floured surface. Knead until smooth and elastic, about 8 to 10 minutes. Cover; let rest 10 minutes.

Divide dough in half. Shape each half into a ball. Roll each into a 12-inch circle. Place each on greased 12-inch pizza pans or baking sheets. Prick dough with fork; let rest 10 minutes.

Parbake at 450°F for 5 minutes. Remove from pans; place on wire cooling racks. Spread Quick Tomato Sauce evenly on each crust; sprinkle with cheese. Bake on wire racks at 450°F for 10 minutes or until done. Cut into wedges and serve immediately.

Makes 2 (12-inch) pizzas

Quick Tomato Sauce: Combine 1 (8-ounce) can tomato sauce and ¼ cup tomato paste. Stir in ½ teaspoon each of crushed oregano and crushed basil.

Cheese-Tomato Pizza

Vegetable Pizza Primavera

New York-Style Pizza Crust (recipe page 286)

1 1/2 cups broccoli florets
1 carrot, cut into julienne strips
1 small yellow squash or zucchini, cut into 1/4-inch-thick slices
6 thin asparagus spears, cut into 1 1/2-inch pieces
10 fresh pea pods *or* 3 tablespoons frozen green peas, thawed
1 green onion, thinly sliced
3/4 cup (3 ounces) shredded Swiss cheese or provolone cheese
1/3 cup slivered fresh basil leaves *or* 2 tablespoons chopped fresh tarragon
leaves
1/4 cup (1 ounce) grated Romano cheese
Black pepper
1/2 teaspoon olive oil

1. Prepare New York-Style Pizza Crust. Move oven rack to lowest position in oven and preheat oven to 500°F.

2. Place steamer rack in large saucepan. Add water to about 1/4 inch below rack. Bring water to a boil over high heat. Add broccoli; cover and steam 6 to 8 minutes or until crisp-tender. Lift broccoli from pan and plunge into large bowl of ice water until chilled. Repeat with remaining vegetables except green onion, adding water to saucepan as needed. Steam carrots 3 to 4 minutes, squash 2 minutes, asparagus 3 to 4 minutes, and pea pods 1 minute. Drain vegetables and pat dry with paper towels.

3. Sprinkle Swiss cheese over dough, leaving 1-inch border. Bake 3 to 4 minutes or until cheese melts and crust is light golden. Place all vegetables on pizza. Top with basil, Romano cheese and pepper. Bake 4 to 6 minutes or until crust is deep golden and cheese is melted. Brush edge of crust with olive oil. Cut into 8 wedges.

Makes 4 servings

Vegetable Pizza Primavera

Ham, Pepper & Onion Pizza
with Two Cheeses

  1   package pizza dough mix *or* 1 prepared (14-inch) pizza crust
  3   cloves garlic, minced
 1/2 cup extra-virgin olive oil, divided
  2   cups chopped plum tomatoes
1 1/2 cups prepared barbecue sauce
 1/4 cup dried oregano leaves
  3   cups (12 ounces) shredded mozzarella cheese
  1   cup freshly grated Parmesan cheese
  2   pounds HILLSHIRE FARM® Ham, cut into strips
  1   red onion, thinly sliced
  1   green bell pepper, thinly sliced
  1   tablespoon pine nuts (optional)

Preheat oven to 425°F. Prepare pizza dough according to package directions; spread dough onto 14-inch round baking sheet. (If using prepared crust, place crust on baking sheet.)

Saute garlic in 1/4 cup oil 5 minutes in medium saucepan over medium heat. Add tomatoes, barbecue sauce and oregano. Bring to a gentle boil; reduce heat to medium. Simmer 20 to 30 minutes or until sauce is thickened.

Brush pizza dough with 2 tablespoons oil. Cover dough with cheeses, leaving 1/2-inch border around edge. Cover cheese with barbecue sauce mixture; arrange Ham, onion and pepper over sauce. Drizzle pizza with remaining 2 tablespoons oil; sprinkle with pine nuts, if desired. Bake 20 minutes. Slice and serve.   *Makes 4 servings*

Thin-Crust Whole Wheat Veggie Pizza

¾ to 1 cup all-purpose flour, divided
½ cup whole wheat flour
1 teaspoon quick-rise dry yeast
1½ teaspoons dried basil leaves, crushed, divided
¼ teaspoon salt
1 tablespoon olive oil
1 large clove garlic, minced
½ cup very warm water (120° to 130°F)
1 teaspoon yellow cornmeal
½ cup no-salt-added tomato sauce
1 cup thinly sliced mushrooms
½ cup thinly sliced zucchini
⅓ cup chopped green onions
1 large roasted red bell pepper,* cut lengthwise into thin strips *or* ¾ cup
  sliced, drained, bottled roasted red peppers
1 cup (4 ounces) shredded part-skim mozzarella cheese
¼ teaspoon red pepper flakes

To roast pepper, cut pepper lengthwise into halves; remove stem, membrane and seeds. Broil 3 inches from heat, skin side up, until skin is blackened and blistered. Place halves in small resealable plastic food storage bag. Seal; set aside 15 minutes. Remove pepper from bag. Peel off skin; drain on paper towel.

Combine ½ cup all-purpose flour, whole wheat flour, yeast, 1 teaspoon basil and salt. Blend oil with garlic in small cup; stir into flour mixture with water. Stir in ¼ cup all-purpose flour until soft, slightly sticky dough forms, adding remaining ¼ cup all-purpose flour to prevent sticking if necessary. Knead dough on lightly floured surface about 5 minutes or until smooth and elastic. Shape dough into a ball. Cover with inverted bowl or clean towel; let rest 10 minutes.

Place oven rack in lowest position; preheat oven to 400°F. Spray 12-inch pizza pan or baking sheet with nonstick cooking spray; sprinkle with cornmeal and set aside. Roll dough into large circle on lightly floured surface. Transfer to prepared pan, stretching dough out to edge of pan. (Too much rolling makes crust heavy and dense; stretching dough to fit pan is best.)

Blend tomato sauce and remaining ½ teaspoon basil in small bowl; spread evenly over crust. Top with mushrooms, zucchini, green onions, roasted bell pepper and mozzarella; sprinkle red pepper flakes on top. Bake 20 to 25 minutes or until crust is golden brown and cheese melts. *Makes 4 servings*

Pizzette with Basil

1 can (6 ounces) CONTADINA® Italian Paste with Italian Seasonings
2 tablespoons softened cream cheese
2 tablespoons chopped fresh basil *or* 2 teaspoons dried basil leaves
1 loaf (1 pound) Italian bread, sliced $1/4$ inch thick
8 ounces mozzarella cheese, thinly sliced
   Whole basil leaves (optional)
   Freshly ground black pepper (optional)

1. Combine tomato paste, cream cheese and chopped basil in small bowl.

2. Toast bread slices on *ungreased* baking sheet under broiler, 6 to 8 inches from heat, turning after 1 minute, until lightly browned on both sides; remove from broiler.

3. Spread 2 teaspoons tomato mixture onto each toasted bread slice; top with 1 slice (about $1/4$ ounce) mozzarella cheese.

4. Broil 6 to 8 inches from heat for 1 to 2 minutes or until cheese begins to melt. Top with whole basil leaves and pepper, if desired.   *Makes about 30 pizzas*

Prep Time: 7 minutes
Cook Time: 10 minutes

Pizzettes are small pizzas that can be served either as appetizers or as main meal accompaniments. They're also a great way to use up bread.

Pizzette with Basil

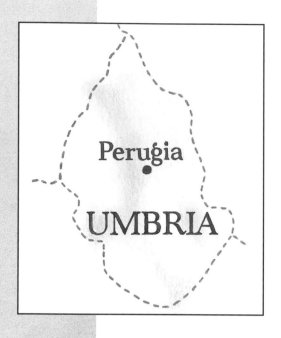

Perugia

UMBRIA

Umbria

FOR CENTURIES UMBRIA WAS STRATEGICALLY IMPORTANT AS THE ROUTE FROM ROME TO THE ADRIATIC SEA, ACTING AS BOTH A BATTLEFIELD AND CROSSROAD FOR TRAVELERS.

*B*ordered by Tuscany, Lazio and Marche, Umbria is the only region in mainland Italy without a seacoast. This rugged land of rolling hills, mountains and rivers is known as "the green heart of Italy" and is rich in medieval culture. As Italy's most rural region, Umbria is often described as having a mystical serenity. The countryside is dotted with monasteries and abbeys and is the birthplace of St. Francis of Assisi and St. Valentine. For centuries Umbria was strategically important as the route from Rome to the Adriatic Sea, acting as both a battlefield and crossroad for travelers. Local lords, wanting to imitate the opulence of the Roman court, created a pleasure-driven lifestyle that was in direct contrast to that of the austere monks. Even today, the region's cuisine reflects this contradiction, fluctuating between two approaches to food: rustic, peasant fare with few ingredients and refined dishes with rich ingredients. The common liquid thread between these culinary traditions is the most widely used agricultural product in the region—olive oil—which gives these varied dishes a shared flavor.

Like Tuscans, Umbrians obsess over the purity of ingredients. Until the twentieth century, Umbrian farmers ate little meat since they had to sell their livestock to make a living. So they devised cucina contadina (peasant cooking) based on seasonal harvests. Today, Perugia's famous beef and Norcia's legendary pork are still important to the local economy. The art of pig farming and meat curing dates back to the Middle Ages in Norcia and the town is known throughout Italy for its pork products: prosciutto di montagna; pancetta (unsmoked bacon); porchetta (suckling pig); salami; sausages. The woods of Norcia are also home to black gold, the prized Umbrian black truffle that tops crostini, eggs and pasta. Other regional specialties include lentils; cardoons or gobbi (a vegetable tasting like a cross between artichokes and celery); woodland game, chestnuts and herbs; white truffles from Orvieto; tagliatelle pasta; and loaves of pane casereccio (unsalted bread).

Umbria has a long wine history dating back to the ancient Etruscans. The region is known mainly for its white wines, such as the pale, dry Orvieto Classico and rich, nutty Grechetto. However it also produces excellent reds, the most prestigious being the aged Torgiano Rosso riserva or Rubesco. Rich, full-bodied Montefalco Sagrantino, made from an ancient local grape variety in both sweet and dry versions, is also highly rated.

In addition to livestock and truffles (Umbria is Italy's leading producer), the region is home to important wheat- and corn-growing areas. Steel production, chemicals and arms manufacturing are found in Narni, Terni and Foligno. Perugia, the capital city, is known for textile and food industries, including dried pastas and the famous Perugina chocolates. Throughout the region artisans carry on ancient handicrafts, the most noted being ceramics and pottery. Umbria has immense tourist potential, but tends to be less visited than other regions due to inadequate rail connections. Tourists who do seek it out discover treasures of medieval and Renaissance art in a setting of relatively unspoiled nature. Every summer the town of Spoleto holds an arts festival. Considered one of Europe's best, it has even spawned a popular twin festival in Charleston, South Carolina.

Marinated Chicken and Pesto Pizza

8 ounces chicken tenders
1/4 cup prepared fat-free Italian salad dressing
   Nonstick cooking spray
1/2 cup sun-dried tomatoes
1 cup chopped plum tomatoes
1 tablespoon prepared pesto
1 teaspoon salt-free Italian herb blend
1/4 teaspoon red pepper flakes
1 (12-inch) prepared pizza crust
1 cup (4 ounces) shredded part-skim mozzarella cheese

1. Cut chicken tenders into 2×1/2-inch strips. Place in resealable plastic food storage bag. Pour Italian dressing over chicken. Seal bag and turn to coat. Marinate at room temperature 15 minutes, turning several times. Remove chicken from marinade; discard marinade. Spray large nonstick skillet with cooking spray; heat over medium heat until hot. Add chicken; cook and stir 5 minutes or until no longer pink in center.

2. Meanwhile, cover sun-dried tomatoes with boiling water in small bowl; let stand 10 minutes. Drain; cut tomatoes into 1/4-inch strips.

3. Preheat oven to 450°F. Combine plum tomatoes, pesto, herb blend and pepper in small bowl. Spread on pizza crust. Add chicken tenders and sun-dried tomatoes; sprinkle with cheese.

4. Bake 8 to 10 minutes or until cheese melts and pizza is heated through.

Makes 6 servings

Marinated Chicken and Pesto Pizza

Italian Covered Deep-Dish Pizza

Thick Pizza Crust (recipe page 302)

2 cups (16 ounces) part-skim ricotta cheese
1 tablespoon cornstarch
1 teaspoon dried basil
1 teaspoon dried oregano
½ teaspoon black pepper
1 jar (7 ounces) roasted red peppers, drained, chopped and divided
1 clove garlic
1 bag (10 ounces) washed fresh spinach leaves
¼ pound thinly sliced lean ham
6 tablespoons (2½ ounces) shredded Romano or Parmesan cheese
½ teaspoon olive oil

1. Prepare Thick Pizza Crust as directed through step 1, adding 1 teaspoon dried rosemary, ½ teaspoon dried oregano and ¼ teaspoon *each* dried thyme and black pepper to flour mixture. Preheat oven to 500°F.

2. Combine ricotta, cornstarch, basil, oregano and pepper in large bowl; set aside. Place ½ cup red peppers and garlic in food processor or blender; process until puréed.

3. Remove stems from spinach leaves. Place half the spinach and 1 tablespoon water in large skillet over medium-high heat. Cover and cook 1 minute. Turn spinach and cook until just wilted. Drain on paper towels. Repeat with remaining spinach. Top spinach with paper towels; press gently to remove moisture.

4. Knead dough on lightly floured surface 2 minutes or until smooth. Roll into even log. Mark in thirds. Cut off ⅓ of dough; cover and set aside. Roll remaining ⅔ of dough into 15-inch disc, following directions in step 2 of Thick Pizza Crust recipe. Spray 14-inch deep-dish pizza pan with nonstick cooking spray. Place dough in pan, easing into edges and up sides; let excess dough hang over lip of pan.

continued on page 302

Italian Covered Deep-Dish Pizza

5. Cover bottom with layer of ham. Spread evenly with ricotta mixture. Cover with spinach. Top with remaining chopped red peppers. Roll remaining dough to 12- to 13-inch round. Place over filling. Brush ½ inch of edge with water. Fold overhanging crust over top and press gently to seal. Bake 10 to 12 minutes or until crust is golden. Spread puréed red peppers over center of top crust. Sprinkle with Romano. Bake 6 to 8 minutes or until crust is deep golden on top and crisp on bottom. Brush edge of crust with olive oil. Garnish with fresh basil, if desired. Cut into 8 wedges.

Makes 8 servings

Thick Pizza Crust

¾ cup warm water (110° to 115°F)
1 teaspoon sugar
½ of ¼ ounce package rapid-rise yeast or active dry yeast
2½ cups all-purpose or bread flour
½ teaspoon salt
1 tablespoon cornmeal (optional)

1. Combine water and sugar in small bowl; stir to dissolve sugar. Sprinkle yeast on top; stir to combine. Let stand 5 to 10 minutes or until foamy. Combine flour and salt in medium bowl. Stir in yeast mixture. Mix until mixture forms soft dough.

2. Remove dough to lightly floured surface. Knead 5 minutes or until dough is smooth and elastic, adding more flour, 1 tablespoon at a time, if necessary. Place dough in medium bowl coated with nonstick cooking spray. Turn dough in bowl so top is coated with cooking spray; cover with towel or plastic wrap. Let rise in warm place 30 minutes or until doubled in bulk. Punch dough down; place on lightly floured surface and knead until smooth, about 2 minutes. Pat dough into flat disk about 8 to 9 inches in diameter. Let rest 2 to 3 minutes. Pat and gently stretch dough from edges until dough seems to not stretch anymore. Let rest 2 to 3 minutes more. Continue patting and stretching until dough is 15 inches in diameter.

3. Spray 12- to 14-inch pizza pan with nonstick spray; sprinkle with cornmeal, if desired. Press crust into pan. Cover with plastic wrap and let stand in warm place 10 to 20 minutes or until slightly puffed. Position oven rack in lowest position. Preheat oven to 500°F. Prick crust with fork at 2-inch intervals. Bake 4 to 5 minutes or until top is dry but not yet golden. Remove from oven. Follow topping and baking instructions for individual recipes.

Makes 1 thick 12-inch crust, 1 medium-thick 14-inch crust, 2 thick 8- to 9-inch crusts, 4 thick 6- to 7-inch crusts or 20 (2½-inch) thick mini pizza crusts

Stuffed Pizza

2 loaves (1 pound each) frozen bread dough, thawed
1 bottle (15 ounces) CONTADINA® Pizza Squeeze Pizza Sauce, divided
1 package (3 ounces) sliced pepperoni, quartered
1 package (10 ounces) frozen chopped spinach, thawed and squeezed dry
1 cup (4 ounces) shredded mozzarella cheese
1 carton (8 ounces) ricotta cheese
1 cup grated Parmesan cheese
1 can (3.8 ounces) sliced ripe olives, drained
1 tablespoon olive oil
1 tablespoon grated Parmesan cheese

1. Roll bread dough into two 12-inch circles on floured surface. Place one circle on greased baking sheet.

2. Spread with 1/4 cup pizza sauce to 1 inch from edge.

3. Combine pepperoni, spinach, mozzarella, ricotta, 1 cup Parmesan cheese and olives in large bowl. Spread mixture over pizza sauce. Squeeze 1/4 cup pizza sauce evenly over filling; dampen outside edge. Place remaining bread dough on top and seal. Cut 8 steam vents.

4. Bake on lowest rack in preheated 350°F oven for 20 minutes. Brush with olive oil; sprinkle with 1 tablespoon Parmesan cheese.

5. Bake for additional 15 to 20 minutes or until well browned. Let stand 15 minutes before cutting. Warm remaining pizza sauce and serve over wedges of pizza.

Makes 8 servings

Prep Time: 20 minutes
Cook Time: 40 minutes
Standing Time: 15 minutes

Pizza Puttanesca

New York-Style Pizza Crust (recipe page 286)

1½ teaspoons olive oil, divided
3 cloves garlic, minced
1 can (8 ounces) tomato sauce
1 teaspoon dried basil leaves
1 teaspoon dried rosemary
½ teaspoon dried oregano leaves
¼ teaspoon fennel seed, crushed
⅛ teaspoon ground red pepper
1 small yellow bell pepper, cored, seeded and cut into strips
3 ounces cleaned squid tubes, cut into ½-inch-wide rings
3 ounces shrimp, peeled, deveined and halved
3 ounces scallops (1¼-inch diameter, about 8)
¾ cup (3 ounces) shredded part-skim mozzarella cheese, divided
2 tablespoons grated Romano cheese
2 teaspoons drained capers (optional)

1. Prepare New York-Style Pizza Crust. Preheat oven to 500°F.

2. Combine oil and garlic in 2- to 3-quart saucepan over medium-high heat. Cook and stir about 1 minute or until garlic is fragrant but not browned. Add tomato sauce, basil, rosemary, oregano, fennel and ground red pepper; bring to a boil. Reduce heat to medium and simmer, uncovered, about 5 minutes or until reduced by about ⅓. Stir in bell pepper; set aside.

3. Bring 1 quart water to a boil in 2- to 3-quart saucepan. Add squid and cook 30 seconds or until edges begin to curl. Transfer to colander. Add shrimp to saucepan; cook 1 minute or until pink and opaque. Transfer to colander with squid. Add scallops to saucepan. Remove from heat and let stand 2 to 3 minutes or until scallops are just slightly transparent in center. Drain.

4. Sprinkle half the mozzarella cheese over prepared crust, leaving 1-inch border. Bake 4 to 5 minutes or until cheese is melted and crust is light golden brown. Spread tomato sauce over cheese. Top with squid, shrimp, scallops, remaining mozzarella cheese and Romano cheese. Bake 3 to 4 minutes or until crust is deep golden brown. Sprinkle with capers, if desired. Cut into 8 wedges.

Makes 4 servings

Pizza Puttanesca

Chunky Three-Cheese and Chicken Pizza

1 cup (½ of 15 ounce can) CONTADINA® Original Pizza Sauce
1 (12-inch) prepared, pre-baked pizza crust
4 ounces cooked chicken, chopped (about 1 cup)
1 cup (4 ounces) cubed mozzarella cheese
½ cup (2 ounces) cubed cheddar cheese
¼ cup (1 ounce) shredded fresh Parmesan cheese
2 tablespoons chopped fresh basil *or* 2 teaspoons dried basil leaves, crushed (optional)

1. Spread pizza sauce onto crust to within 1 inch of edge.

2. Top with chicken, mozzarella cheese, cheddar cheese and Parmesan cheese.

3. Bake according to pizza crust package directions or until crust is crisp and cheese is melted. Sprinkle with basil.   *Makes 8 servings*

Pizza Blanco

½ cup grated Parmesan cheese
1 (12-inch) prebaked pizza crust
3 plum tomatoes, thinly sliced
½ cup HIDDEN VALLEY® The Original Ranch® Dressing
½ cup roasted red pepper strips, rinsed and drained
1 can (2¼ ounces) sliced ripe olives, drained
¼ cup sliced green onions
1 cup (4 ounces) shredded mozzarella and Cheddar cheese blend

Preheat oven to 450°F. Sprinkle Parmesan cheese on pizza crust; cover with a single layer of tomato slices. Drizzle dressing over tomatoes. Arrange red pepper, olives and onions on pizza; sprinkle with cheese blend. Bake at 450°F. for 15 minutes or until cheese is melted and crust is hot.   *Makes 8 servings*

Turkey Calzones

1 package (1¼ pounds) BUTTERBALL® Lean Fresh Ground Turkey
1 cup prepared pizza sauce
2 tablespoons chopped fresh parsley
2 tubes (12 ounces each) refrigerated large biscuits (10 per tube)
¾ cup low fat ricotta cheese
1¼ cups (5 ounces) shredded low fat mozzarella cheese
1 egg white
1 tablespoon water
Grated Parmesan cheese

Cook ground turkey according to package directions for crumbles. Remove from heat. Stir in pizza sauce and parsley. Place biscuits on lightly floured surface; flatten each into 3- to 4-inch circle. Place dollop of turkey mixture, ricotta and mozzarella cheese on half of each circle. Lightly moisten edges with water; fold circles in half. Gently press to seal and enclose filling. Combine egg white and water. Place filled calzones on baking sheet. Brush with egg white mixture; sprinkle with Parmesan cheese. Bake in preheated 400°F oven 10 to 15 minutes or until golden brown. Serve with additional pizza sauce. *Makes 20 calzones*

Note: These can be baked and reheated later in preheated 400°F oven 6 to 8 minutes.

Preparation Time: 30 minutes

Classic Pepperoni Pizza

1 cup (¹/₂ of 15 ounce can) CONTADINA® Original Pizza Sauce
1 (12-inch) prepared, pre-baked pizza crust
1¹/₂ cups (6 ounces) shredded mozzarella cheese, divided
1¹/₂ ounces sliced pepperoni
1 tablespoon chopped fresh parsley

1. Spread pizza sauce onto crust to within 1 inch of edge.

2. Sprinkle with 1 cup cheese, pepperoni and remaining cheese.

3. Bake according to pizza crust package directions or until crust is crisp and cheese is melted. Sprinkle with parsley.   *Makes 8 servings*

BelGioioso® Provolone Pan Pizza

1 loaf refrigerated French or Italian bread dough
2 cups tomato sauce
12 to 14 ounces BELGIOIOSO® Mild Provolone Cheese, sliced
1 teaspoon dried oregano leaves
1 teaspoon dried basil leaves
  Salt and pepper to taste
3 to 4 tablespoons olive oil
  BELGIOIOSO® Parmesan Cheese (optional)

Roll out dough in lightly oiled 12- or 14-inch pizza pan. Spread with tomato sauce. Top with BelGioioso Mild Provolone Cheese, oregano, basil, salt and pepper. Sprinkle with oil. Sprinkle with BelGioioso Parmesan Cheese, if desired. Bake in preheated 400°F oven 20 minutes. Serve hot.   *Makes 4 servings*

Classic Pepperoni Pizza

Homemade Pizza

½ tablespoon active dry yeast
1 teaspoon sugar, divided
½ cup warm water (105°F to 115°F)
1¾ cups all-purpose flour, divided
¾ teaspoon salt, divided
2 tablespoons olive oil, divided
1 can (14½ ounces) whole peeled tomatoes, undrained
1 medium onion, chopped
1 clove garlic, minced
2 tablespoons tomato paste
1 teaspoon dried oregano leaves, crushed
½ teaspoon dried basil leaves, crushed
⅛ teaspoon black pepper
½ small red bell pepper, cored and seeded
½ small green bell pepper, cored and seeded
4 fresh medium mushrooms
1 can (2 ounces) flat anchovy fillets
1¾ cups shredded mozzarella cheese
½ cup freshly grated Parmesan cheese
⅓ cup pitted ripe olives, halved

1. To proof yeast, sprinkle yeast and ½ teaspoon sugar over warm water in small bowl; stir until yeast is dissolved. Let stand 5 minutes or until mixture is bubbly. (If yeast does not bubble, it is no longer active. Always check expiration date on yeast packet.)

2. Place 1½ cups flour and ¼ teaspoon salt in medium bowl; stir in yeast mixture and 1 tablespoon oil, stirring until a smooth, soft dough forms. Place dough on lightly floured surface; flatten slightly. Knead dough, using as much of remaining flour as needed to form a stiff elastic dough.

3. Shape dough into a ball; place in large greased bowl. Turn to grease entire surface. Cover with clean kitchen towel and let dough rise in warm place 30 to 45 minutes until doubled in bulk. Press two fingertips about ½ inch into dough. Dough is ready if indentations remain when fingers are removed.

continued on page 312

Homemade Pizza

4. For sauce, finely chop canned tomatoes reserving juice. Heat remaining 1 tablespoon oil in medium saucepan over medium heat. Add onion; cook 5 minutes or until soft. Add garlic; cook 30 seconds more. Add tomatoes with juice, tomato paste, oregano, basil, remaining $\frac{1}{2}$ teaspoon sugar, $\frac{1}{2}$ teaspoon salt and black pepper. Bring to a boil over high heat; reduce heat to medium-low. Simmer, uncovered, 10 to 15 minutes until sauce thickens, stirring occasionally. Pour into small bowl; cool.

5. Punch dough down. Knead briefly on lightly floured surface to distribute air bubbles; let dough stand 5 minutes more. Flatten dough into circle on lightly floured surface. Roll out dough, starting at center and rolling to edges, into 10-inch circle. Place circle in greased 12-inch pizza pan; stretch and pat dough out to edges of pan. Cover and let stand 15 minutes.

6. Preheat oven to 450°F. Cut bell peppers into $\frac{3}{4}$-inch pieces. Trim mushroom stems; wipe clean with damp kitchen towel and thinly slice. Drain anchovies. Mix mozzarella and Parmesan cheeses in small bowl. Spread sauce evenly over pizza dough. Sprinkle with $\frac{2}{3}$ of cheeses. Arrange bell peppers, mushrooms, anchovies and olives over cheeses. Sprinkle remaining cheeses on top of pizza. Bake 20 minutes or until crust is golden brown. To serve, cut into wedges.   *Makes 4 to 6 servings*

*P*izza Romano

1 (10-inch) prepared pizza crust *or* 4 rounds pita bread
1 cup (4 ounces) shredded mozzarella cheese
4 slices HILLSHIRE FARM® Ham, cut into $\frac{1}{2}$-inch strips
1 jar (8 ounces) marinated sun-dried tomatoes, drained (optional)
1 jar (6 ounces) oil-packed artichokes, drained and cut into eighths
1 jar (4 ounces) roasted red peppers, drained and cut into strips

Preheat oven to 425°F. Place pizza crust on cookie sheet; top with remaining ingredients. Bake on lower rack of oven 15 to 20 minutes or until crust begins to brown lightly and cheese is melted.   *Makes 4 servings*

Vegetable-Cheese Pizzas

2½ cups chopped tomatoes
1 cup thinly sliced onion
1 cup chopped green bell pepper
6 tablespoons water, divided
2 cloves garlic, minced
1½ teaspoons dried Italian seasoning
1 teaspoon sugar
2 tablespoons cornstarch
4 large pita bread rounds, split horizontally, or 8 (7-inch) flour tortillas
½ cup (2 ounces) shredded part-skim mozzarella cheese
⅓ cup (1½ ounces) shredded reduced-fat sharp Cheddar or colby cheese
2 tablespoons grated Parmesan or Romano cheese

Preheat oven to 375°F. Combine tomatoes, onion, bell pepper, 2 tablespoons water, garlic, Italian seasoning and sugar in 2-quart saucepan. Bring to a boil over medium-high heat. Reduce heat to medium-low. Cover; simmer 8 to 10 minutes or until onion is tender.

Combine remaining 4 tablespoons water and cornstarch in small bowl; add to tomato mixture. Cook and stir until mixture boils and thickens. Cook and stir 2 minutes more.

Meanwhile, place pita bread halves on ungreased baking sheets. Bake 8 to 10 minutes or until edges just start to brown.

Spread vegetable mixture over pita bread halves. Sprinkle with mozzarella, Cheddar and Parmesan cheeses. Bake about 5 minutes more or until cheeses melt and pizzas are heated through. *Makes 4 servings*

Pepper Pita Pizzas

1 teaspoon olive oil
1 medium onion, thinly sliced
1 red bell pepper, cut in thin strips
1 green bell pepper, cut in thin strips
4 cloves garlic, minced
2 tablespoons minced fresh basil *or* 2 teaspoons dried basil
1 tablespoon minced fresh oregano *or* 1 teaspoon dried oregano
2 Italian plum tomatoes, coarsely chopped
4 pita breads
1 cup (4 ounces) shredded reduced fat Monterey Jack cheese

Preheat oven to 425°F. Heat olive oil in medium nonstick skillet over medium heat until hot. Add onion, peppers, garlic, basil and oregano. Partially cover and cook 5 minutes or until tender, stirring occasionally. Add tomatoes. Partially cover and cook 3 minutes. Place pita breads on baking sheet. Divide tomato mixture evenly among pita breads. Top each pita bread with ¼ cup cheese. Bake 5 minutes or until cheese is melted. *Makes 4 servings*

BelGioioso® Provolone Pita Pizzas

1 pita bread
²⁄₃ cup pizza sauce
¼ cup diced onion
¼ cup diced green bell pepper
10 to 12 thin slices pepperoni
1 cup shredded BELGIOIOSO® Provolone Cheese

Split pita into 2 rounds. (If pita doesn't separate, use 2 whole pitas.) Place pitas cut-side up on baking pan. Layer each pita with pizza sauce, onion, bell pepper, pepperoni and BelGioioso Provolone Cheese. Bake in preheated 400°F oven 7 to 8 minutes. Cut each pita into 4 pieces. *Makes 2 servings*

Pepper Pita Pizza

ronto Pizza

6 ounces lean fresh ground American lamb
$\frac{1}{2}$ teaspoon onion salt
$\frac{1}{2}$ teaspoon fennel seeds
$\frac{1}{4}$ teaspoon dried oregano leaves, crushed
$\frac{1}{4}$ teaspoon dried basil leaves, crushed
$\frac{1}{8}$ teaspoon red pepper flakes
$\frac{1}{2}$ cup chopped bell pepper
$\frac{1}{2}$ cup chopped Italian plum tomatoes
1 (10- to 12-inch) prebaked pizza shell
$\frac{1}{2}$ cup pizza sauce
1 tablespoon grated Parmesan cheese
$\frac{1}{4}$ cup thinly sliced fresh basil leaves, optional
$\frac{1}{2}$ cup (2 ounces) shredded part-skim mozzarella cheese

Preheat oven to 450°F.

Combine lamb, onion salt, fennel seeds, oregano, dried basil and red pepper flakes in small bowl; knead until well blended.

Spray nonstick skillet with nonstick cooking spray. Cook and stir lamb over medium-high heat, stirring to separate lamb, until lightly browned. Drain on paper towel. In same skillet, cook and stir bell pepper 3 to 4 minutes, stirring occasionally. Add tomatoes; cook and stir 1 minute. Place pizza shell on cookie sheet or pizza pan; top with pizza sauce and vegetables. Sprinkle with Parmesan cheese, fresh basil, cooked lamb and mozzarella cheese. Bake 8 to 10 minutes. Cool 5 minutes and slice into wedges. *Makes 6 to 8 servings*

Microwave Directions: Cook lamb mixture in 2-quart microwavable dish on HIGH (100% power) 3 minutes, stirring several times to crumble lamb. Add bell pepper and tomatoes; microwave on HIGH 2 minutes, stirring once. Drain well. Assemble pizza as directed above.

Favorite recipe from *American Lamb Council*

Pronto Pizza

Herbed Chicken with Boursin Pizza

Cornmeal Crust (recipe page 320) or New York-Style Pizza Crust
(recipe page 286)

- $^1/_4$ cup dry white wine
- 1 tablespoon lemon juice
- 2 tablespoons olive oil, divided
- 1 clove garlic, minced
- $^1/_2$ teaspoon dried oregano leaves
- $^1/_2$ teaspoon dried basil leaves
- $^1/_2$ teaspoon black pepper
- 1 pound boneless skinless chicken breasts
  Nonstick cooking spray
- $^3/_4$ cup crumbled light Boursin cheese
- $^1/_2$ cup chopped fresh basil
- 2 tablespoons chopped fresh chives

1. Prepare Cornmeal Crust.

2. Combine white wine, lemon juice, 1 tablespoon olive oil, garlic, oregano, basil and pepper in medium bowl. Transfer wine mixture to large resealable plastic food storage bag. Add chicken to bag; seal bag and knead to coat chicken with marinade. Place in refrigerator and marinate at least 2 hours or overnight.

3. Remove chicken from marinade; discard remaining marinade. Spray large nonstick skillet with cooking spray; heat over medium heat until hot. Add chicken; cook and stir 12 to 15 minutes or until chicken is golden brown and no longer pink in center. Remove chicken to cutting board. When chicken is cool enough to handle, cut into $^1/_2$-inch pieces.

4. Preheat oven to 450°F.

5. Brush dough with remaining 1 tablespoon olive oil. Top with chicken, Boursin cheese, basil and chives.

6. Bake 18 to 20 minutes or until crust is golden brown and cheese is melted.

Makes 8 servings

Herbed Chicken with Boursin Pizza

Cornmeal Crust

1 cup warm water (110° to 115°F)
2 tablespoons sugar or honey
1 package (1/4 ounce) active dry yeast or rapid-rise yeast
2 to 2 1/2 cups all-purpose flour
1 cup plus 1 tablespoon cornmeal, divided
1/4 teaspoon salt (optional)

1. Combine water and sugar in small bowl; stir to dissolve sugar. Sprinkle yeast on top; stir to combine. Let stand 5 to 10 minutes or until foamy.

2. Combine 2 cups flour, 1 cup cornmeal and salt, if desired, in large bowl. Stir in yeast mixture. Mix until mixture forms soft dough. Remove dough to lightly floured surface. Knead 5 to 10 minutes, adding remaining 1/2 cup flour, if necessary, until dough is smooth and elastic.

3. Place dough in large bowl coated with nonstick cooking spray. Turn dough in bowl so top is coated with cooking spray; cover with towel or plastic wrap. Let dough rise in warm place about 1 1/2 hours or until doubled in bulk. Punch down dough and pat into disk. Gently stretch dough into 14- to 15-inch circle.

4. Spray 14-inch pizza pan with nonstick cooking spray; sprinkle with remaining 1 tablespoon cornmeal. Press dough into pan. Follow baking directions for individual recipes.

Makes 1 thick 14-inch crust (8 servings)

Pizza crusts come in a variety of shapes and sizes. Some are round, some square, some big and some small. There are thick, chewy crusts, thin, crispy crusts and those in between. Anyway you slice it, though, it's all pizza!

Italian Turkey Sausage and Veggie Pizza

1 pound ITALIAN TURKEY SAUSAGE, casings removed if necessary
1 (12-inch) thin-crust pizza shell
  Vegetable spray
2 cups sliced onions
1 cup shredded carrots
1 cup sliced green or red pepper
1 cup sliced mushrooms
1 cup broccoli florets
1 cup sliced artichoke hearts
10 cherry tomatoes, cut in half
$\frac{1}{2}$ cup shredded Cheddar cheese
$\frac{1}{2}$ cup shredded mozzarella cheese

1. In large, nonstick skillet over medium-high heat, cook sausage, breaking up large pieces, until browned (about 5 to 6 minutes); drain and place on pizza shell on large cookie sheet.

2. Spray skillet with vegetable spray. Over medium-high heat, cook onions until tender and golden brown. Spread over pizza crust.

3. Re-spraying pan with vegetable oil as necessary, individually cook carrots, pepper slices and mushrooms, scattering each over onions.

4. Arrange broccoli, artichokes and tomato halves on top of pizza.

5. Sprinkle pizza with cheeses and bake in preheated 450°F oven for 10 to 15 minutes, or until cheeses are melted. *Makes 6 servings*

Favorite recipe from *National Turkey Federation*

Vegetable Pizza

2 to 3 cups BIRDS EYE® frozen Farm Fresh Mixtures Broccoli, Red
    Peppers, Onions and Mushrooms
1 Italian bread shell or pizza crust, about 12 inches
1 to 1¹⁄₂ cups shredded mozzarella cheese
    Dried oregano, basil or Italian seasoning

∾ Preheat oven according to directions on pizza crust package.

∾ Rinse vegetables in colander under warm water. Drain well; pat with paper towel to remove excess moisture.

∾ Spread crust with half the cheese and all the vegetables. Sprinkle with herbs; top with remaining cheese.

∾ Follow baking directions on pizza crust package; bake until hot and bubbly.

Makes 3 to 4 servings

Prep Time: 5 minutes
Cook Time: 15 minutes

Pepperoni Pepper Pizza

1 can (5 ounces) pizza sauce
1 prepared (12-inch) pizza crust
2 cups (8 ounces) shredded mozzarella cheese
¹⁄₂ red bell pepper, cut into thin strips
¹⁄₂ green bell pepper, cut into thin strips
2 ounces HILLSHIRE FARM® Pepperoni, sliced

Preheat oven to 450°F. Spread pizza sauce on pizza crust. Layer sauce with 1 cup cheese, bell peppers and pepperoni; top with remaining 1 cup cheese. Bake, on ungreased cookie sheet, 10 to 12 minutes or until pizza crust is crisp and cheese is melted.

Makes 4 to 6 servings

Vegetable Pizza

Roma Tomato Pizzas

  2 loaves (1 pound each) frozen bread dough, thawed
  ⅓ cup olive oil
  2 cups thinly sliced onions
  2 cloves garlic, minced
12 Roma (Italian plum) tomatoes, sliced ⅛-inch thick
  1 teaspoon dried basil leaves, crushed
  1 teaspoon dried oregano leaves, crushed
     Black pepper
  ½ cup grated Parmesan cheese
  1 can (2¼ ounces) sliced, pitted ripe olives, drained
     Green and yellow bell pepper strips

Preheat oven to 450°F. Roll out each loaf on lightly floured surface into 15-inch circle; press each into greased 15-inch pizza pan or stretch into 15×10-inch baking pan. Crimp edges to form rim; prick several times with fork. Bake crusts 10 minutes. Remove from oven; set aside.

Reduce oven temperature to 400°F. Heat oil in large skillet over medium-high heat until hot. Add onions and garlic; cook and stir 6 to 8 minutes or until onions are tender. Divide onion mixture (including olive oil) between crusts. Arrange tomato slices evenly over onion mixture. Sprinkle each pizza with ½ teaspoon basil leaves, ½ teaspoon oregano leaves and black pepper to taste. Sprinkle each pizza with ½ cup parmesan cheese. Top with olives and desired amount of bell peppers. Bake 10 to 15 minutes or until toppings are heated through.   *Makes 2 (15-inch) pizzas*

Roma Tomato Pizza

Basil Parmesan Pizza

1 cup water
2 tablespoons olive or vegetable oil
¾ teaspoon salt
3 cups bread flour
¼ cup grated Parmesan cheese
1 teaspoon sweet basil
2 teaspoons FLEISCHMANN'S® Bread Machine Yeast
1 tablespoon cornmeal
   Favorite toppings

BREAD MACHINE DIRECTIONS

Add water, oil, salt, bread flour, cheese, basil and yeast to bread machine pan in the order suggested by manufacturer. Select dough/manual cycle. When cycle is complete, remove dough from machine to lightly floured surface. If necessary, knead in enough flour to make dough easy to handle.

Grease pizza pan (see Pizza Pan Tip for pan size) and sprinkle with cornmeal. Roll out dough and place on pan or pat dough in pan. Top with favorite toppings. Bake at 425°F for 15 to 25 minutes or until edges of crust are golden and cheese is bubbly.

Makes 1 or 2 pizzas

Pizza Pan Tip: Bake your pizza in any of the pan sizes listed: Two 12-inch round pans (thin crust), one 14-inch round pan (thick crust), or one 15×10-inch baking sheet (thin crust).

Basil Parmesan Pizza

Le Insalate

Unlike its American counterpart, the salad course in Italy typically comes towards the end of a meal. Salads eaten after main courses tend to aid in digestion and cleanse the palate for the dessert course that follows. Italian salads feature a wide variety of salad greens that grow in the region, including radicchios, arugula, and, believe it or not, dandelion leaves. Some salads include pastas while others have no greens, as is the case with the traditional combination of tomatoes, fresh mozzarella and prosciutto.

Bow Tie Pasta Salad (page 332)

Tomato, Mozzarella & Basil Salad

2 tablespoons red wine vinegar
1 clove garlic, minced
$^1/_2$ teaspoon salt
$^1/_4$ teaspoon dry mustard
Generous dash black pepper
$^1/_3$ cup olive or vegetable oil
4 Italian plum tomatoes
6 ounces mozzarella cheese
8 to 10 fresh basil leaves

1. For dressing, combine vinegar, garlic, salt, mustard and pepper in small bowl. Add oil in slow steady stream, whisking until oil is thoroughly blended.

2. Slice tomatoes and cheese into $^1/_4$-inch-thick slices. Trim cheese slices to size of tomato slices.

3. Place tomato and cheese slices in large, shallow bowl or glass baking dish. Pour dressing over slices. Marinate, covered, in refrigerator at least 30 minutes or up to 3 hours, turning slices occasionally.

4. Layer basil leaves with largest leaf on bottom, then roll up jelly-roll fashion. Slice basil roll into $^1/_4$-inch-thick slices; separate into strips.

5. Arrange tomato and cheese slices alternately on serving plate or 4 individual salad plates. Sprinkle with basil strips; drizzle with remaining dressing.

Makes 4 servings

Tomatoes, mozzarella and basil make a classic combination that has withstood the test of time. All are important ingredients that show up throughout traditional Italian cuisine. After all, there's nothing more Italian than finishing a great meal with a salad of these three ingredients.

Tomato, Mozzarella & Basil Salad

Bow Tie Pasta Salad

1 package (16 ounces) uncooked bow ties, rotini, ziti or other shaped pasta
1 bag (16 ounces) BIRDS EYE® frozen Farm Fresh Mixtures Broccoli, Cauliflower and Carrots*
1 cup Italian, creamy Italian or favorite salad dressing
1 bunch green onions, thinly sliced
1 cup pitted ripe olives, halved (optional)

*Or, substitute any other Birds Eye® frozen Farm Fresh Mixtures variety.

❧ Cook pasta according to package directions; drain.

❧ Cook vegetables according to package directions; drain.

❧ Combine pasta and vegetables with remaining ingredients in large bowl. Cover and chill until ready to serve.   *Makes about 8 side-dish servings*

Serving Suggestion: Use this recipe as the base for a variety of main-dish salads, adding sliced salami and small cubes of cheese or cooked chicken, turkey or seafood to the pasta and vegetables.

Prep Time: 5 minutes
Cook Time: 20 minutes

Mixed Spring Vegetable Salad

8 ounces fresh green beans, trimmed and cut into thirds
1 medium zucchini (about ½ pound), sliced
1 large tomato *or* 3 plum tomatoes, sliced
3 tablespoons FILIPPO BERIO® Extra Virgin Olive Oil
3 tablespoons lemon juice
Salt and freshly ground black pepper

Cook or steam green beans and zucchini separately until tender-crisp. Cover; refrigerate until chilled. Stir in tomato. Just before serving, drizzle olive oil and lemon juice over vegetables. Season to taste with salt and pepper.

Makes 6 servings

Chicken, Tortellini & Roasted Vegetable Salad

Sun-Dried Tomato & Basil Vinaigrette (recipe follows)
- 3 cups whole medium mushrooms
- 2 cups cubed zucchini
- 2 cups cubed eggplant
- ¾ cup red onion wedges (about 1 medium)
  Nonstick olive oil cooking spray
- 1½ packages (9-ounce-size) reduced-fat cheese tortellini
- 6 cups bite-size pieces leaf lettuce and arugula
- 1 pound boneless skinless chicken breasts, cooked and cut into 1½-inch pieces

1. Prepare Sun-Dried Tomato & Basil Vinaigrette. Heat oven to 425°F.

2. Place mushrooms, zucchini, eggplant and onion in 15×10-inch jelly-roll pan. Spray generously with cooking spray; toss to coat. Bake 20 to 25 minutes or until vegetables are browned. Cool to room temperature.

3. Meanwhile, cook tortellini according to package directions; drain. Cool to room temperature.

4. Combine vegetables, tortellini, lettuce and chicken in large bowl. Drizzle with vinaigrette; toss to coat. *Makes 8 servings*

Sun-Dried Tomato & Basil Vinaigrette

- 4 sun-dried tomato halves, not packed in oil
  Boiling water
- ½ cup fat-free low-sodium chicken broth
- 2 tablespoons finely chopped fresh basil *or* 2 teaspoons dried basil leaves
- 2 tablespoons olive oil
- 2 tablespoons lemon juice
- 2 tablespoons water
- 1 clove garlic, minced
- ¼ teaspoon salt
- ¼ teaspoon black pepper

1. Place tomatoes in small bowl. Cover with boiling water. Let stand 5 to 10 minutes or until soft. Drain well; chop.

2. In small jar with tight-fitting lid, combine tomatoes and remaining ingredients; shake well. Chill until ready to use; shake before using. *Makes about 1 cup*

Sicilian-Style Pasta Salad

1 pound dry rotini pasta
2 cans (14.5 ounces each) CONTADINA® Recipe Ready Diced Tomatoes
   with Italian Herbs, undrained
1 cup sliced yellow bell pepper
1 cup sliced zucchini
8 ounces cooked bay shrimp
1 can (2.25 ounces) sliced pitted ripe olives, drained
2 tablespoons balsamic vinegar

1. Cook pasta according to package directions; drain.

2. Combine pasta, undrained tomatoes, bell pepper, zucchini, shrimp, olives and vinegar in large bowl; toss well.

3. Cover. Chill before serving. *Makes 10 servings*

Pizza Salad

3 cups torn lettuce
3 small tomatoes, sliced
2 cups (8 ounces) shredded mozzarella cheese
6 ounces fresh mushrooms, sliced
2 ounces thinly sliced pepperoni
$^1/_2$ cup chopped green bell pepper
$^1/_2$ teaspoon LAWRY'S® Garlic Powder with Parsley
$^1/_2$ teaspoon LAWRY'S® Seasoned Pepper
$^1/_2$ to $^3/_4$ cup Italian salad dressing
1 cup croutons

In large salad bowl, place lettuce, tomatoes, cheese, mushrooms, pepperoni, bell pepper, Garlic Powder with Parsley and Seasoned Pepper; mix lightly. Add dressing; toss to coat. Sprinkle with croutons just before serving. *Makes 4 servings*

Sicilian-Style Pasta Salad

Fennel, Olive and Radicchio Salad

11 Italian- or Greek-style black olives, divided
 ¼ cup olive oil
 1 tablespoon lemon juice
 1 flat anchovy fillet *or* ½ teaspoon anchovy paste
 ¼ teaspoon salt
   Generous dash black pepper
   Generous dash sugar
 1 fresh fennel bulb
 1 head radicchio*
   Fennel greenery for garnish

*Radicchio, a tart red chicory, is available in large supermarkets and specialty food shops. If not available, 2 heads of Belgian endive can be used; although it does not provide the dramatic red color, it will give a similar texture and its slightly bitter flavor will go well with the robust dressing and the sweet anise flavor of fennel.

1. For dressing, cut 3 olives in half; remove and discard pits. Place pitted olives, oil, lemon juice and anchovy in food processor or blender; process 5 seconds. Add salt, pepper and sugar; process until olives are finely chopped, about 5 seconds more. Set aside.

2. Cut off and discard fennel stalks. Cut off and discard root end at base of fennel bulb and any discolored parts of bulb. Cut fennel bulb lengthwise into 8 wedges; separate each wedge into segments.

3. Separate radicchio leaves; rinse thoroughly under running water. Drain well.

4. Arrange radicchio leaves, fennel and remaining olives on serving plate. Spoon dressing over salad. Garnish, if desired. Serve immediately.   *Makes 4 servings*

Italian Bread Salad

1 loaf (about 12 ounces) hearty peasant-style bread (such as sourdough, rosemary-olive oil or roasted garlic)
1 cup sliced red onion
1 teaspoon minced garlic
1/3 cup bottled balsamic and olive oil vinaigrette
1 1/2 cups grape tomatoes or cherry tomatoes, halved
1/3 cup pitted oil- or salt-cured black and green olives
1 bag European salad mix or pre-washed baby spinach
   Freshly ground black pepper to taste

1. Preheat oven to 250°F. Tear bread into large cubes, about the size of marshmallows. Place on baking sheet. Bake 10 to 15 minutes or until slightly dry but not browned. Set aside to cool.

2. Place onion slices and garlic in large salad bowl. Add vinaigrette and stir to coat. Set aside a few minutes to allow flavors to mellow.

3. Add tomatoes and olives; stir gently to coat with dressing. Add greens, bread cubes and Parmesan; toss gently. Add more vinaigrette if needed and season with black pepper.

Makes 4 servings

Tip: You can use day-old bread that has started to dry out for this recipe. Bread that is a little too hard or stale can be softened by sprinkling it with water. Gently squeeze the bread in your hands to remove excess moisture.

Fresh Seafood and Linguine Salad

1½ pounds small squid
4 pounds mussels, cleaned*
1½ to 3 dozen clams*
8 ounces linguine
Olive oil
¼ cup freshly squeezed lemon juice
2 cloves garlic, minced
Salt
¼ teaspoon black pepper
1 red onion, thinly sliced and separated into rings for garnish
⅓ cup finely chopped Italian parsley for garnish

*Discard any opened clams or mussels.

1. Clean squid. (See tip on page 244 for detailed directions on cleaning squid.) Cut bodies crosswise into ¼-inch rings; finely chop tentacles and fins. Pat pieces dry with paper towels.

2. To steam clams and mussels, place 1 cup water in large stockpot. Bring to a boil over high heat. Add clams and mussels. Cover stockpot; reduce heat to low. Steam 5 to 7 minutes until clams and mussels are opened. Remove from stockpot with slotted spoon. Discard any clams or mussels that remain closed.

3. Meanwhile, cook pasta according to package directions. Drain. Place in large bowl and toss with 2 tablespoons olive oil.

4. Add just enough olive oil to large saucepan to cover bottom. Heat over medium heat; add squid. Cook and stir 2 minutes until squid is opaque. Place squid in large glass bowl. Add pasta, mussels and clams.

5. Combine ½ cup olive oil, lemon juice, garlic, ½ teaspoon salt and pepper in small bowl; blend well. Pour over salad; toss gently to coat.

6. Cover; refrigerate at least 3 hours. Season with additional lemon juice, salt and pepper, if necessary. Garnish with onion rings and parsley, if desired.

Makes 6 servings

Fresh Seafood and Linguine Salad

Marinated Vegetable Salad

3 tablespoons plus 1 1/2 teaspoons white wine vinegar
2 tablespoons minced fresh basil *or* 1/2 teaspoon dried basil leaves
1/2 teaspoon salt
1/8 teaspoon black pepper
   Dash sugar
6 tablespoons olive oil
2 ripe medium tomatoes
1/3 cup pitted green olives
1/3 cup Italian- or Greek-style black olives
1 head green or red leaf lettuce
1 small head curly endive
2 heads Belgian endive

1. For dressing, place vinegar, basil, salt, pepper and sugar in blender or food processor. With motor running, add oil in slow steady stream until thoroughly blended.

2. Cut tomatoes into wedges. Combine tomatoes and green and black olives in medium bowl. Add dressing; toss lightly. Cover and let stand at room temperature 30 minutes to blend flavors, stirring occasionally.

3. Rinse leaf lettuce and curly endive; drain well. Refrigerate greens until ready to assemble salad. Core Belgian endive and separate leaves; rinse and drain well.

4. To serve, layer leaf lettuce, curly endive and Belgian endive leaves in large, shallow serving bowl.

5. Remove tomatoes and olives with slotted spoon and place on top of greens. Spoon remaining dressing over salad. Serve immediately or cover and refrigerate up to 30 minutes. *Makes 6 servings*

Marinated Vegetable Salad

Rigatoni Salad

12 ounces uncooked rigatoni pasta, cooked
1 to 2 cups chopped greens, such as arugula, frisée or any crisp lettuce
1 bag (10 ounces) frozen snowpeas or sugar snap peas, thawed
1/2 pound cherry tomatoes, halved
1 medium red or yellow bell pepper, cut into narrow strips
1/2 red onion, cut into thin strips
1/3 cup sliced black olives
1/3 to 1/2 cup Italian salad dressing
Grated Parmesan cheese (optional)

Combine all ingredients except Parmesan in large salad bowl. Toss gently to mix and coat all ingredients. Sprinkle with Parmesan, if desired.

Makes about 8 servings

Note: Vary the amounts of each ingredient according to your taste. Substitute steamed green beans (whole or cut) for the peas; or add steamed, sliced carrots, zucchini or yellow squash.

Tomato Parsley Salad

1/2 cup FILIPPO BERIO® Extra Virgin Olive Oil
3 tablespoons white wine vinegar
2 cloves garlic, minced
1/4 teaspoon salt
1/4 teaspoon freshly ground black pepper
4 cups fresh parsley leaves
1/2 cup grated Parmesan cheese
4 tomatoes, thinly sliced

In small bowl, whisk together olive oil, vinegar, garlic, salt and pepper. Place parsley in large bowl. Add olive oil mixture and cheese; stir well. Add tomatoes; toss until lightly coated.

Makes 4 to 6 servings

Rigatoni Salad

Orzo and Summer Squash Salad

1 1/3 cups (8 ounces) uncooked orzo pasta
  3 cups diced zucchini and/or yellow summer squash (1/2-inch pieces)
  1 cup diced tomato
  1/2 cup prepared light or regular Caesar salad dressing
  1 teaspoon dried basil leaves*
    Fresh spinach leaves
    Salt and black pepper

*You can substitute 1/4 cup julienned fresh basil leaves for dried basil leaves.

1. Cook orzo according to package directions, adding squash for last 2 minutes of cooking. Drain well; rinse under cold water to stop cooking.

2. Place mixture in large bowl; stir in tomato. Pour dressing over salad; sprinkle with basil. Toss gently to coat. Cover and refrigerate until cool. Serve salad over spinach leaves. Season to taste with salt and pepper. *Makes 6 (1-cup) servings*

Serving suggestion: Serve alongside simply grilled poultry, pork or fish.

Prep and Cook Time: 25 minutes

Pasta Pesto Salad

8 ounces BARILLA® Penne or Mostaccioli, cooked according to package
    directions and chilled
1 container (about 7 ounces) prepared pesto sauce
4 plum tomatoes, cut into large chunks
1 cup roasted red peppers, cut into strips*
1 cup (4 ounces) crumbled feta cheese
  Salt and pepper

*Roasted red peppers are available in jars in Italian, deli or produce sections of supermarkets.

1. Combine chilled penne and pesto sauce in large serving bowl.

2. Add tomatoes and red peppers; toss gently. Sprinkle with cheese. Add salt and pepper to taste. *Makes 6 to 8 servings*

Tomato & Mozzarella Salad with Sun-Dried Tomato Dressing

DRESSING

⅓ cup water

¼ cup *French's*® Worcestershire Sauce

¼ cup balsamic vinegar

¼ cup sun-dried tomatoes packed in oil, drained

2 tablespoons *French's*® Napa Valley Style Dijon Mustard

2 cloves garlic, minced

½ cup olive oil

SALAD

6 cups washed and torn mixed salad greens

2 large ripe tomatoes, sliced

8 ounces fresh mozzarella cheese,* sliced

1 bunch asparagus, trimmed and blanched**

1 tablespoon minced fresh basil leaves

*Look for fresh mozzarella in the deli section of your supermarket.

**To blanch asparagus, cook asparagus in boiling water 2 minutes. Drain and rinse with cold water.

Place water, Worcestershire, vinegar, sun-dried tomatoes, mustard and garlic in blender or food processor. Cover and process until well blended. Gradually add oil in steady stream, processing until smooth. Set aside.

Place salad greens on large platter. Arrange tomatoes, cheese and asparagus on top. Sprinkle with basil. Serve with dressing.

Makes 6 to 8 side-dish servings (about 1½ cups dressing)

Prep Time: 30 minutes

Before canning became popular, the most common method of preserving tomatoes in Italy was to dry them on the tiled roofs of homes. These sun-dried tomatoes, as they came to be called, allowed Italians to cook with their favorite ingredient all winter long.

LAZIO

•Rome

Lazio

UNLIKE THE LAVISH BANQUETS OF THE ROMAN EMPIRE, THE TRUE FOOD OF LAZIO IS SIMPLE, PEASANT FARE FROM THE GHETTOS AND RURAL SUBURBS OF ROME.

Also known by its ancient Latin name Latium, Lazio is located between the Apennines and the Tyrrhenian Sea and is considered the "open door" to southern Italy. Umbria and Tuscany lie to the north and northwest and in ancient times the Tiber River was the cultural boundary between the Etruscans of those northern regions and the Latins. With Rome as its capital, one might expect Lazio's cuisine to reflect the lavish banquets of the Roman Emperors. But the fall of the Roman Empire was accompanied by a similar fall of extravagant cooking traditions. Even the papal legacy did little to define the region's culinary style since each new pontiff arrived at the Vatican with his own cooks and provincial recipes. Instead, the true food of Lazio—and Rome—is simple, peasant fare that some gastronomes insist was born in the Jewish ghettos, unaffected as they were by changes in the Vatican.

Lazio's hearty, country dishes that from the ghettos and rural suburbs of Rome include coda alla vaccinara (stewed oxtails and vegetables); stracciatella (beef broth with eggs and cheese); and saltimbocca alla romana (veal fillets with prosciutto and sage). The region is noted for a variety of green vegetables, including artichokes tender enough to eat raw. The Jewish specialty, carciofi alla giudia, consists of whole cooked artichokes flattened into flowerlike shapes and deep-fried to crispy perfection. Arugula or ruchetta, which grows wild and has a stronger, tarter flavor than cultivated varieties, often appears in salads with garlic and olive oil. While rice and grains are both grown in southern Italy, grains thrive best in the arid climate making wheat flour—and pasta—a staple. And in Lazio one of the most popular pastas is spaghetti. Two well-known dishes are spaghetti all'amatriciana (tomato sauce flavored with chiles, bacon, onion and oil) and spaghetti alla carbonara (egg and cheese sauce flavored with bacon, garlic and chiles). Sheep provide milk for pecorino romano cheese and meat for abbacchio alla cacciatora (baby lamb cooked with rosemary, garlic and anchovies). Other regional specialties include extra-virgin olive oil from the hills of northern Lazio, fresh buffalo milk mozzarella, gelato (ice cream), and porchetta (roast suckling pig).

An important wine-producing area, Lazio is known for its white wines. The Castelli Romani area in the Alban hills southeast of Rome is famous for the dry white Frascati and Mariano. Still, some connoisseurs claim that better reds, such as Fiorano, Cabernet and Merlot, are produced there.

As with most southern Italian regions, Lazio is not known as an industrial area, though some chemical, food and paper manufacturers are located there. Tourism and the government provide most of the employment in Rome, which is also the center of Italy's film industry. It almost goes without saying that in Lazio you are never more than a few minutes from an archaeological wonder: temples, aqueducts and majestic villas embodying the glory that was the Roman Empire have left their mark everywhere.

Zesty Romaine and Pasta Salad

6 ounces bowtie pasta
1 cup broccoli florets
¼ cup water
¼ cup red wine vinegar
2 tablespoons sugar
1 tablespoon finely chopped fresh basil
1 tablespoon lemon juice
1 tablespoon prepared Dijon mustard
1 clove garlic, minced
½ teaspoon black pepper
6 cups washed and chopped romaine lettuce
1 can (15 ounces) dark red kidney beans, drained and rinsed
1 cup carrot slices
1 small red onion, cut into halves and thinly sliced
½ cup grated Parmesan cheese

1. Cook pasta according to package directions, adding broccoli during last 3 minutes of cooking; drain. Rinse with cold water; drain.

2. To make dressing, combine water, vinegar, sugar, basil, lemon juice, mustard, garlic and pepper in small bowl until well blended.

3. Combine lettuce, pasta, broccoli, beans, carrots and onion in large bowl. Add dressing; toss to coat. Sprinkle with Parmesan cheese.   *Makes 4 servings*

Zesty Romaine and Pasta Salad

Tuna Pasta Primavera Salad

2 cups cooked and chilled small shell pasta
1½ cups halved cherry tomatoes
½ cup thinly sliced carrots
½ cup sliced celery
½ cup chopped seeded peeled cucumber
½ cup thinly sliced radishes
½ cup thawed frozen peas
¼ cup slivered red bell pepper
2 tablespoons minced green onion, including tops
1 (7-ounce) pouch of STARKIST® Premium Albacore or Chunk Light Tuna
1 cup salad dressing of choice
Bibb or red leaf lettuce
Fresh herbs, for garnish

In large bowl, combine all ingredients except lettuce and herbs. Chill several hours. If using oil and vinegar dressing, stir salad mixture occasionally to evenly marinate ingredients. Place lettuce leaves on each plate; spoon salad over lettuce. Garnish with fresh herbs, if desired. *Makes 6 servings*

Prep Time: 25 minutes

Tuna Pasta Primavera Salad

Dessert

As varied as the Italian countryside, dessert might be a rich, creamy ricotta cheesecake common in the south or a marvelous chocolate creation typical of the north. Pasta has even been known to find its way into a pie as a surprisingly effective filling base. Italian desserts, both cake and pies as well as biscotti and cookies, have always been influenced by the ingredients available. For instance, tiramisu was originally made with a basic custard of eggs and cream, both readily available in the dessert's region of origin, Friuli-Venezia. It wasn't until tiramisu gained popularity that chefs in Lombardy added a local cheese, marscapone. This version became the accepted classic tiramisu.

Minted Pears with Gorgonzola
(page 359)

Quick Tiramisu

1 package (18 ounces) NESTLÉ® TOLL HOUSE® Refrigerated Sugar Cookie Bar Dough
1 package (8 ounces) ⅓ less fat cream cheese
½ cup granulated sugar
¾ teaspoon TASTER'S CHOICE® 100% Pure Instant Coffee dissolved in ¾ cup cold water, *divided*
1 container (8 ounces) frozen nondairy whipped topping, thawed
1 tablespoon NESTLÉ® TOLL HOUSE® Baking Cocoa

PREHEAT oven to 325°F.

DIVIDE cookie dough into 20 pieces. Shape into 2½×1-inch oblong shapes. Place on ungreased baking sheets.

BAKE for 10 to 12 minutes or until light golden brown around edges. Cool on baking sheets for 1 minute; remove to wire racks to cool completely.

BEAT cream cheese and sugar in large mixer bowl until smooth. Beat in *¼ cup* Taster's Choice. Fold in whipped topping. Layer *6* cookies in 8-inch-square baking dish. Sprinkle each cookie with *1 teaspoon* Taster's Choice. Spread *one-third* cream cheese mixture over cookies. Repeat layers 2 more times with *12 cookies, remaining* coffee and *remaining* cream cheese mixture. Cover; refrigerate for 2 to 3 hours. Crumble *remaining* cookies over top. Sift cocoa over cookies. Cut into squares.

Makes 6 to 8 servings

Legend has it that Venetian lace makers created this delicious dessert while resting from the rigours of their detailed work.

Quick Tiramisu

Mocha Biscotti

2½ cups all-purpose flour
½ cup unsweetened cocoa
2 teaspoons baking powder
1¼ cups sugar
¾ cup egg substitute
¼ cup margarine or butter, melted
4 teaspoons instant coffee powder
½ teaspoon vanilla extract
⅓ cup PLANTERS® Slivered Almonds, chopped
  Powdered sugar, optional

1. Mix flour, cocoa and baking powder in small bowl; set aside.

2. Beat sugar, egg substitute, melted margarine or butter, coffee powder and vanilla in large bowl with mixer at medium speed for 2 minutes. Stir in flour mixture and almonds.

3. Divide dough in half. Shape each portion of dough with floured hands into 14×2-inch log on a greased baking sheet. (Dough will be sticky.) Bake in preheated 350°F oven for 25 minutes.

4. Remove from oven and cut each log on a diagonal into 16 (1-inch) slices. Place biscotti, cut-side up, on baking sheets; return to oven and bake 10 to 15 minutes more on each side or until lightly toasted.

5. Remove from sheets. Cool completely on wire racks. Dust biscotti tops with powdered sugar if desired. Store in airtight container.   *Makes 32 biscotti*

Preparation Time: 20 minutes
Cook Time: 35 minutes
Total Time: 1 hour and 5 minutes

Mocha Biscotti

Cannoli Pastries

18 to 20 Cannoli Pastry Shells (recipe follows)
2 pounds ricotta cheese
1$\frac{1}{2}$ cups sifted powdered sugar
2 teaspoons ground cinnamon
$\frac{1}{4}$ cup diced orange peel, minced
1 teaspoon grated lemon peel
  Powdered sugar
2 ounces semisweet chocolate, finely chopped
  Orange peel strips and fresh mint leaves for garnish

1. Prepare Cannoli Pastry Shells; set aside.

2. For cannoli filling, beat cheese in large bowl with electric mixer at medium speed until smooth. Add 1$\frac{1}{2}$ cups powdered sugar and cinnamon; beat at high speed 3 minutes. Add orange peel and lemon peel to cheese mixture; mix well. Cover and refrigerate until ready to serve.

3. To assemble, spoon cheese filling into pastry bag fitted with large plain tip. Pipe about $\frac{1}{4}$ cup filling into each reserved cannoli pastry shell.*

4. Roll Cannoli Pastries in additional powdered sugar to coat. Dip ends of pastries into chocolate. Arrange pastries on serving plate. Garnish, if desired.

Makes 18 to 20 pastries

*Do not fill Cannoli Pastry Shells ahead of time or shells will become soggy.

Cannoli Pastry Shells

1$\frac{3}{4}$ cups all-purpose flour
2 tablespoons granulated sugar
1 teaspoon grated lemon peel
2 tablespoons butter, cold
1 egg
6 tablespoons marsala
  Vegetable oil

1. Mix flour, granulated sugar and lemon peel in medium bowl; cut in butter with 2 knives or pastry blender until mixture resembles fine crumbs. Beat egg and marsala in small bowl; add to flour mixture. Stir with fork to form ball. Divide dough in half; shape into two 1-inch-thick square pieces. Wrap in plastic wrap and refrigerate at least 1 hour.

2. Heat 1½ inches oil in large saucepan to 325°F. Working with 1 piece of dough at a time, roll out on lightly floured surface to ¹⁄₁₆-inch thickness. Cut dough into 9 or 10 circles using appropriate sized cutout.

3. Wrap each circle around a greased metal cannoli form or uncooked cannelloni pasta shell. Brush one edge of rectangle lightly with water; overlap with other edge and press firmly to seal.

4. Fry, 2 or 3 cannoli pastry shells at a time, 1 to 1½ minutes until light brown, turning once. Remove with tongs; drain on paper towels.

5. Cool until easy to handle. Carefully remove fried pastries from cannoli forms or pasta shells; cool completely. Repeat with remaining piece of dough.

Makes 18 to 20 pastry shells

ℳinted Pears with Gorgonzola

    4   whole firm pears with stems, peeled
    2   cups Concord grape juice
    1   tablespoon honey
    1   tablespoon finely chopped fresh mint
    1   cinnamon stick
  ¼   teaspoon ground nutmeg
  ¼   cup Gorgonzola cheese, crumbled

1. Place pears in medium saucepan. Add grape juice, honey, mint, cinnamon stick and nutmeg. Bring to a boil over high heat. Cover and simmer 15 to 20 minutes, turning pears once to absorb juices evenly. Cook until pears can be easily pierced with fork. Remove from heat; cool. Remove pears with slotted spoon; set aside. Discard cinnamon stick.

2. Bring juice mixture to a boil; simmer 20 minutes. Pour over pears. Sprinkle Gorgonzola around pears.

Makes 4 servings

Sfince Di San Giuseppe
(St. Joseph's Ricotta Puffs)

FILLING

- 1 pound ricotta cheese, drained
- ¹/₂ cup confectioners' sugar
- 4 ounces grated dark chocolate
- ¹/₄ cup candied fruit, finely chopped
- 1 teaspoon orange extract
- 1 teaspoon vanilla

PUFFS

- 1 cup water
- ¹/₂ Butter Flavor CRISCO® Stick or ¹/₂ cup Butter Flavor CRISCO® all-vegetable shortening
- 1 tablespoon granulated sugar
- ¹/₂ teaspoon salt
- 1 cup sifted all-purpose flour
- 4 large eggs, beaten
- 1 teaspoon fresh grated lemon peel
- 1 teaspoon fresh grated orange peel
- Confectioners' sugar

1. For filling, combine all filling ingredients in large bowl; mix well. Refrigerate while making puffs.

2. For puffs, heat oven to 450°F. Combine water, shortening, granulated sugar and salt in medium saucepan. Bring to a boil over medium-high heat; stir well. Add flour, stirring vigorously, until mixture leaves sides of pan. Remove from heat; let cool.

3. Slowly add eggs, beating vigorously, to cooled flour mixture. Add lemon and orange peel; mix well.

4. Spray baking sheets with CRISCO® No-Stick Cooking Spray. Drop tablespoonfuls of batter 2 inches apart onto baking sheets.

5. Bake at 450°F for 15 minutes. *Reduce oven temperature to 350°F.* Bake an additional 15 to 20 minutes or until golden. Cool completely on cooling rack.

6. To assemble, cut puffs in half horizontally. Spoon ricotta filling into bottom half. Cover with top half. Drizzle with melted chocolate, if desired.

Makes about 18 puffs

Sfince Di San Giuseppe

.Potenza

BASILICATA

Basilicata

IN THE EIGHTH CENTURY B.C., GREEK SETTLERS LEFT THEIR INDELIBLE FINGERPRINT ON BASILICATA IN THE FORM OF GRAPEVINES, SHEEP AND GOATS, AS WELL AS INTENSE FLAVORS.

*B*asilicata is also known as Lucania, derived either from the Latin word for "woodland" or from the prehistoric Lyki people that migrated there. Lucania became Basilicata in the twelfth century, the name based on the word for a Byzantine governor (basilikos). Located in the instep of Italy's boot, this mostly mountainous region possesses two tiny coastlines along the Ionian and Tyrrhenian Seas. The harsh, though picturesque, landscape is sparsely populated and impoverished. Despite a lack of arable land, this is the only Italian region where farmers outnumber industrial workers. While agriculture has not been a prosperous endeavor, recent technological improvements along the fertile Ionian coast have yielded excellent results with vegetables, citrus fruits, sugar beets and hothouse strawberries.

The cooking in Basilicata emanates a warmth and vitality that belies its austere surroundings. Greek settlers arrived around the eighth century B.C. and left their indelible fingerprint on the culinary heritage in the form of grapevines, sheep and goats, and intense flavors. The integrity of Basilicatan cuisine abides in the isolation of the mountains. Historically, communication and travel were nearly impossible—it was difficult for people to leave even if they wanted to—so local cuisine has remained fairly unchanged within families and villages. Meat is too costly to eat often, but when it is lamb is the first choice. Two of the regions most popular dishes are agnello al forno (oven-roasted lamb with vegetables and herbs) and cazmarr (stew of lamb organs with cheese, garlic and onions). Pork is thriftily preserved in elaborate sausages that are known throughout Italy, such as lucanega and soppressato (flavored with ginger). Game hunting is prevalent with partridge, quail, hare and boar prepared from ancient recipes that reflect an earlier hunter society. Hard, durum wheat is the major crop and is used to make the pervasive pasta dishes—lasagne with beans, strascinati with a sauce of chickpeas or lentils, and fusilli with ricotta. Sauces are highly seasoned and spicy hot with ginger and the fiery diavolicchio chile pepper as favorite flavorings. Wheat (grano) is also cooked and served with a sauce in place of pasta or as a dessert pudding (grano dolce) with chocolate, walnuts and sweet wine. Cheeses are very important to the region and the aged Lucanian pecorino made from 70% sheep's and 30% goat's milk is especially prized. And vegetables of all kinds are baked in the oven and eaten in great quantities, including eggplants, potatoes, zucchini, peppers, broccoli and tomatoes.

As they did in Campania, the ancient Greeks brought Aglianico grapevines to Basilicata. Grown on the slopes of Mount Vulture (an extinct volcano) these vines produce the robust, aged Aglianico del Vulture, considered by some to be the best red wine in southern Italy. Also from the Vulture area and the eastern Bradano valley are the sweet white Moscato and Malvasia wines.

While Basilicata's economy is still fairly weak, there have been some improvements in the last forty years. The discovery of methane gas deposits in the 1960's along with the rise in the chemical industry has transformed parts of the Basento valley. Recently the Italian automaker, Fiat, opened a new plant near Melfi. Potenza, the capital, is a center for engineering and building materials. Other industries include sugar, textiles and foodstuffs. Tourism is limited to coastal resort areas, namely Maratea on the Tyrrhenian and Matera on the Ionian. However, there is potential to develop the region's tourism as it offers a great variety of scenery and ancient attractions within a relatively small territory.

talian Ice

1 cup sweet or dry fruity white wine
1 cup water
1 cup sugar
1 cup lemon juice
2 egg whites*
  Fresh berries (optional)
  Mint leaves for garnish

*Use clean, uncracked eggs.

1. Place wine and water in small saucepan; add sugar. Cook over medium-high heat until sugar has dissolved and syrup boils, stirring frequently. Cover; boil 1 minute. Uncover; adjust heat to maintain simmer. Simmer 10 minutes without stirring. Remove from heat. Refrigerate 1 hour or until syrup is completely cool.

2. Stir lemon juice into cooled syrup. Pour into 9-inch round cake pan. Freeze 1 hour.

3. Quickly stir mixture with fork breaking up ice crystals. Freeze 1 hour more or until firm but not solid. Meanwhile, place medium bowl in freezer to chill.

4. Beat egg whites in small bowl with electric mixer at high speed until stiff peaks form. Remove lemon ice mixture from cake pan to chilled bowl. Immediately beat ice with whisk or fork until smooth. Fold in egg whites; mix well. Spread egg mixture evenly into same cake pan. Freeze 30 minutes. Immediately stir with fork; cover cake pan with foil. Freeze at least 3 hours or until firm.

5. To serve, scoop Italian Ice into fluted champagne glasses or dessert dishes. Serve with berries. Garnish, if desired.

Makes 4 servings

Italian Ice

Rum and Spumone Layered Torte

1 package (18 to 19 ounces) moist butter recipe yellow cake mix
3 eggs
$^{1}/_{2}$ cup butter, softened
$^{1}/_{3}$ cup plus 2 teaspoons rum, divided
$^{1}/_{3}$ cup water
1 quart spumone ice cream, softened
1 cup whipping cream
1 tablespoon powdered sugar
  Chopped mixed candied fruit
  Red and green sugars for decorating (optional)

Preheat oven to 375°F. Grease and flour $15^{1}/_{2} \times 10^{1}/_{2} \times 1$-inch jelly-roll pan. Combine cake mix, eggs, butter, $^{1}/_{3}$ cup rum and water in large bowl. Beat with electric mixer at low speed until moistened. Beat at high speed 4 minutes. Pour evenly into prepared pan.

Bake 20 to 25 minutes or until toothpick inserted in center comes out clean. Cool in pan 10 minutes. Turn out of pan onto wire rack; cool completely.

Cut cake into three 10×5-inch pieces. Place one cake layer on serving plate. Spread with half the softened ice cream. Cover with second cake layer. Spread with remaining ice cream. Place remaining cake layer on top. Gently push down. Wrap cake in plastic wrap and freeze at least 4 hours.

Just before serving, combine cream, powdered sugar and remaining 2 teaspoons rum in small chilled bowl. Beat at high speed with chilled beaters until stiff peaks form. Remove cake from freezer. Spread thin layer of whipped cream mixture over top of cake. Place star tip in pastry bag; fill with remaining whipped cream mixture. Pipe rosettes around outer top edges of cake. Place candied fruit in narrow strip down center of cake. Sprinkle colored sugars over rosettes, if desired. Serve immediately.

Makes 8 to 10 servings

Rum and Spumoni Layered Torte

 Tiramisu

6 egg yolks
½ cup sugar
⅓ cup Cognac or brandy
2 cups (15 ounces) SARGENTO® Whole Milk Ricotta Cheese
1 cup whipping cream, whipped
32 ladyfingers, split in half
1 tablespoon instant coffee dissolved in ¾ cup boiling water
1 tablespoon unsweetened cocoa
Chocolate curls (optional)

In top of double boiler, whisk together egg yolks, sugar and Cognac. Place pan over simmering water in bottom of double boiler. Cook, whisking constantly, about 2 to 3 minutes until mixture is thickened. Remove top of double boiler; cool yolk mixture completely. In large bowl of electric mixer, beat yolk mixture and Ricotta cheese on medium speed until blended. Fold in whipped cream.

Place half the ladyfingers in bottom of 13×9-inch pan, cut sides up. Brush with half the coffee; spread with half the Ricotta mixture. Repeat layers. Refrigerate 2 hours. Just before serving, dust with cocoa using fine sieve; cut into squares. Garnish with chocolate curls, if desired. *Makes 16 servings*

Chocolate Curls: To prepare chocolate curls, combine ½ cup semisweet chocolate chips with 2 teaspoons vegetable shortening in 2-cup microwave-safe bowl. Microwave at HIGH (100%) 1 minute. Stir until chocolate is completely melted. Spread evenly into a thin layer on small cookie sheet. Let stand until firm. (Do not chill in refrigerator.) Hold small pancake turner upside down at 45° angle to cookie sheet. Run pancake turner across chocolate, allowing chocolate to curl.

Cheesecake Cannoli

1 container (15 ounces) POLLY-O® Whole Milk Ricotta Cheese
½ cup cold milk
1 package (4-serving size) JELL-O® Cheesecake Flavor Instant Pudding & Pie Filling
1½ cups thawed COOL WHIP® Whipped Topping
2 squares BAKER'S® Semi-Sweet Baking Chocolate, finely chopped
12 prepared cannoli shells

BEAT ricotta cheese and milk in medium bowl with wire whisk until well blended. Add pudding mix. Beat with wire whisk 2 minutes or until well blended. Gently stir in whipped topping. Stir in chocolate and add-ins, if desired. Using pastry bag fitted with large straight tip, pipe mixture into cannoli shells.

REFRIGERATE until ready to serve.   *Makes 12 servings*

Note: Waffle bowls or cones may be substituted for cannoli shells.

Prep Time: 5 minutes

Suggested Add-ins:

¼ cup chopped pistachio nuts
¼ cup chopped toasted almonds
¼ teaspoon almond extract
½ teaspoon grated lemon peel
2 tablespoons each finely chopped citron and candied orange peel

Tips: This filling mixture can be used to fill ice cream cones. For a smoother filling, puree mixture in food processor before adding whipped topping and chocolate.

Chocolate Almond Biscotti

1   package DUNCAN HINES® Moist Deluxe® Dark Chocolate Cake Mix
1   cup all-purpose flour
$\frac{1}{2}$ cup butter or margarine, melted
2   eggs
1   teaspoon almond extract
$\frac{1}{2}$ cup chopped almonds
    White chocolate, melted (optional)

1. Preheat oven to 350°F. Line 2 baking sheets with parchment paper.

2. Combine cake mix, flour, butter, eggs and almond extract in large bowl. Beat at low speed with electric mixer until well blended; stir in almonds. Divide dough in half. Shape each half into 12×2-inch log; place logs on prepared baking sheets. (Bake logs separately.)

3. Bake at 350°F for 30 to 35 minutes or until toothpick inserted in center comes out clean. Remove logs from oven; cool on baking sheets 15 minutes. Using serrated knife, cut logs into $\frac{1}{2}$-inch slices. Arrange slices on baking sheets. Bake biscotti 10 minutes. Remove to cooling racks; cool completely.

4. Dip one end of each biscotti in melted white chocolate, if desired. Allow white chocolate to set at room temperature before storing biscotti in airtight container.

Makes about 2$\frac{1}{2}$ dozen cookies

Chocolate Almond Biscotti

Lemon Raspberry Tiramisu

2 packages (8 ounces each) fat-free cream cheese, softened
6 packages artificial sweetener *or* equivalent of ¼ cup sugar
1 teaspoon vanilla
⅓ cup water
1 package (0.3 ounce) sugar-free lemon-flavored gelatin
2 cups thawed frozen fat-free nondairy whipped topping
½ cup all-fruit red raspberry preserves
¼ cup water
2 tablespoons marsala wine
2 packages (3 ounces each) ladyfingers
1 pint fresh raspberries or frozen unsweetened raspberries, thawed

1. Combine cream cheese, artificial sweetener and vanilla in large bowl. Beat with electric mixer at high speed until smooth; set aside.

2. Combine water and gelatin in small microwavable bowl; microwave at HIGH 30 seconds to 1 minute or until water is boiling and gelatin is dissolved. Cool slightly.

3. Add gelatin mixture to cheese mixture; beat 1 minute. Add whipped topping; beat 1 minute more, scraping side of bowl. Set aside.

4. Whisk together preserves, water and marsala in small bowl until well blended. Reserve 2 tablespoons of preserves mixture; set aside. Spread ⅓ cup preserves mixture evenly over bottom of 11×7-inch glass baking dish.

5. Split ladyfingers in half; place half in bottom of baking dish. Spread half of cheese mixture evenly over ladyfingers; sprinkle 1 cup of raspberries evenly over cheese mixture. Top with remaining ladyfingers; spread remaining preserves mixture over ladyfingers. Top with remaining cheese mixture. Cover; refrigerate for at least 2 hours. Sprinkle with remaining raspberries and drizzle with reserved 2 tablespoons of preserves mixture before serving. *Makes 12 servings*

Lemon Raspberry Tiramisu

Florentine Cookies

¼ cup unsalted butter

¼ cup sugar

1 tablespoon heavy or whipping cream

¼ cup sliced blanched almonds, finely chopped

¼ cup walnuts, finely chopped

5 red candied cherries, finely chopped

1 tablespoon golden or dark raisins, finely chopped

1 tablespoon crystallized ginger, finely chopped

1 tablespoon diced candied lemon peel, finely chopped

3 tablespoons all-purpose flour

4 ounces semisweet chocolate, chopped

1. Preheat oven to 350°F. Grease 2 large baking sheets.

2. Combine butter, sugar and cream in small heavy saucepan. Cook, uncovered, over medium heat until sugar dissolves and mixture boils, stirring constantly. Cook and stir 1 minute more; remove from heat. Stir in nuts, fruit, ginger and lemon peel. Add flour; mix well.

3. Spoon heaping teaspoonfuls batter onto prepared baking sheets. Repeat, placing 4 cookies on each baking sheet to allow room for spreading.

4. Bake cookies, 1 baking sheet at a time, 8 to 10 minutes or until deep brown. Remove baking sheet from oven to wire rack. (If cookies have spread unevenly, push in edges with metal spatula to round out shape.) Cool cookies 1 minute or until firm enough to remove from sheet; then quickly and carefully remove cookies to wire racks. Cool completely.

5. Repeat with remaining batter. (To prevent cookies from spreading too quickly, allow baking sheets to cool before greasing and spooning batter onto sheets.)

6. Bring water in bottom of double boiler just to a boil; remove from heat. Place chocolate in top of double boiler and place over water. Stir chocolate until melted; immediately remove top of double boiler from water. Let chocolate cool slightly.

7. Line large baking sheets with waxed paper. Turn cookies over; spread chocolate on bottoms. Place cookies, chocolate side up, on prepared baking sheets; let stand until chocolate is almost set. Score chocolate in zig-zag pattern with tines of fork. Let stand until completely set or refrigerate until firm. Serve or store in airtight container in refrigerator.   *Makes about 2 dozen cookies*

Florentine Cookies

Acknowledgments

The publisher would like to thank the companies and organizations listed below for the use of their recipes and photographs in this publication.

A.1.® Steak Sauce

American Lamb Council

Barilla America, Inc.

Bays English Muffin Corporation

BelGioioso® Cheese, Inc.

Birds Eye®

Bob Evans®

Butterball® Turkey Company

Cucina Classica Italiana, Inc.

Del Monte Corporation

Duncan Hines® and Moist Deluxe® are registered trademarks of Aurora Foods Inc.

Egg Beaters®

Filippo Berio® Olive Oil

Fleischmann's® Yeast

The Golden Grain Company®

Grey Poupon® Dijon Mustard

Hebrew National®

The Hidden Valley® Food Products Company

Hillshire Farm®

The Kingsford Products Company

Kraft Foods Holdings

Lawry's® Foods

McIlhenny Company (TABASCO® brand Pepper Sauce)

National Fisheries Institute

National Turkey Federation

Nestlé USA

New Jersey Department of Agriculture

Norseland, Inc. / Lucini Italia Co.

North Dakota Wheat Commission

Perdue Farms Incorporated

PLANTERS® Nuts

The Quaker® Oatmeal Kitchens

Reckitt Benckiser Inc.

RED STAR® Yeast, a product of Lasaffre Yeast Corporation

Riviana Foods Inc.

Sargento® Foods Inc.

The J.M. Smucker Company

Sonoma® Dried Tomatoes

StarKist® Seafood Company

Uncle Ben's Inc.

Unilever Bestfoods North America

Walnut Marketing Board

Wisconsin Milk Marketing Board

Index

Index

Index

Index